Old Bushman

A Spring and Summer in Lapland

With Notes on the Fauna of Luleå Lapmark

Old Bushman

A Spring and Summer in Lapland
With Notes on the Fauna of Luleå Lapmark

ISBN/EAN: 9783337274368

Printed in Europe, USA, Canada, Australia, Japan

Cover: Foto ©Andreas Hilbeck / pixelio.de

More available books at **www.hansebooks.com**

A SPRING AND SUMMER

IN

LAPLAND

WITH

NOTES ON THE FAUNA OF LULEÄ LAPMARK.

BY

AN OLD BUSHMAN,

AUTHOR OF "BUSH WANDERINGS IN AUSTRALIA."

> "Away, away, from men and towns,
> To the wild woods and the downs.
> To the silent wilderness,
> Where the soul need not suppress
> Its rapture, lest it should not find
> An echo in another mind."—SHELLEY.

LONDON:
GROOMBRIDGE AND SONS,
5, PATERNOSTER ROW.
MDCCCLXIV.

TO THE EDITOR OF

THE "FIELD" NEWSPAPER,

AS A SLIGHT ACKNOWLEDGMENT OF THE

KIND AND COURTEOUS TREATMENT

WHICH HE HAS INVARIABLY RECEIVED DURING A THREE YEARS'

CONNECTION WITH THAT PAPER,

THIS WORK

Is Respectfully Dedicated,

BY

AN OLD BUSHMAN.

GARDSJÖ, SWEDEN.

PREFACE.

THE following work on the Fauna of Lapland is compiled from notes kept during a season's collecting up at Quickiock in 1862. These notes have, for the greater part, already appeared in the columns of the "Field" Newspaper; but the Editor having kindly given back to the Author the right of republishing, he has, at the request of several friends, collected them in the shape of a volume, with some slight alterations and additions, and again brings them before the public in another form, fancying that they may now be of more service to the naturalist and traveller than in the columns of a newspaper. As the Author's sole object in going up to Lapland was for the purpose of collecting birds and eggs, the present work will be found rather as a guide to the ornithologist than any other class of reader, although at the same time it is to be hoped that the general reader will find something in it to interest him. In conclusion, the Author can only express his sincere hope that the work in its present form will be as kindly and favourably received as the notes from which it is compiled were, when they first appeared in the columns of the "Field."

CONTENTS.

CHAPTER I.
A FEW PRELIMINARY REMARKS ON THE GENERAL FAUNA AND LANDSCAPE OF SCANDINAVIA . . . 6

CHAPTER II.
PREPARATIONS FOR THE JOURNEY, AND HINTS TO THE TRAVELLER 18

CHAPTER III.
THE JOURNEY UP 33

CHAPTER IV.
LAPLAND 75

CHAPTER V.
NOTES FROM MY DIARY KEPT AT QUICKIOCK . . 116

CHAPTER VI.
HINTS TO SPORTSMEN AND NATURALISTS IN LAPLAND . 144

CHAPTER VII.
ON THE FISH PECULIAR TO THESE WATERS, THE REPTILES, AND THE INSECTS OF LAPLAND . . . 156

CHAPTER VIII.

A CHAPTER ON THE MAMMALIA BELONGING TO THIS DISTRICT 172

CHAPTER IX.

ON THE ORNITHOLOGY OF LAPLAND . . . 241

CHAPTER X.

A CHAPTER ON THE ORNITHOLOGY AROUND VARDOL, IN EAST FINLAND, LYING CONTIGUOUS TO THE NORTH CAPE 371

CHAPTER XI.

THE JOURNEY DOWN, AND CONCLUSION . . 387

A SPRING AND SUMMER IN LAPLAND.

CHAPTER I.

A FEW PRELIMINARY REMARKS ON THE GENERAL FAUNA AND LANDSCAPE OF SCANDINAVIA.*

It is no easy task to give even a good general account of the fauna, climate, or scenery of this wide-stretched continent, which extends from about 55° to 71° of north latitude, and covers an area of nearly 300,000 English square miles, diversified with every description of landscape, from the low peat sandy plains and open turf mosses of the south, and the dense pine forests of the midland districts, to the barren fells of the north, whose snow-capped summits afford a scanty sustenance to scarcely any other living creature than the reindeer and the ptarmigan. Over so wide a surface we shall expect to find soil and

* By Scandinavia is meant Sweden and Norway, not including Denmark.

vegetation of every description; and it is the diversity of scenery which meets the traveller's eye at every turn, that gives a charm to wandering through these northern climes. Still, rich as it is in natural productions, rich as it is in every branch of its fauna, this is a land comparatively but little known to the British traveller; whilst almost every other part of the European continent, whose natural beauties can scarcely surpass this magnificent country in the summer, are as well known to the English tourist as the woods and glades of his own merry England.

Scarcely any other country in Europe possesses so many attractions to the naturalist as Scandinavia, for the varied nature of the landscape, with so few inhabitants scattered over its surface, marks it as a fitting home for such of the rarer species of quadruped and bird as delight in solitude and retirement; while its vast extent of coast, its magnificent rivers, and innumerable inland lakes must render it one of the greatest interest to the ichthyologist. Most of the larger and wilder species of the European mammalia are to be met with in one part or another of this immense continent. The elk finds shelter in the midland forests; the reindeer on the northern fells; the bear, the lynx, the glutton, the wolf, and the Arctic fox, are no strangers in the midland and northern districts; and the marten cat, the fox, and the squirrel, besides many species of bats and field-mice, abound in every part of the country. Unfortunately, the beaver is now nearly extinct, and almost the only memento we meet with here at the present day of this interesting animal (which was once so common in the north of Europe) is an occasional deserted beaver dam, in one or other of the wildest and most secluded northern forests.

It is on account of this country presenting so wide and varied a surface, that we find so manifest a difference in its fauna, and this is still further supported when we consider the nature of the lands—open downs, deep forests, sandy flats, cultivated fields, meadow, marsh, and morass, and in the very north, snow-covered fells. These last must exercise a great influence on the fauna of the north, for every species of animal must have its well-defined limit from the region of perpetual snow. Messon, with his usual acumen, divides Scandinavia into separate regions for different animals and plants.

Beginning from the very tops of the fells, and following, by degrees, in a southerly direction, the tracks that lie below them, we shall find that certain species of animals, as well as of plants, are only to be met with on the highest fells, amongst perpetual snow-drifts; and also that other species are found only in those tracts far removed from the fells themselves, and this will hold good, whether we divide these regions in a vertical or horizontal direction, with this difference, that the regions in the latter are much broader than in the former.

After these remarks we will divide the land into the following regions for plants and quadrupeds, taking a fell tract in West Norway, 60° north latitude.

1. *The Perpetual Snow Region,* which extends from the tops of the highest snow fells down to the first bushes. In this region the only vegetations are a few ice plants, lichens, and mosses; and the only quadrupeds that belong to them are the glutton, the white fox, the reindeer, the northern hare (*Lepus borealis*), and the common weazel.

2. *To the Willow and Birch Region* belong the lemming, two or three species of field-mice, the fox, the wolf, the bear, the stoat, the common field-mouse, the *Lorex pygmæus,* and one bat (*Vesp. borealis*).

3. *In the Pine and Fir Region* we meet with the long-eared bat, parti-coloured bats, the water-shrew, the lynx, the marten, the otter, the long-tailed field-mouse, the common mouse, two or three species of vole, the squirrel, the elk, and the red deer.

4. *In the Oak Region,* reckoning from that tract where the oak-tree first grows, the great bat, the hedgehog, the common rat, the grey hare (*Lepus Canescens*), the polecat, and the badger.

5. *The Beech Region,* the Barbastell bat, the mole, the dormouse, and the Roedeer.

6. *In such Tracts* as the black mulberry can ripen in (*skåne*) are found fossil remains of the wild boar, the large bear (*Ursus spelæus*), the southern species of reindeer, the *Bos urus, Bos frontosus, Bos longifrons,* and the bison.

And as regards the ornithology of the country, we shall see the limits of the several birds just as clearly defined. For—

1. *In the Snow Region* we meet with the snow bunting, Buffon's skua, the wheatear, the raven, rough-legged buzzard, the gyrfalcon, the snowy owl, the short-eared owl, the ptarmigan, the white-fronted goose, the dotterel, the golden plover, the redshank, the dunlin, the purple landpiper, the common gull, the herring gull (by the fell lakes), and three or four species of diving duck.

2. *In the Willow and Birch Region* — the meadow pipit, the blue-throated warbler, the brambling, the mealy redpole, the black-headed bunting, the yellow wagtail, the willow wren, the redwing, the ring ouzel, the redstart, marsh tit-

mouse, Siberian titmouse, water ouzel, willow grouse, common sandpiper, common snipe, hooper, bean goose, pintail, scoter, widgeon, wild duck, and teal.

3. *In the Pine and Fir Region*—the Siberian jay, the waxwing, pine bullfinch, the hawk owl, the fieldfare, the greenfinch, the siskin, chaffinch, hedge-sparrow, bullfinch, crested tit, coal tit, great black woodpecker, three-toed woodpecker, goldcrest wren, the crossbills, redbreast, garden warbler, song thrush, tree pipit, capercailzie, black grouse, and hazel grouse.

4. *In the Cultivated Districts* — the hooded crow, magpie, ortolan bunting, yellow bunting, white wagtail, common sparrow, swallow, and martin, etc.

Thus we shall see, as might naturally be expected, that the vegetation, as well as the fauna of this land, has its defined limits; for, beginning with the cultivated districts at the bottom of the fells, where many of the trees and shrubs peculiar to Britain are met with, we come first (ascending the fell sides) to the fir districts, and then to the pine. Above these we meet with the common birch, and higher up with the willow and the fell birch. Above this we reach a district where little save mosses and lichens can grow, and above all lies the region of perpetual snows.

The botanist can judge for himself how wide a field is here open to him, and it is no wonder that Sweden is able to boast of so many well versed in this science, and the study of the entomologist goes hand in hand with it. But to the geologist and lover of antiquarian lore Scandinavia posseses still richer attractions. Judging from the fossil remains preserved in the museums of the country, many animals (long since outrooted from this land, and some altogether extinct) in former days inhabited the south of Sweden, and the bones of antediluvian monsters which are occasionally dug up in the turf mosses of "Skania," are evidences of by-gone ages. It is easy, while gazing on these interesting relics, to carry the reflective mind back to the period before man appeared on the face of the globe; when, probably, the waves rolled over the greater part of this continent, and we can picture to the mind's eye monstrous cartilaginous fishes then peopling the waters, and reptiles of misshapen and hideous growth drawing their slow length over the slimy oozes of the Fens. Pass we on to a later day, and the whole face of the country has gradually changed. The wild bull tossed his mane in the then secluded forest; the wild sow farrowed in security in regions as yet untrodden by the foot of man, and hundreds of gigantic elk and red deer roamed at will through the oak and beechen forests, and over the wide prairies of southern Scandinavia.

"Whatever," observes Dr. Johnson, "withdraws us from the power of our senses, whatever makes the past, the distant, or the future predominate over the present, advances us in the dignity of thinking beings." And whoever takes an interest in the early ages of mankind will here find much to occupy his attention and his thoughts. The rude implements of the chase and the barbarous weapons of warfare which are still preserved, carry the mind back to distant ages, when the battle and the chase formed man's constant or only employment. Huge barrows and cairns, and rude but stupendous monuments of stone mark the site of many an ancient battle-field, or the last resting-place of the old Scandinavian warrior and king; whilst rude hieroglyphics, cut on the rocks in many places of these coasts, are mementos at the present day, of those savage barbarians who in the early ages of Christianity spread fire and desolation over so great a portion of Europe; when the "Viking" or pirate vessel spread her sails to the wind, and bore the "Vikinger" or dreaded sea pirate to the opposite shores of Britain.

Our task, however, is with the present, and not the past; and it only remains for us to add, that let his taste be what it may—whether he be a sportsman, a naturalist, or merely a wanderer in search of the beauties of nature—the traveller here will find full employment; and there is, probably, scarcely another country in Europe, through which (especially during the summer months) a stranger can travel with so much cheapness, security, and freedom as in this.

But to return to our more immediate subject. As regards the mammalia of Scandinavia, two hypotheses have been framed respecting their introduction into this land. It is supposed by some, and with good reason, that this continent was at an early period landlocked with the rest of Europe before the Baltic and the Bothnia formed a dividing line of sea; and according to their idea, most of the southern species came over the dry land where the Baltic now flows, and the more northern ones, such as the glutton, Arctic fox, reindeer, flying squirrel, and some others, came from the tracts lying north-east of the Bothnian Gulf. Be this, however, as it may, each species appears to be pretty well confined to its assigned limits, and only makes occasional migrations to other districts, induced by an instinct which it baffles man's ingenuity to account for.

Not so, however, with the ornithology of the north. The migrations of the feathered race to these climes are much more regular and certain; but it may be remarked that many individuals of the different families, which as a general rule are only summer migrants to the north of the country, remain stationary in the south of Sweden during the winter, especially if the weather be open; and many ducks, although the majority leave the country, are to be seen off the southern coast, and even on the open midland waters, during that season. Some other species are only partial migrants in the winter from the northern and midland districts to the south of the country, where they remain during the coldest season, and return to their more northerly breeding haunts in the spring. Among these we may mention the hooded crow, one or other of the falcons and hawks, the jackdaw, mealy redpole, greenfinch, siskin, goldfinch, mountain linnet, chaffinch, purple sandpiper, spotted crake, dabchick, and some of the diving ducks and gulls.

The few that remain in the middle and north of the country throughout the most inclement winters are the eagles, the gyrfalcon, goshawk, all the owls (with the exception of the short-eared), the raven, magpie, all the woodpeckers (except the middle-spotted), which is confined at all seasons to the south of the country; the crossbills, pine grosbeak, waxwing, jay, Siberian jay, the titmice, yellow bunting, sparrow, bullfinch, a few redwing and fieldfare, and a diving duck or two, if there be any open water. And we may notice three others, whose slender frames appear ill fitted to withstand the rigours of a northern winter, but which I have seen in the Wermland forests during the severest weather—the tree-creeper, the wren, and the gold-crest. Why these little stragglers should remain behind, after all their glad companions of summer have flitted to warmer climes, has always been a mystery to me. Some few species, such as the hen harrier, the pigmy curlew, the knot, the sanderling, the bernacle goose, the brent, and the grey plover, have not yet, in my knowledge, been detected breeding in any part of Scandinavia, but are only seen during their migrations, as it is supposed, to and from more north-easterly latitudes; but as I have shot the grey plover, the knot, and the pigmy curlew, on the southern coast of Skånia, very early in August, in full summer dress, as well as birds of the year, there is every reason to suppose that these individuals had bred somewhere on this continent. With the exception of, perhaps, a rare sea-fowl, whose peculiar home is in high northern latitudes, there are no regular winter migrants to Scandinavia.

Some birds are becoming yearly more scarce

in the north. For instance, the sheldrake, bittern, ruff, lapwing, black tern, black-headed gull, and golden plover; and as all these, with the exception of the last-named, are southern species, this fact may be accounted for by the increase of cultivation. On the contrary, one or two other species are gradually spreading themselves more widely over the face of the country—such as the shore lark, Siberian tit, etc. Many of the summer migrants do not appear in the same quantities in each succeeding year. The nutcracker is a striking instance of this fact; and in certain winters, when the supply of fir cones and berries runs short, fewer of the partial migrants are to be seen in the midland forests.

That the British fauna is far richer in accidental varieties than the Scandinavian, is easily accounted for by the fact of the former country being so densely populated and closely examined, that it is next to impossible for a strange bird to show itself on the British shores without being at once noticed. Whereas, such is the wild nature of the Scandinavian landscape, and so thinly are the habitations of man scattered over its surface, that a rare bird may come and go, year after year, without being noticed by any one. But that Scandinavia is much richer in indigenous species and individuals of those species, during the breeding season, may be supposed, when we consider the wide tracts of uninhabited country between Falsterbo Reef and the North Cape, abounding in suitable localities for the wilder, and to the British fauna rarer, species of birds, whose shy and retired habits lead them to seek securer and more secluded breeding haunts than any part of Great Britain can afford. We find, therefore, that out of the 357 species included in the British fauna, not one-half are known to breed in that country; whereas, out of about 300 Scandinavian species, about 230 breed in the north.

With regard to the Danish fauna, it may be regarded as intermediate—between that of Great Britain and Scandinavia; but comparatively fewer birds breed there than in either of the above-named lands. In climate and general appearance the country much resembles the British isles; and I thought I never gazed upon a quieter, richer, or lovelier landscape, than when passing through the Belts a few summers ago. The country is well adapted to the habits of the southern warblers, and many of the common waders and water fowl, and lying in a direct line, as it were, between England and Sweden, it is more frequently visited by the rarer northern birds than the former country. The south of Denmark is highly cultivated, and the whole land has a far more pastoral appearance than the opposite shores of Sweden. In the north of Zealand, however, are many miles of barren moorland, which, without possessing the rich appearance of the bonny purple heather of Scotland, are well adapted to the habits of the curlew, golden plover, and many other birds which frequent the British moors. The country, however, is level, and, therefore, we never meet in Denmark either with the ptarmigan or the willow grouse, both which abound in Sweden and Norway; and the absence of the pine and fir forests renders it an unfitting residence for some of the large birds of prey. That noblest of all game birds, the capercally, as well as the hazel grouse, are unknown here, and the blackcock is rare; otherwise the Danish fauna much resembles that of the south of Sweden, from which it is only separated by the Sound, a narrow channel but a few English miles broad. There are no rivers to speak of in Denmark, but many large ponds, well stocked with the commoner species of fresh-water fish. However much the agriculturist and the admirer of pastoral scenery may love to linger among the neat enclosures and rich pastures of the Danish farmers, this country affords but little interest to the naturalist or the sportsman, who will eagerly hasten on to the wilder and less inhabited districts.

I consider the British coasts, generally speaking, to be much richer in sea fowl than the southern coast of Sweden; but the wild "Skar Gard," or cluster of rocky islands that skirt the northern shores of Scandinavia is the peculiar home of these birds, which resort, every spring, in countless thousands, to their breeding haunts on the western and northern coasts; whilst the immense swamps and morasses, and innumerable inland lakes with which the whole of Scandinavia is studded, afford secure shelter and breeding places for every species of inland aquatic birds. In the very south of Sweden, where the oak, the beech, and the hazel usurp the place of the pine and the fir, kings of the northern forest, the different species of warblers find a home as congenial to their habits as the groves and plantations of England; and as regards the general fauna of this part of the country, it differs but little from that of Britain. The severity of the northern winter is here but little felt, and the spring migrants make their appearance nearly as early as in England, and generally a fortnight earlier than they are to be seen in the midland districts, where snow frequently covers the ground in the end of April.

In the midland districts, where pine and fir forests of boundless extent rise on high stony ranges, intersected with plains and valleys of meadow and cultivated land and dells, where the willow and the alder vegetate in great luxuriance, nearly every species of land birds finds a congenial home. Whilst vast morasses, many of which can never be traversed by the human foot, rivers, and inland lakes of every size, fringed with the reed, the bulrush, and the candock, and thousands of acres of low meadow land, covered with thick coarse grass, abound in every species of water and aquatic birds, which resort to the north in hundreds at the commencement of the breeding season. It is here that the British naturalist begins to meet with rare and new specimens, and it is here that the eye of the traveller first gazes on the fine scenery of the north; and more beautiful scenery than Scandinavia displays during the summer months it would be hard to find. I have wandered over many lands, but scarcely ever saw a European landscape to vie with this.

In the very north, the appearance of the whole country becomes gradually more wild and rugged, and high mountains and barren fells, covered with perennial snows, rise above the limits of vegetation, and towering over the forests which skirt their bases, are the home of some few of the very scarcest and wildest species, whose haunts during the breeding season are but little known to us.

It is therefore not to be wondered at that the

southern naturalist should fondly long to wander in the secluded regions of the far north, which contain treasures so eagerly coveted for his collection at home, and it is to be hoped that a perusal of the following pages will give him a slight insight into the fauna of this magnificent land, and prove that the task of reaching it is neither so arduous or troublesome as he might at first be led to suppose.

CHAPTER II.

PREPARATIONS FOR THE JOURNEY, AND HINTS TO THE TRAVELLER.

THE tourist who visits Lapland merely for the sake of seeing the country will find little difficulty in effecting his object. He will not require to leave England before the end of May; he can perform the whole journey from Hull to Happaranda (the most northerly town in the Bothnian Gulf), *viâ* Gothenburg and Stockholm, by steam. The Bothnian steamers start from Stockholm as soon as the sea is free from ice. Of course this is dependent upon the season; but we cannot reckon with any certainty that they can run the whole way up until early in June. He will require no passport, and neither guide nor interpreter, till he reaches Happaranda, from which place he can branch off in any direction he pleases. His journey will then be performed in boats or on foot, and he will find far less difficulty in reaching the wildest spot in Lapland than he would anticipate. But if his object is merely to visit the North Cape, his better plan will be to go from Hull to Christiana in Norway, thence to Bergen, and from that place he will obtain a passage by steamer right up to Hammerfest or Vardoe. The journey from Hull to Gothenburg will occupy three days; from that place to Stockholm, three more; thence to Happaranda, four more.

But it is a very different affair for the naturalist or collector, especially if eggs are his principal object. He will require to be up at his headquarters early in April, and he must necessarily steam up in the autumn, before the winter sets in, and brave the rigours and monotony of a Lap winter; or he must adopt my plan, and sledge up during the winter—taking care that he is not too late, for the snow melts all at once when the thaw sets in (and this happens long before the ice goes in the rivers); and just at this time travelling is dangerous, troublesome, and laborious. I was lucky enough to hit the identical time. I left Gardsjö on March 24, and reached Quickiock on April 16, and the sledging was good the whole way up, save for six English miles. Had I waited another week I should have had little or no sledging till I reached Hernosand; and such a journey at this time of year, on these dreadful peasants' carts, over bad roads, could have been scarcely borne by any one save a Swedish mailman or a genuine " gutta-percha" boy.

It is not my intention to occupy more space than I can possibly help with the details of my journey, and, in fact, throughout my whole notes, will endeavour to be as concise as possible; but this little work being intended as a guide for any future traveller or naturalist who may wish to visit this interesting land, of which comparatively so little is known in England, I shall, perhaps, notice some matters which may appear trivial to the general reader, yet prove of great service to the traveller. As my trip, however, was solely for the purpose of collecting and obtaining a better knowledge of the habits of the rarer British birds during the breeding season, my notes on the ornithology of the districts which I visited may probably assume a more lengthened form; and the reader may rely implicitly on what I write; for, as I ever have done, I shall state nothing as a fact which does not come under my own personal observation. I shall, in the first place, give a short sketch of the journey up, and make a few remarks on life in Lapland, as it struck me; and I shall carefully avoid tiring the reader with anecdotes related to me by others; for I look upon a narrative or book filled with anecdotes, unless the writer can himself vouch for their truth, as little better than a work of fiction. And let me remark at starting, that if I state any fact at variance with other naturalists, it does not follow that I wish to infer that they are wrong, or that I know more than they do. The habits of birds differ much in different localities; and it is never fair to condemn a man for stating a fact relative to the habits of any bird or animal because we may not happen to have observed it ourselves.

I shall commence by making a few remarks on the manner of posting through these northern countries. The roads throughout Sweden are generally excellent—hilly, it is true, and rough in many places, owing to the nature of the country, but well looked after by the "landsman," or chief magistrate of each district. A toll-bar is never seen, except occasionally at the entrance of a town. At a distance of about every Swedish mile ($6\frac{3}{4}$ English), or perhaps $1\frac{1}{2}$ mile, is a post-station, the master of which is bound to furnish horses and conveyances for travellers, as well as accommodation. Diligences run between many of the principal towns, and in the summer steamers ply through the whole country; but the posting is all done by the peasants' little horses; and, if the traveller has no conveyance of his own, he rides in winter on a peasant's sledge—at other times, in one of their little carts. The post-master has seldom any horses in his stable; and "A pair out, quick!" is not the order of the day here. The horses are furnished by the neighbouring farmers, each in his turn, and the postmaster has sometimes to send a distance of two English miles for horses; consequently, the traveller is often delayed a couple of hours at each station, but by the law he must not be kept more than three. If he sends forward a messenger or "forbud" in advance (which will cost him, perhaps, 6*d.* the Swedish mile), the horses will be ready for him; but he must not keep them waiting, or he will have to pay for the peasant's time. I observed, however, on my journey up, that at most of the stations now the mileage is a little higher, and they were bound to furnish us with horses in a quarter of an hour, so that a "forbud" is unnecessary. The rate of travelling may be estimated at one Swedish mile in the hour; and what with delays, bad horses, and hilly roads, the traveller may truly be said to *crawl* through the country. The charge, per Swedish mile, is about 1*s.* for each horse, and 1*d.* for the cart or sledge. The drivers are generally little peasant lads — sharp, merry, rosy-cheeked urchins; and capitally they drive; and if they receive 1*d.* per Swedish mile as postilion fee, they are more than satisfied. The horses are small, but always in good condition (for the Swedish peasant looks after his little horse like a child), and a galled back or broken knee is rarely seen in the north. At each post-station is a day-book, in which the traveller enters his name, where he is bound for, etc.; and if he has any complaint to make here, he books it. In each day-book is entered the distance to the next stage, and the charge; so there is not half the trouble in posting through Sweden that the stranger would imagine. This day-book is sent in to the landsman at the end of each month, and a new one issued. The postmaster is usually a better class of peasant, always civil and well-behaved, especially towards a foreigner. Most of the inns are furnished with a bill of fare hung up in the travellers' room; and, as it may not be uninteresting to the English reader, I insert a tariff (dated Sept. 12, 1861) which I copied from an inn a little north of Herinosand:—

	s.	d.		s.	d.
A best meal (three dishes)	1	0	A kanna of small beer	0	1½
One not quite so good	0	8	A bread cake	0	1
Twenty eggs	1	0	Two feeds of oats	0	4
A cup of coffee	0	1	20lb. clover hay	0	9
Best bed (down mattress)	1	0	Do. meadow hay	0	4½
One not quite so good	0	8	A tallow candle, 6 to the lb.	0	1½
A bed of straw	0	4	Four bottles sweet milk	0	3
A fire of birch wood	0	1½	Do. sour	0	1
One of fir or pine	0	1	1lb. butter	0	9
A kanna (4 bottles) ale	0	4	Stabling for a horse	0	1½

Robbery or extortion is rarely, if ever, heard of on the Swedish roads. In the summer the roads are excellent, in the spring and autumn bad; but it is when the frozen snow covers them that the travelling is best. The reader may perhaps wonder how the roads are kept clear of snow; and it is done after this fashion:—As soon as the first snow falls, and the roads are covered pretty deeply, the snow-plough is brought out. This is a kind of triangular machine, built of three boards, a foot deep, 14 feet long, 10 feet wide behind, and coming to a point in front, like the bows of a ducking-punt. Cross-bars extend across the plough, and upon these a lot of peasants perch themselves to give it weight; four or six oxen are yoked to it, and by dragging it backwards and forwards from one station to another, the loose snow is shovelled up in banks on each side, and, as it always comes on to freeze as soon as the snow-storm is over, an excellent road, level as a bowling-green, is formed throughout the whole country, which stands, without any repairing, till the spring thaw; and if the snow falls again, the snow-plough is again brought into requisition. Each gentleman opens a road from his house to the high road; and he must be careful not to let the snow fall too deep before he brings out his snow-plough, or he may be snowed in. Roads are set out across all the frozen lakes by bushes stuck in the snow; gaps are made in fences, and straight short cuts made from one village to another. The travelling is now by sledge; and if he is only well wrapped up, the traveller rolls along as comfortably as in a first-class railway carriage; not so, however, when he travels on the bare roads in one of these peasant carts—for of all the bone-setting, jolting, infernal machines that a traveller ever rode in, these are the worst. Talk of the old English coach-box before springs were invented, it was nothing to them; and certainly Sweden can boast of the worst public conveyances of any country in the world. Imagine a little shallow box, about 6 feet long and 4 feet wide, fixed upon a wooden axle, with two of the most rickety wheels that ever hung together, and in the middle of this box a seat placed upon two slanting ash-poles, about 1 foot above the axle—and the reader can form an idea of a Swedish peasant's cart. There is not a spring about the whole concern; and as for an apron, such a thing was never dreamt of here. The jolting of such a machine over bad roads, with deep ruts, can be better imagined than described. The peasants, who are hard as nails, don't feel it a bit; but the poor traveller, especially if he be one of the soft-wooled kind, is kept in a constant state of agony and fear wherever the roads are bad (and in spring and autumn the ruts are often up to the axle), obliged to hold on like grim Death, otherwise he is sure to be shot off his perch, every bone in his skin aching with pain. Not a bit of use complaining to the phlegmatic driver, who seems to pick out the worst bits of road, just to try the traveller's mettle. All the answer you get is the usual long-drawn "Soo." If you don't like it, you can get out and walk; and, as this saves his horse, this just pleases him. What with bad harness and rickety carts, it is a wonder we don't hear of more accidents on these roads. Much as I have travelled in Sweden, I never had but one accident; this was, however, an awful smash.

Each horse is by law obliged, if the traveller wishes it, to draw 400lb., exclusive of the cart and driver. The passenger is weighed in at 200lb., and he can have 200lb. of luggage. By diligence he can only have 30lb. No box that ever was made, unless strongly iron-bound, can stand the wear and tear of a long journey in one of these carts. A strong English leather trunk (but mind and cover it with sail cloth) and carpet bag are as good as anything; but the passenger must be careful not to have his trunk too large, or it won't fit into the box—about $2\frac{1}{2}$ feet long, $1\frac{1}{2}$ broad, and 18 inches deep is the best size. A small glazed carpet bag to hold his money, map, and other little odds-and-ends, must not be forgotten. The

Swedish travellers adopt a very useful plan, they have a kind of large leather "reticule" attached to the neck by a strap, with a snap lock; this holds their loose change, tobacco, etc., and very useful it is, for when a man is tightly enveloped in a huge skin cloak, he can't well get at his pockets.

As my object in visiting Lapland was to obtain a good insight into the natural history of the country, and to collect, I determined to leave nothing to chance. I therefore took up one of my best collecting lads as servant; and as three can travel as cheaply as two, as far as posting goes (for two must have two sledges, and three require no more, one driver sufficing to bring back the two empty sledges), I also had a young Swede as companion, to help me in any difficulty on the road. In this respect I acted foolishly, for I could have managed just as well by myself; and when he got up to Lapland he was seized with such a fit of home-sickness, that I was obliged to send him home by the first open water, thus entailing a great and unnecessary expense. And here let me give a bit of advice to any naturalist visiting Lapland. If he must have a guide or interpreter, let him take a regular travelling servant from Stockholm. Such a man knows his work, and keeps his place as a servant. I may, however, mention that at most of the towns, if he wishes it, the traveller will have no difficulty in obtaining a young student who will willingly accompany him for a trifle on such a trip. In collecting, let him trust to the help of the natives in the district which he visits; they will be too glad to help him to earn a little money. They know the country, and the haunts and localities of the different birds and beasts in their neighbourhood, and will do more for him in a week than a strange servant, let him be ever so good, will in a month. But I did not know at first that I could procure so much assistance, and it was all important that I should have one man upon whom I could trust, for I could not explain to the Laps in what state of plumage I wanted the different birds, and I knew my lad could be depended upon, for he has been in my service some years. He certainly worked well, but every specimen he procured for me cost me four times as much as those I bought of the natives.

We travelled in two sledges. Our baggage weighed about 360lb., which I computed thus, and, so that we should have no trouble on the road, I weighed every package before we started:—Dog, 35lb.; shot and powder, 100lb. (but this was barely sufficient); trunk with clothes, books, etc., 80lb.; double gun in case, etc., 25lb.; double gun for my lad, 14lb.; spare single ditto, 7lb.; small carpet bag, with money and things for road, 20lb.; clothes for my

PREPARATIONS FOR THE JOURNEY.

two mates, 60lb. We could, by law, have taken 40lb. more; and, in fact, the sledging runs so light in the winter, that not one of the drivers would have grumbled if we had had a little overweight. I could have bought very good shot (at 3*d.* per lb. if I had taken 1 cwt.) and fair powder at 1*s.* 6*d.* in Gefle, through which town I must pass; and even at Quickiock we could buy coarse powder (I mention this as a guide to the stranger); but, as I had plenty at home, I thought it best to take it. Moreover, the English powder is far cleaner and stronger than any you can buy in Sweden. *Small* shot, however, is never to be procured up in the country, as it is not used by the shooters here.

I should, however, advise every naturalist or sportsman to bring over powder and caps (for he cannot procure these here), and a spare gun, for if an accident happens up in these wilds he cannot repair it.

I took care to provide lots of small silver and copper money for the roads, and an excellent little travelling map by Strom, which sets out all the roads in Sweden, and marks the distance between the post stations. This I found most useful. A good map of Lapland itself is, however, hard to procure. A good cloak lined with sheepskin over my pea jacket, a pair of outer cloth-lined boots, my old Australian "possum rug" round my knees, a fur cap to cover the head and ears, and warm gloves, without fingers, completed my equipment; and not one of these articles should the traveller omit who undertakes a journey through these northern climes in the winter, when the quicksilver varies from 15° to 40° below zero, Celsius. Wrapped up as I was, with the thermometer never lower than 25° (13° below zero Fahr.), I was "none too warm," and at times when the bleak north wind came howling through the forests, dashing the cutting sleet into my face, I fancied my nose would snap off "like a carrot."

The cap I wore was an old tiger-skin one, which I picked up south of the Line; and a most imposing figure I cut as I sledged up to the doors of the country public-houses, the "admired of all admirers." My cap was an object of veneration to all the peasant lads that drove us. I believe there was nothing about me that they envied except this; but certainly, like the grandfather's stick in Eliza Cook's beautiful poem, this cap "was the coveted relic of all."

Of course many inquiries were made by the postmasters up the road as to who I was and what was my business, and one and all firmly believed that I was some rich Englishman or other, travelling up to buy the great Gellivare iron mines. One brandy-nosed old sinner was exceedingly inquisitive, and when I assured him my visit to Lapland was solely for the purpose of collecting, he took his pipe out of his mouth, looked at me for a little while, more " in sorrow than in anger," and left the room with this comment: " Well, surely you Englishmen *are* mad!" It was clear he had already got some such notion into his muddled, brandified old head, and now he was perfectly convinced.

The dog I took up was a young unbroken setter, and although I should advise every sportsman visiting Lapland to take up, at least, one good general-purpose dog, I should never recommend him using a first-class dog in the Lap forests, where the steadiest dog that ever was shot over would be spoilt in a month, for of all the birds to try a young dog's temper, these willow grouse are the worst. For the ptarmigan, on the fells, a high ranging well-broken setter is of course the dog, but in the forests and bushes, a slow, heavy, close-hunting, retrieving spaniel would be by far more useful. Although included in the weight of baggage, my dog seldom rode in the sledge; and out of the 1000 English miles, I am sure he ran by our side about 800. I was rather afraid of the wolves, which often snap up a dog by the road. However, we never saw a wolf during our whole journey; but I always had my revolver ready, for it is just when the winter is going that wolves are most to be feared. We also were each provided with a small tomahawk (which on a journey of this kind may prove very useful in more ways than one). Nor did we forget a coil of rope, and some large nails, and a small canteen filled with the common brandy of the country to give an occasional dram to the drivers, on the principle that " a spur in the head is worth two in the heel "— and it is wonderful how a stimulant like this acts on these roads.

CHAPTER III.

THE JOURNEY UP.

The morning of March 24, the day I left Gardsjö, was about as miserable a one as ever I turned out in. The snow lay deep on the ground, and the dark pine-forests looked doubly gloomy in the sickly light of the waning moon. A drizzling sleet was falling; the thermometer was just 17° below zero, Celsius ($1\frac{1}{2}$° Fahr.), and the prospect of a journey of about a thousand English miles in open sledges, in such weather, looked cheerless enough. However, the horses were put to, and about five we got under weigh, and reached Philipstad, a little town sixty miles distant, by midnight. This was our first stage, and the journey passed without a single incident on the road worth recording, save that, for the last Swedish mile into that town, the road was quite bare, for the snow was so cut up with the sledges which transport the iron ore from the mines in this neighbourhood, that we had to change our sledges for carts, the only time throughout our whole journey. The cold was intense throughout the day—in fact, the first was the worst day we had all the way up.

We had now come into the mining country, and the character of the landscape just to the north of the town where the great Persberg iron mines lie, was bleak and barren in the extreme. A mining district is always dreary enough, and as we drove by these mines in the morning, and looked down the dark yawning chasms, which we passed within a few feet, icicles twenty feet long hanging down from their sides, I fairly shuddered, for a slip of the horse's feet on the ice-covered road might have precipitated us down a pit many hundred feet deep.

The next day was a kind of holiday, a sort of "bye Sunday," of which they have many in Sweden during the course of the year; not that anybody appears to consider it a religious day, but only a sort of excuse for knocking off work and wearing their Sunday clothes. The weather was fine and clear, and as soon as we had left the iron mines a much prettier country opened upon our view; and on this day we passed through the only really deep forest on our road. The sledging was first-rate, but we made a poor day's journey, for, on arriving at a very pretty village (a thing rather unusual to see in Sweden) called Gulsjö, where we had excellent night-quarters at a first-rate inn, we discovered that my lad had lost his gun on the road, and I had to send him back to look after it. He returned at midnight, but without the gun, which had been left at Philipstad, and I recovered it afterwards with a broken stock. We left at five next morning, the air clear and frosty, 22° cold, Celsius (about 8° below zero Fahr.), and we this day passed through the finest and prettiest country we saw during our whole journey; and although now the landscape was covered with a sheet of snow, it was easy to guess what it must be in the summer. Fine, clean, well-built gentlemen's seats, iron-foundries, and neat farmhouses studded the whole face of the country; and the jolly "brukspatrons," or owners of the foundries, and the well-fed, well-clothed peasants, whom we met on the road, proved that we were now travelling through one of the richest districts in Sweden. We made about fifty miles this day, and at night slept in a very comfortable inn at a little place called Bomarsbo. We had now come into Dalecarlia, a province renowned in past ages for the loyalty, and at the present day for the industry and honesty, of its inhabitants. This is, I believe, the only province in Sweden which owns a national costume. The people are great pedlars, and go throughout the whole country with their goods; and no one can have travelled in Sweden without having met some of these stalwart fine-looking Dalecarlians, in their sheepskin coats, knee breeches, and stockings; and the cheerful, rosy-cheeked, blue-eyed Dalecarlian girls, in their Bloomer dress, with red or blue stockings, trotting merrily along with their packs on their backs.

The country was now magnificent. High mountains covered with deep forests and but little cultivated land, timber and iron being the principal riches of this district. The next day we started at daylight, and by dinner reached Fahlun, certainly the very ugliest and dirtiest little town I have ever seen in my life. It is, however, the capital town in Dalecarlia, and famous for being the site of the largest copper mines in Sweden; and as the traveller approaches the town he needs little warning to tell him he is in the vicinity of the copper mines. Every trace of vegetation has been destroyed by the noxious vapours of copper and brimstone. Large masses of stone, the accumulation of ages, are scattered over the plain in which the pits are sunk, and the fumes from the piles of ore which were then being calcined were most oppressive. I think I never saw so complete a picture of desolation as this district presented: we saw not a living creature, the occupation of the men keeping them under ground; not a bird was to be seen, and the only sound which we heard was the shrieking and groaning of the machinery from the different works. The town itself seemed plague-struck; dirty little houses, the residences of the miners, ran out in irregular streets up to the mouths of the pits; and as most of the houses in the town were covered with sheet copper, the very air was impregnated with its noisome exhalations. There was, however, a very curious old church here, with copper doors. As usual, I found out the museum, in the town, which was in a very primitive condition, and on my making inquiries of one of the professors whether he knew how many species of charr used to be met with in the lakes round here, he candidly confessed that he knew nothing at all about the charr, except that it was an excellent fish for the table. We had to pass more than half a day and a night in this very nasty disagreeable little town, for the railway train to Gefle only runs once a day, at 9 A.M., and we arrived too late to catch this. In the afternoon, for want of something to do, I walked out to inspect the site of the mines; but I will not weary the reader with a description of what I saw. If he has never seen a copper mine district he has lost very little; and if he has, he knows exactly what I saw. I believe formerly the yield of these mines was very great, something like

25,000 tons of copper yearly; now, however, it has gradually decreased to a quarter of that amount. At nine the next morning we started by the railway to Gefle, a clean, neat seaport town on the Bothnia, about sixty miles to the east, and by taking this route, instead of going by Stockholm, we saved a considerable bend. We reached Gefle by one; the train was slow and made many stoppages, but all things were conducted with as much order and regularity as on an English line. I remarked that all the engines and carriages were English. Gefle is one of the principal seaport towns in Sweden, containing about 9,000 inhabitants, well-built and clean, with neat granite quays, and presents a strange contrast to the dingy little town we had left in the morning. A good trade is carried on in the summer, both with England and America. I had two or three naturalist friends in the town, upon whom I called —one of them a keen oologist; and the sight of his cabinet, enriched with many rare Lapland eggs, given to him by the late Mr. Wooley, on his way from Lapland, only made me the more anxious to reach that (to the naturalist) "promised land." We were told now we should have no sledging, as the roads were bad, for eight Swedish miles out of the town, and such was the case. This was annoying: we had hitherto travelled comfortably enough, and our baggage rode well, for the sledges were large; and to exchange this for the shaking of the peasant's cart was not a pleasant prospect. However, luckily, a heavy fall of snow came on in the night, and next morning on waking we had the satisfaction of seeing a deep snow cover all the road, and we sledged out of the town in triumph. We were now on the straight high road to Lapland, but with above 600 dreary miles between us and Lulea.

The day was dull, the wind a cutting north-easter, and glad enough was I when, about six in the evening, we drove up to the door of the excellent " Gäst Gifure Gård" at Mo-Myske, after a short day's work of only forty miles. But we had had quite enough of it; and even had daylight served us, I could hardly have passed by this comfortable inn, which in appearance, appointment, and accommodation more nearly approached one of the jolly old roadside English inns of our youthful coaching days than I have seen out of England. We had this day passed through a flat but rather pretty country, and by the roadside I remarked two of the neatest new-built churches I have ever seen in Sweden. But at this time of the year a man does not travel in search of the picturesque; the same dull monotony pervades the whole landscape, and the traveller may well be excused in exclaiming, "All is barren." On the road we met certainly more than 100 carts laden with reindeer skins, coming down from a large fair in Lyksell Lapland.

Any one who has read Bayard Taylor's "Northern Journey" will recollect his mentioning having stopped at this very public-house, and being in a jocular mood, and thinking, as the vulgar saw has it, "to take a rise" out of the old landlord, he accosted him in Arabic. However, it seemed that two could play at that game; and to Taylor's astonishment he received an answer in the same tongue. It appears that the landlord had spent seven years in Tripoli, and, as he told Taylor afterwards, had waited twenty years in this public without ever meeting a guest with whom he could converse in the Eastern tongue. I had a great curiosity to see this old gentleman, and upon going into the kitchen on pretence of seeing my dog fed, I met one of the finest, halest, and most venerable white-headed old men I have ever seen. Had he been seated cross-legged on an ottoman, with a pipe in his mouth and a turban on his head, I could well have fancied myself in the presence of the Dey of Algiers himself. I took off my cap, and making a low salaam, accosted him with "Allah Akbar." He stared with astonishment, and exclaimed in Swedish, "What, another Arabian!" But before he could answer I addressed him in English, of which language he was perfect master—in fact, he spoke seven languages fluently. I was invited into his bar-parlour, where I dined off a capital beef-steak, and a bottle of real London porter. I found the old boy excellent company—in fact, I never spent a pleasanter evening in my life. He had evidently feathered his nest well, for his house lay at the junction of four roads, and I saw by his day-book that more than 300 horses had gone from his inn during the last month.

The next day was Sunday, and we did not leave very early, for old " Allah Akbar" would have a crack with me before I started. The country round here was much more open—in fact, much the same as Wermland, and I found that land was fully as dear. The ground was now becoming very bare, and the patches of young rye which were uncovered looked green and healthy. The horses in this district are excellent, and all the peasants seemed of a better class than those of Wermland. In our first stage from Mo-Myske the old peasant who drove my sledge was a very chatty, intelligent, inquisitive old man, and hearing that I was English, was very curious to know something of " Ye manners and customes of ye English." We conversed on various topics, till at length we touched upon religion ; and after a long controversy the old gentleman turned suddenly round, and to my astonishment asked me how we *swore* in English. As he was very pressing I gave him a specimen of "the nucleus of England's native eloquence." He seemed to think it not half energetic enough, and he then treated me also to a Swedish oath almost as long and bitter as the oath of excommunication in Sterne's "Tristram Shandy." After allowing me a minute or so to see what effect it would have upon me, he triumphantly turned round and observed, "There, that's *grim*, isn't it? You can't swear like that in England;" and truly I could have almost said with my Uncle Toby—"I could scarce have found it in my heart to curse the devil so."

As we entered a little village about sundown this evening, I was struck by seeing something flaming red on the roadside in the distance before us, and on coming up we overtook two pretty little girls, dressed in full fig—pork-pie hats, and short crimson cloaks; much after the fashion, I should suppose, of the two young ladies in Regent Street, whose pugnacious father wrote to the *Times* a short time back, denouncing vengeance on some one or other unknown, who had insulted the young ladies by staring at them. Much as such a costume might have been out of place in Regent Street, it seemed doubly so in these wilds, and, having no fear of Paterfamilias before our eyes, we had a good stare at the young damsels. They were worth looking at, and they seemed to know it; their red healthy cheeks, bright eyes, and scarlet cloaks, were quite refreshing to our eyes after having gazed so long on nothing but dark pines and snow-covered fields. Whoever set the fashion I can't say, but I observed that there was quite a run upon these pork-pie hats up here; and to crown all, I saw right up at Quickiock a great chubby Lap boy with one stuck upon his bullet head.

We did not make more than forty miles this day, and at night we slept at a small roadside public-house where the accommodation was very inferior to that of Mo-Myskie.

From Mo-Myskie the road branches off to Soderhamn, another of the small seaports which stand on the shores of the Bothnia; but we avoided this town, and kept the straight road on to Sundswall. We reached one stage beyond Hudiskwall the day we left Mo-Myskie, and the little village we slept in was called "Sanna." The morning we left Sanna was dreary and chill, and the cold throughout the whole day intense. We intended to reach Sundswall that night, which we did about 11 P.M., after passing through a flat but barren and wooded country, no incident on the road worth recording—in fact, our journey the whole way up was about as monotonous as can well be imagined. The last stage into Sundswall was two and a half Swedish miles, nearly the whole way over ice, on a bight in the Bothnia; and of all the trotters I ever sat behind in Sweden, I think the little mare that I had for this stage was the best. She was a little, scratching, lop-eared, vicious-looking thing, with a mouth like iron, and the peasant who drove me said it was no use trying to hold her; so, wrapping the rope reins round his wrist, he just let her go her own pace. Having no watch I could not time her, but, when we reached Sundswall, I looked at the clock, and our second sledge came in just three-quarters of an hour after us, and yet she upset us three times on the road! However, a roll in the snow breaks no bones, for, as the old song has it,

> "There's more to be feared from a slip on the green,
> Than a fall on a frozen river."

I am certain we must have done the distance well under the hour, and this with a mare which no one in England, to buy her by her looks, would have given a five-pound note for. The chap who drove me said that he would willingly take £7 for her.

When we got to Sundswall she was neither "sick nor sorry;" he never took her from the sledge, but let her stand and pick a bit of hay which he had brought with him; and when he started to go home, off she went at the same pace. Truly these little Swedish horses must be as hardy as their native mountains.

On leaving Sundswall in the morning, at daybreak, a heavy snow was falling, but it was not cold (about 8° Celsius). The country now became more rugged and wild, but yet nothing like Lap scenery; in fact, the whole country by the side of the Bothnia is flat, and the forests small. Further in from the coast the forests are deeper, and the timber heavier; but it is not until one travels many miles inland, and reaches the great dividing fell range between Sweden and Norway, that the traveller sees anything like real Lap scenery. Sundswall seemed to be a pretty little town, and does a brisk summer trade in timber. The country round is little adapted for agriculture, and they have to bring nearly all their provisions from Stockholm. Living is consequently dear, and the price of provisions increases the further we come north. A drove of Laps had wandered as far down as Sundswall in the winter, and camped for some time with their reindeer close to the town. In the afternoon we passed through Hernosand, a clean, well-built little town, but we pushed on twelve miles further, and at nightfall reached a little place called "Wedga," situate on the great Angerman river, which is here nearly two English miles broad. On crossing this, next morning a new scene broke upon our view; the country became wilder and wilder, and, in the summer, must be as beautiful as any in Europe. Mountains, clothed with forests, overtopped each other, and the deep gullies which lay between them forcibly reminded me of Australia. I was struck with the fine gentlemen's houses which we saw by the roadside; while furnaces and water-mills denoted the mineral and timber wealth of this part of Sweden. Sweden is, indeed, a grand country, and there must be some great mismanagement that a land with such internal wealth should be so poor.

Although the country around seemed little adapted to agriculture, they do manage to grow some wheat and rye, both of which must be sown by the middle of June. I saw sheep at nearly every place where we stopped, and at one observed a primitive and curious mode of threshing. The corn is spread out on the floor of a long, narrow shed, and a horse draws a kind of machine, very much resembling a patent clod-crusher, backwards and forwards, which knocks out the grain. A great deal of linseed is sown here, which, when cut, is not carried into the house, but hung up to dry on the cross-bars of what appears to be a gigantic six-barred gate, about twenty feet high. We now began to see fire-places in all the cow-byres; and on this day I noticed the last gooseberry tree, which appeared to grow further north in the gardens than any other fruit. The country appeared to be well peopled, and the peasants well fed and clothed. At a little village, called Akstå, we passed by the most curious little church I ever saw, and close by it a house, with, I am sure, as many windows in it as there are days in the year. The last twelve miles of our journey, this day, lay over a bay by the side of the Bothnia; and it was here that we saw the first drove of reindeer. There were about 400 of them, attended by a Lap family, all on "skiddor," or snow-skates; and they were seeking pasture. Their little sledges, spears —in fact, all their worldly gear—were piled up together on the ice. The men were wild, gipsy-looking fellows, by no means so small as I had expected to see. They formed altogether a wild, picturesque group, which I longed for an artist's talent to depict. They told us to hurry on, for the reindeer were fast heading to the fells—a sure sign that spring was at hand. This was by far the worst night we were out in, for we faced a cutting north-east wind, and the drifting snow nearly blinded us. By midnight we reached our night-quarters, at a little place called Hornäs, so completely frozen, that my legs and arms were paralyzed. We were half an hour before we could knock the people up, and when we did get in there was no fire in our room, and no supper to be had. So we just cast ourselves on the bed in our clothes, and lay till morning. Any shelter was better than being out on so wild a night. I quite pitied the peasant lad who had to take our sledges back, but he did not seem to care a pin, and he had no great-coat. In the night the weather completely changed; and when we started in the morning it was as mild as spring. I saw the first northern jay this day. By breakfast we arrived at a little sea-port, called Ornskoldsvik—certainly one of the prettiest little places (half town and half village) we passed through on our road up; and in summer it must much resemble one of the secluded little bathing villages we see on the English coast. It seemed quite an oasis in the desert, and the only wonder is how such a sweet little spot ever got into this wilderness. I ferreted out a jolly baker here, who understood a little English, of whom we bought some pork for the road, for which we paid 9d. per lb. (the price in Wermland is 3d.) But, if pork was dear, game was cheap enough: the price they asked for a large capercailzied cock being 1s., and for a willow grouse 2d.

We now began to see at every station that

peculiar breed of thick-coated dogs, whose skins are valued so much in the north for lining cloaks or "pells." They appear to be peculiar to this district, are not unlike an Esquimaux dog in appearance, but the coat is very fine and thick, and of a rich black-brown colour. They are evidently a very different race from the little prick-eared, mangy-looking curs which the Laps use to guard their reindeer; nor are they identical with the little, stumpy, pointed-nosed, curly-tailed bear-dogs, which show such sagacity and pluck in the chase of old Bruin. They all appeared to be in excellent condition, as sleek as moles, but seem to be of little or no use when living. There is something very repulsive in the idea, especially to a sportsman, in fattening so faithful and useful a companion as the dog to slaughter him merely for the sake of the skin. We slept this night at a little place called Lefuar, in certainly the finest inn we had entered on the road, with carpeted floors (a thing most unusual even in the Swedish gentlemen's houses), and a travellers' room, furnished as well as any parlour in England. In fact, the further north, the better appeared to be the inns; but none came up to this. They, however, did not forget to charge, and I paid 2s. for a bottle of English porter. The last stage into Lefuar was about nine English miles; and as we were waiting for our sledges, a gentleman who was just starting for that place politely offered me a seat in his sledge. This I gladly accepted, as much for the sake of the company as anything, and we started long before the other sledge was ready (which, by the way, was driven by a remarkably handsome peasant girl; and this circumstance probably accounted for my mates not reaching Lefuar till nearly two hours after myself). Arrived at Lefuar, I could not do less than stand a bottle of punch for my ride, for I could not think of offering post money to a gentleman. When the bottle was out, I thought he would go home, for the sledge stood at the door, and he lived a short distance from the inn. However, he loitered about the room; so, fancying he would like to "wet the other eye," I proposed another half bottle, which, however, he refused, but remarked that it was the post-money (1s. 8d.) which he was waiting for. This would have seemed strange in England; but these sons of the north are "practical men." I remember, in my day, that the rule of the road at home used to be that the odd man should pay "the pikes" for his ride; and as there are no toll-bars here, I reckoned the punch instead.

When we left next morning at day-break, although the thermometer only showed 2° of cold, Celsius ($28\frac{1}{2}$° Fahr.), the wind was more cutting and bitter than ever I remember it, and, coming from the N.E., we had it right in our teeth. But we had a good sign that mild weather was at hand, in the blackcock, which sat perched in the birch-trees by the roadside, and would scarcely fly away, although we drove close by them, very different from their wild habits, when they are waiting for cold. I saw two woodlarks fly over, and I observed a sparrow with a straw in his beak, evidently nesting. The country was barren, the woods stunted, and the landscape wore the same monotonous aspect throughout the whole day. At a small road-side station we got three cups of coffee and a large basin of warm bread-and-milk (the very best thing to travel on in cold weather), for 4*d*. In the afternoon we passed through Umeä, a little, dirty old town, with a remarkably fine white church, and the largest prison I have seen in the north. I take it, neither are ever full. We had now above 150 dreary miles before us ere we reached the next town, Piteä. We pushed on this day, and did our seventy miles, for the roads were getting bad, and I was much afraid that the frost was breaking up. In fact, many of the little trout streams which we crossed were open in places; and I must say, often, when we were sledging over the ice, I felt very ill at ease; for the ice always begins to thaw under the water, and in patches, so that, although it appears perfectly safe to the eye, a sledge may pop through without any previous warning; and then, where are you? I care nothing for open water; but I have a great fear of being taken under the ice. I think no journey can be so dreary as over a frozen lake—perhaps six English miles—the monotony of the view only broken by the fir branches, which are stuck up on each side to mark the line of road. Many lives are yearly lost in the north, just when the ice is breaking up; and the recklessness of these peasants at this time is past belief. At midnight we reached a little village called Deckneboda, where we got capital night-quarters, and our whole expenses not more than 2s. When we left at five next morning we found that it had frozen hard in the night, and the snow carried well. Bad horses, however, throughout the whole day; the country flat and ugly; and I was not sorry when at night we pulled up at a little village called Bureä, after having done our fifty English miles. The cold was intense, and I quite envied the hardihood of the little peasant lads who drove us. *They* had no fur cloaks or comforters—sometimes no gloves—and yet they were merry and cheerful, and their little cheeks looked as rosy as apples. Bad as the conveyances may be, it would be hard to find a more careful or better class of drivers than these lads. They have a curious fashion up here—no whips, but the reins about six feet longer than is necessary. This answers all the purpose of a whip; and that horse must indeed be a slug who won't spring when he feels this drawn across his quarters. The next day was Sunday. The sun rose bright and clear; the country became prettier; and as we neared Sunnäna the splendid white church of Skellefteä—which place lies on the other side of the river—burst suddenly upon our view. The fine, deep-toned bell was tolling for church; groups of well-dressed peasants were standing round the door, and all at once thoughts of youth and home flashed across my mind, and I could hardly suppress a sigh as I thought in how far different a manner, and among what far different scenes, the quiet Sabbath morning of twenty years ago was spent. We breakfasted at Sunnäna on reindeer flesh, reindeer cheese, and a bottle of real Burton ale. I crossed the river to Skellefteä, to call upon an old naturalist friend in that town. It was nearly half an English mile across, and, seeing a large crack in the ice, I had the curiosity to measure its thickness. My stick showed four feet and I did not touch water, for the crack did not go quite through the ice; and this was on the 5th of April, when, I suppose, at home they were gathering cowslips and violets, and thinking that the hedges were getting too blind for hunting. The sledging was now becoming very bad, for less snow had fallen here this year than usual, and all the fields by the roadside were bare. We saw very little arable land, nothing but rough tussocky meadows, filled with little sheds or barns, in which they put the hay when it is made. This is a good plan, for it is much easier to bring it home in the winter on sledges than in the summer. As soon as we left Skellefteä the country again became flat and ugly; a deep snow set in towards the afternoon, and, had there been anything worth seeing by the roadside we could not have seen it, for we were quite blinded by the falling snow. We did little more than forty miles this day, and at night slept at Iäful, where we had humble but very comfortable night quarters. We were now only about twelve miles from Piteä, and less than fifty from Luleä, which town we meant to reach by the following night.

Next morning, when we left, we found that a deep snow had fallen in the night, and the sledging was first-rate. We reached Piteä by breakfast time —a dingy, little, old town, with neither a barber nor a bookseller in it, both of whom I much wanted to consult. There was, however, as good an inn here as any country inn in England, and

English porter and reindeer venison was our bill of fare. As usual, the coffee-room was filled with well-dressed men, though the hour was early. It seems to me that all the business in these little country towns is transacted in the public-houses. We pushed on through a country remarkable for nothing but its ugliness, and reached New Luleä (which lies a Swedish mile nearer to the sea than the old town) by three in the afternoon. It is a curious fact, but it appears that the waters of the Bothnia have so much receded, that the old town of Luleä, which now stands a Swedish mile from the new town, was at one time the port, and the sea then was had over the site of the present town of New Luleä. When we set off I had hardly made up my mind which part of Lapland I would visit; but, as I had an introduction to a good old doctor in Luleä, who knew Lapland well, I determined to act upon his advice. When I called upon him in the evening, he strongly recommended Quickiock as easy of approach, and a good station for the naturalist. For Quickiock, therefore, I determined to steer. This place lies about two hundred English miles due west from Luleä, right under the great dividing fell range between Norway and Sweden. We rested the whole day in Luleä, and we needed it, as we had now been fifteen days on the road. Nothing much to see in this little town. We made the acquaintance here of a jolly sporting parson, who had the cure of Old Luleä, and we called and breakfasted with him on our way up to Quickiock next morning. They have a corps of sharpshooters up here, and I saw a stand of very fair rifles at the house of the parish clerk, who is chief of the company. The country around Luleä looked flat and dreary, the forests stunted and small; in fact, I was altogether disappointed with the landscape the whole way up—nothing at all like what I imagined Lap scenery would be. But, hold hard! we are hardly in Lapland yet.

It was a lovely morning when we left Luleä, and our whole day's journey lay over the ice. As yet we had no trouble about horses, for our road had all along been on the king's highway, and the postmasters up were bound to furnish us with horses at day-book price. But when we reached a little village called Boden, about twenty-eight miles from Luleä the posting ended, and we were then obliged to trust to the civility of the peasant to furnish us with horses. Boden is the post town for Iockmock and Quickiock; the post comes from Luleä twice a week to Boden; goes from Boden to Iockmock every fortnight, and from Iockmock to Quickiock once a month. In winter the post is carried by a man on skiddor, in the summer it is rowed in a boat; and although the letters are carried in this precarious manner for 180 miles, you never hear of one being lost, and as to a mail robbery, such a thing is never dreamt of. We were now obliged to pay a little more for our horses; in fact, it was only by sufferance that we obtained them at all, and what surprised me was that the peasants did not " claw " us more (to use an expressive Swedish term), for we were totally dependent on them, and unless they furnished horses, must have stayed where we were. I am certain in Britain we should not have come off so cheap. However, by the aid of a little "soft sawder," which goes a long way with a northern peasant, and an intimation that we were on a visit to the priest at Iockmock, we managed pretty well. The word "priest" has a talismanic effect upon these peasants. The day was dull and cold, but the sledging capital. We made fifty English miles, and the last twelve were about the best of our journey, for the horses were fresh and the whole distance over the frozen Luleä river. Still no signs of Lapland. But now the peasants all began to speak Lap, and this day we had the first specimen of a Lap settler's cottage; and very neat and clean it was, with a carpet on the floor. We slept at a place called "Suart Lo" at a peasant's house, and paid 2s. for our night's quarters. When we reached the house night had set in, and the full moon was riding high in a cloudless sky as blue as steel, the snow on the river glistening in its soft beams as if millions of diamonds were scattered over it. It was a lovely scene—the high forest-covered mountains frowning over the river, " for the whole appearance of the country was fast becoming wilder and more rugged," and, as first impressions are always most lasting, so my first night in Luleä-Lapland will long be remembered after many others are forgotten. There is a large iron foundry here belonging to the great Gellivare mines, which lie about one hundred miles to the north, and as I had an introduction to the manager we had no difficulty in getting horses for the first twelve miles from here. Two days more of the same monotonous travelling brought us to Iockmock, which place we did not reach until the morning of the 12th, for we met with a most unaccommodating settler on the road, who would only let us have one horse; so we piled the baggage in a sledge, and walked twelve miles by its side. We could not, therefore, reach Iockmock that night, but slept on the road. Just round Iockmock the forests were deeper and better timbered than any we had seen since we left Sundswall; in fact, the whole character of the landscape was becoming more like Lapland. A lot of Laps were quartered in the cottage where we slept, with their reindeer camped outside; and in the evening our room was filled with them, for they all flocked in to have a look at the foreigners. Our host was a very nice old settler, and we had comfortable quarters. We reached Iockmock by twelve next day. We had now only about eighty miles further, and our journey was done. It was winter market at Iockmock, and the place was crowded with Laps, who had come down to sell their skins, etc., and buy their summer necessaries; and I had a very good opportunity of observing the habits of these little vagabonds when they were out for a spree, and it is needless to say that two-thirds of them were drunk, for, like all other bushmen, who, perhaps, never see a glass of spirits for six months, they do not lose their time when they come down to a town or a place where spirits are to be got.

It would be scarcely worth while to waste much space in a description of the Laplanders. Every child of ten years old must be familiar with their dress and their habits, from what he has read; but I may add that the original Lap, in his frowzy old reindeer pells and dirty old peaked blue cap, scarcely realizes the idea that we have formed of the Laplander whom we have seen depicted in story books. In the winter their whole dress is formed of reindeer-skin, except the cap, which, in all we saw, was high, and peaked like a sugar-loaf, and of blue cloth. But I believe the Laps of each district have their peculiar dress. Men and women dress nearly alike; and as in both the straight hair flows lankily down the back and sides of the head, and as I never observed any beards or whiskers among them, it is hard at first sight to distinguish a man from a woman. The dress is rather in Bloomer style—a short skin coat, generally with the hair outside, buckled round the middle, and a pair of tanned reindeer breeches, which fit tight round their spindled shanks (and many a London groom would give a year's wages if he could only sport a Laplander's leg). These breeches are fastened round the ankle, and a pair of tanned reindeer boots, fashioned much like a Chinese shoe, with peaked and turned-up toes, are drawn over them; and a long list thong, wound thickly round the top of the boot, renders them nearly perfectly waterproof. What surprised me was, that in the depth of winter their necks are always bare; and this is the case generally throughout Sweden. They wear no stockings, but in lieu thereof these boots, which are roomy, and stuffed full of soft hay. This keeps their feet always warm; and the soles being rather pliable, no shoe in the world could be better adapted for climbing the rugged fells. Body linen I don't believe they wear; but I never examined one to see. They have splendid gloves, like mittens, some of them ornamented with great taste. The summer dress is much after the same fashion, only the material, at least of the coat (for both men and women stick to the skin breeches all the year round), is of a coarse blue cloth—in the richer Laps ornamented with silver braid. A pair of long snow-skates, or "skiddor" (without which the Lap could do nothing in winter); a spear, with a four-edged spike a foot long, as sharp in the edges as a razor, on a stout six-foot aspen shaft; an old skin knapsack on his back, which holds his provisions and all his small personal gear; a rude case-knife at his side, and a little iron pipe in his mouth—form the Laplander's winter equipment. The sledges very much resemble a small boat cut off in the middle—just large enough to hold one; and although I suppose they know their own business best, I fancied I never saw worse-planned harness than that which fastens the reindeer to these sledges, for they have no shafts, and the driver seems not to have the slightest power of guiding his animal; and if you asked a Lap, at starting, which way he was going, he might well answer you like the Cambridge youth when he mounted his tandem— "Can't tell—ask my leader." The driver is obliged to have a short pole in his hand like a sprit, to keep the sledge on its balance, which goes jolting along, now over on one side, now on the other; and what with steering his reindeer and keeping his sledge upright, he has plenty to do. He is so packed in with skins, that he is part and parcel of the sledge, and if he upsets he can't roll out. It is rare fun to see, when a sledge does go over, how viciously the reindeer turns round to attack the driver, or sets off at full speed, dragging sledge and man along in one confused heap through the snow, in spite of all the latter's oaths and imprecations, which a foreign tongue appears to the English ear to make "still more horrid and awful." I never rode in one of the sledges, and when I saw the Laps start from Iockmock, on their homeward journey to the fells, I did not fancy that I had lost much.

There was nothing picturesque in the appearance of Iockmock, seen as it was by us in its winter dress; but when we returned in the summer it looked very different. A cluster of little, low wooden houses stuck up here and there without any regularity, and half the village seemed to consist of empty sheds for the accommodation of the Laps when they come down from their distant homes to the church three or four times in the year. The parish of Iockmock is twenty Swedish miles long and three broad, so that many of the Laps and settlers have far to come to church; and this is the case with most of these northern parishes, for between Umeä and Piteä we passed peasants' carts on the Friday afternoon travelling to church on the following Sunday. The northern peasant is not over religious, but there are certain holy days in the year when he would as soon miss his dinner as his visit to the church, and then no distance stops him.

The church at Iockmock was a curious, eight-cornered, old wooden building, and close to it stood the "watch-house." What on earth they could want for such a building in this wild track I could not make out, certainly not to put the drunken Laps in, for the church would scarcely have held them.

We took up our quarters with the priest, a real, nice little specimen of a Lap pastor. He had been located in Lapland forty years, and his whole little world seemed truly to be centred in this rude spot. Save one journey down to Luleä, he told me he had never left Iockmock, for, as the poor old man observed, "travelling is expensive. I can't go down to Luleä and back under 50s." Still he seemed happy and contented, and if it is true that a man's children are his greatest riches in this world, and that he is most happy who "has his quiver full of them," I take it my old friend must have been among the happiest of mortals, for he had managed not only to bring into the world, but respectably to bring up, eighteen children on an income of perhaps less than £50 a year, and a finer, healthier sample than those which he had at home I never saw. I did not indulge my curiosity so far as to inquire exactly what his real income might be, but he told me that in his parish were about eighty Laps, each family of whom pay him yearly two pairs of gloves, 20lb. of reindeer meat, two squirrel-skins, and a reindeer cheese. Besides this, he had his house and a little bit of land, and I suppose what few settlers there are in his parish all pay him a trifle.

Musing on the inequality of earthly riches, I strolled down the village street in the afternoon, and, as I saw all the Laps hurrying towards the church, I thought I might as well look in also, and here I saw a sight which I would not have missed for a trifle. Although not Sunday, there was a kind of bye-service on this afternoon, for the special benefit of the Laps who would wish to receive the sacrament before they departed to their native fells.

The church was full of Laps, and, although here and there I saw as fine a young fellow as I would wish to meet, the major part of them were little, brown, weather-beaten pigmies, standing about five feet nothing, all clad in real Lap costume. Has it ever been the reader's luck to attend a benefit at a low fighting-house in London, and take a note of the countenances of the smaller class of fighting men who form the principal actors in the scene? If so, he can form a very good idea of the general character of Lap physiognomy. One and all seem to have been cast in the same pugilistic mould—bullet heads, high cheek-bones, low foreheads, bright sunken eyes, and flattened noses. In fact, if they had only been cropped close, and dressed in tight trowsers and Newmarket coats, I would have challenged all London to have picked out a bunch of more thoroughpaced-looking little blackguards than I could have collected from this congregation. The women were ranged in pews on one side, the men on the other (and this is the fashion in all the Swedish churches), and, except that the former kept their high-peaked sugar-loafed caps on during the service, you could see little difference between the two. None of these ladies could boast of much personal attraction—their countenances being exactly like those of the men, and quite as brown and knotty. But there was one face, which peeped down from the gallery, from which I could hardly take my eyes, and which even haunts me to this day. It was that of a little flaxen-haired Lap girl, about seven years

F

old, and a sweeter or more cherub-looking face I never set my eyes on, and the little blue-peaked cap, braided with silver, perched jauntily on her head, gave a lively kind of expression to perhaps the sweetest face I ever saw in my life. I never yet saw a child so beautiful as this wild Lap, and a painter might have made his fortune if he could only have transferred the expression of that countenance to his canvas. Certainly there can be no truth in breeding if such a little angel came from the rough stock that filled the body of this church. The service passed off quietly enough—the communion began, and a curious sight it was to see these little vagabonds run along the tops of the pews, like so many rats on a plank, in hot haste to reach the altar; and now commenced a scene such as I never witnessed in the house of God, and trust I shall never witness again. It seems that within the last few years a kind of fanaticism has crept in among these Laps, and the word of God, instead of "pouring oil upon a bruised spirit," as everyone is taught to believe who will read the Scriptures aright, only fills them with imaginary terrors, and, far different from the creed of the real Christian, they seem to think the best atonement they can make for their sins lies in outward show. I have seen a little of this kind of humbug in other churches in Sweden, where at certain parts of the service the women all commence groaning and sobbing so loud that you can scarcely hear the clergyman. This, however, soon passes off, and is scarcely worth notice. These Laps, however, must have been far more susceptible, or far more wicked, for all at once, when the communion service began, two or three women sprung up in different parts of the church, and commenced frantically jumping, howling, shrieking, and clapping their hands. I observed one middle-aged female particularly energetic, and who sank down in a kind of fit after about ten minutes' exertion. The infection soon spread, and in a few minutes two-thirds of the congregation "joined in the cry," and all order was at an end. Five or six would cluster round one individual, hugging, kissing, weeping, and shrieking till I really thought some would be smothered. One old patriarch in particular, who sat close behind me, seemed an object of peculiar veneration, and the Laps crowded from all parts of the church to hug him. How he stood it I can't imagine; but he sat meekly enough, and at one time I counted no less than seven "miserable sinners" hanging about the old man, all shrieking and weeping. The religious orgies of the wild aborigines in Australia round their camp fire are not half so frightful as this scene, for they at least do not desecrate a place of worship with their mad carousals. As the Yorkshireman would say, "I fairly *trimbled*" lest my turn should come next; or I might even have been regarded as a heathen by these poor deluded wretches (for I was a foreigner and did not communicate), and there is no saying to what excesses their fanaticism might have led them. I had quietly ensconced myself in a comfortable pew furthest from the door, and to *bolt* would have been impossible. Strange as it may appear to the English reader, I must say I felt great satisfaction in having my revolver in my pea-jacket pocket; and my fears were not altogether groundless, for it is not long ago that the Laps, in just such a fit of fanaticism as this, barbarously murdered one if not two settlers up at the altar, flogged the priest nearly to death with willow rods, and would have taken his life if assistance had not arrived. Meanwhile, during all this uproar, the priest went on with the communion service as if nothing was taking place, the clerk and the choristers kept up their monotonous chants amid such an uproar as I'll be bound to say was never before heard in a place of worship. I would give something to see the countenance of a fashionable London beadle if the spirit was suddenly to move his congregation in this way; and if it is true, as these fanatics tell us, that when the spirit moves them they can't help it, such a scene is as likely to occur in St. George's, Hanover-square, as in this wild Lap church. Had they been drunk I should not have been much surprised, but they all appeared perfectly sober; and it only proves how dreadfully religious fanaticism can work upon the human mind when we see it convert these Laps—probably the most apathetic and cold-blooded race under the sun—into a lot of maniacs. The riot never once ceased till the service had ended; and I must confess that I felt well pleased when I found myself once again outside the door of the church. The priest told me that this fashion had only crept upon these Laps within the last few years.

We stayed at Iockmock over the Sunday; and, as we were now only about eighty miles from Quickiock, we hired horses for one rixdaler per mile to take us through the whole distance. We left on the Monday morning. Our whole day's journey lay over ice, and, after passing through a wild but far prettier country than we had yet seen, we came at night to a place called Granudden, about half way, where we slept. We paid 3s. 6d. for our night's lodging, supper, and breakfast. The lodging was very comfortable, and the people civil and obliging—in fact, we found this the case the whole way up. The next morning was mild but hazy. The loud, hoarse cackle of the ripa was heard in every wood, and the Siberian jay was now our constant companion. Spring was evidently fast setting in. When we left in the morning I saw something indistinctly looming in front of us, in the distant horizon, which I at first took to be huge masses of cloud, but my driver, pointing with his whip, exclaimed, "There are the fells!" Just now the mist cleared away, and the distant snowfells gradually became more distinct, rising above each other like huge billows of ice upon a frozen sea. I now felt that I was in Lapland; that I had realized the heartfelt wish of years; and that I had at length reached a country possessing more attractions to the naturalist than perhaps any other in Europe. The nearer we approached Quickiock the grander became the scenery; and now Waldi Speken—the highest fell in this range—towered many hundred feet above the rest, like an enormous sugar-loaf. It was perhaps the sudden manner in which these fells appeared to burst upon the view that added much to the grandeur; and I will fairly confess that, for once in my life, reality far exceeded anticipation.

No steeple-chase rider ever looked more anxiously over the course which he is about to cross than my lad and myself did over the country as we neared Quickiock. "Let's see the field and mark it well, for here will be the battle." This was to be our station for months. We knew nothing of the fauna of the district, and it remained to be proved what rarities we should find in the solitudes of the forests and fells in which this little village is embedded. The country certainly looked unpromising at present. The woods were small, and the huge snow-capped fells rising above the limits of all vegetation, seemed to offer no fitting home for any other bird than the ptarmigan; but we little imagined how the whole face of the country would change as by magic when spring once fairly set in, for it seemed to us almost an impossibility that in a few weeks these huge snow masses would " dissolve in silent dew," and the river which we were now crossing over a coat of ice four feet thick would be all open water.

About three we drove up to the little village of Quickiock, and our long, monotonous journey was at an end. The village itself has not much to boast of except its naturally beautiful situation, which in summer is about as romantic as can well be imagined. Four dwelling-houses constitute the whole village, but, as is always the case in the north, there are so many outhouses, sheds, and buildings, attached to each dwelling, that one house with its offices seems to form half a village.

Nothing can be uglier than the generality of the northern villages, and it really seems as if man tried all he could to mar the beauty of the landscape when he sets up his dwelling-house here. The farm-houses are in general low, built of wood, painted either a flaming red colour, or else miserably dilapidated, and the roof or thatch scarcely ever in repair. The out-houses, cow-houses, barns, granaries, etc., are all huddled together, stuck here, there, and everywhere, without the slightest order; and those offices which in general we endeavour in England to keep as much out of sight as possible, always in the most conspicuous place, often right in front of the parlour window. Quickiock was no exception to the general rule. There is a little more fashion about the gentlemen's houses, some of which for neatness of building and the taste in which the grounds are laid out, would equal any in England; but even here the condition and position of the outhouses often spoils the effect. The country around Quickiock in the summer is perhaps as beautiful as any in Lapland, for the village lies in a valley on the banks of a magnificent river, surrounded on all sides by forests and fells. But there is as much difference between Quickiock in its winter dress and Quickiock in its summer dress as there is between a withered old French dowager in her morning dishabille and curl-papers, and the same old lady "figged" out in the evening in opera costume. The fells do not, however, long wear their summer livery, and the Spaniard was perhaps not so far wrong when he described the climate of the north as six months white winter, three months black winter, and three months green winter.

The dull haze of a winter's afternoon (for although it was the middle of April it was just as much winter here as December in England) hung over the village, and the whole prospect looked cheerless enough as we drove on the ice up to the priest's house, which was to be our head-quarters for the season. We had now come as far into the country as we could on sledge, and we could not have travelled a Swedish mile further if we had wished, anyhow except on foot.

To sum up our journey, we left Gardsjö on March 24, and reached Quickiock on April 16, having been little more than three weeks on the road; and although the journey at this time of the year is very monotonous, with but little change of scene, it was far less troublesome than I had imagined it would have been. We met with every attention on the road, and good night-quarters and excellent provisions wherever we stopped. The distance in all was a little more than 1,000 English miles. About fifty miles per day was our general journey, and although we could perhaps have done a little more by travelling at night, it was hardly worth our while. It certainly was sad crawling work, and I suppose old Mountjoy in his best day would have walked up in less time. I reckoned that the expenses of the three and the dog averaged 6*s.* per day, and the posting came to about 1*s.* 2*d.* the Swedish mile for each sledge. Altogether the journey up cost us near £25. The horses and sledging were pretty good throughout. Luckily we had no rain, but the cold at times was intense. We had scarcely an incident on the road worth recording, and the scenery through which we passed on the whole journey may be summed up in three words, " Snow and pines." We found the posting stations in the north far superior to those in the middle of Sweden, and the living appeared to become better the further north we came.

I could not help remarking how very few birds of any description we saw on our road up—one Ural owl, one blackcock, and one Siberian jay were all that we shot, and we always had a loaded gun ready in the sledge, but neither heard of nor saw a single wolf.

We got capital quarters in the priest's house at the rate of one rixdaler banco, or 1*s.* 8*d.* per day for each man.

CHAPTER IV.

LAPLAND.

As we are now in Lapland, before I touch upon the natural history of the country, I will make a few remarks on life in Lapland in general.

When I set off for my Lap trip, I had made my mind up to two things—the first was that we should have to "rough it," and live upon bark bread and reindeer cheese; the other, that our living would cost next to nothing, and that one rixdaler would go further in these wild regions than two in Wermland. In both these surmises I was egregiously mistaken. Nowhere in Sweden have I found better quarters than with the priest at Quickiock (in fact, all things were far too fine for a collector, whose room can never be kept clean); but nowhere, except in towns, have I found living dearer, or paid so much for a day's wages to men whom I had to help me. 3s. per day was the wages I paid to men up here to do the same work as the Wermland peasant will for 1s. 1s. 8d. a day for board and lodging does not seem much to an Englishman—nor is it; but I can live equally well in Wermland for 1s.: and as our principal fare here consisted of game and fish, which were to be had for the fetching, it was quite enough. It is true groceries were dear, as all have to be brought up from Luleå, and rye may be quoted as dear again as in Wermland. As to bark bread, I never saw it; and reindeer cheese we scarcely ever tasted.

And now the reader must bear in mind that, although I am giving him an idea of life in Lapland, I perhaps saw as little of Lapland as any man who has travelled up there. I was obliged to be stationary in one spot the whole time. I rarely wandered more than three Swedish miles from Quickiock, and my occupation kept me much indoors, for I skinned more than 1,000 specimens during four months, besides collecting a great many eggs and butterflies. My hints are therefore chiefly intended to assist any naturalist who, like myself, wishes to visit Lapland, and remain stationary in one spot for the purpose of collecting, more than for the man who pays a flying visit to the country merely for the purpose of seeing the land and the character of its inhabitants.

As to living, our bill of fare for the table was not very varied. While the snow lay on the ground we lived on dried reindeer venison and ptarmigan, both about as dry and tough as a gamekeeper's old leather gaiter; and when the river opened we tasted nothing but fish until the young ducks came in. Fresh meat—such as beef or mutton—we never saw. It is true the fish were of the best kind—trout, charr, and gwynniad; and, doubtless, a London alderman would vote such a bill of fare as "none so bad;" but, *toujours perdrix*. Moreover, everything was plain boiled, and we scarcely ever got a vegetable. A good cook might have made something out of such materials; but condiments of all kinds, save salt, were wanting; and I should strongly recommend every English traveller who visits these remote regions to bring up with him a little Cayenne pepper and a bottle of "Burgess's Original;" and, above all, if he be a smoker, to provide himself with some real cavendish before leaving England, for, of all the bad tobacco which I ever smoked, that which we procured at Quickiock was the worst—in fact, the Swedish tobacco in general, although cheap, is not good; for you must put up either with a sort of stuff which has no real tobacco flavour, but smokes like chopped hay, or with a strong, rank, roll tobacco, such as the peasants chew and smoke. We had plenty of good coffee (with excellent milk and cream); and this and cold water—certainly the clearest and purest I ever drank in my life—formed our "every-day drain." Strange to say, I never saw a drop of "the cratur" the whole while I was at Quickiock. The good old doctor in Luleä strongly recommended us to freight up a few bottles of cognac, and take a "nip" every morning, to keep the raw fell air out of our stomachs, and as an excellent preventive against "diarrhœa," which, he said, was very prevalent in Lapland; but *I* knew, from old experience, how long such a kind of medicine would last in the bush, and how apt the stomach is to be out of order with so palatable a remedy at hand: so I took up instead a pound of English salts, which was recommended as a secondary specific, and, strange to say, I was never once asked for a dram, and I left them behind just as I brought them up. I wonder how it would have been with a case of French brandy!

It is all very well to visit Lapland for a few summer months, and know that you can leave the country when you are tired of it; but, somehow or other, I should not like to live here my whole life. The same monotonous scenery. North, south, east, and west, the view was shut in by barren fells, the tops of most of them covered with perennial snows. It is strange how soon one tires of this kind of wild scenery. There are pastoral landscapes in Old England upon which one is never weary of gazing; and even if a man's life be spent among them, he can always find some new feature in the landscape which he never descried before: but not so with the rugged scenery of the far north. The first time such a scene bursts upon the traveller's view it leaves an impression which he probably never forgets; but the effect is sadly lessened the second time he sees it; and, as the novelty wears off, the landscape appears to lose half its charms. Moreover, the monotony of such a life, shut out, as it were, from the rest of the world, with a seven months' winter, during which you can't stir out of doors unless you can use the "skiddor," with not a book to turn to, and a monthly post, would soon wear me out. I never felt dull and weary in the Australian bush, and could have passed my life there cheerfully and contentedly. The sport there was sport indeed, and you shared it with men of your own stamp. Frequent visitors from town to the old "kangaroo tent" would bring us out an occasional book or a newspaper, and we at least knew what our old sporting friends at home were doing, though we could not participate in their sports. During the short time, however, that I was in Lapland the time never hung heavy on my hands, for I was fully occupied; and in the spring and summer, a collector here requires a day of forty-eight instead of twenty-four hours. But I much wanted a good mate. The peasant lad whom I took up, however good he might be on the fell or in the forest, was no companion. The good priest with whom we boarded was a man of few words, rather morose in his disposition; and had it not been for the jolly old parish clerk—who was a perfect contrast to all the rest of our neighbours, and was, moreover, a bit of a collector—I should scarcely have had a man to speak to. Doubtless the inclinations and tempers of the inhabitants of every land are much affected by the climate and scenery of the country in which they live, and the Lap settlers are just what you would expect men to be who live for more than half the year snowed in, with no companionship but their own. They never see the sun during the depths of winter; and by referring to a Lap almanac, I see that it is supposed to rise here on Christmas day at forty minutes after ten, and to set at twenty minutes after one. In describing a Lap winter to me, the old clerk wound up with—"For forty-two days in the dead of winter we can't see to kill a bird at a hundred yards with a rifle." There is nothing jolly about these settlers. Men and women are the same. If you speak to them you get a half civil answer, but nothing more; and although the stranger is sure to be treated with civility, and, no doubt, what they consider kindness, their manner is very different from the hearty welcome he receives in old Wermland. Luckily, they are exceedingly covetous, and will do almost anything for money; so if you have but the circulating medium you are sure to get all the assistance you require, and anything the country affords. And as a hint to the traveller, let me advise him, before reaching Lapland, to change his notes into silver. Small silver money will often save a rixdollar; and a specie dollar, or "blank," as they call it here, will rouse the apathy and greed of a Lap when paper currency will have no effect. With plenty of silver money, and a few notes of 100 rix-dollars (or £5) to fall back upon—and he will have no difficulty in changing them, provided that they are new notes of the Stockholm bank—a stranger will have no trouble about money matters. Although covetous to a degree, I always found both settlers and Laps strictly honest; and when a bargain was once made, I never knew them wish to back out.

The reader will, perhaps, be curious to know what these settlers do to occupy their time in a country where they can scarcely reckon on more than three months' summer; and this question is soon answered. Their whole life (to use a homely but forcible expression of my old Australian mate) appears to be one perpetual struggle for "grub."

G

One-half of their time seems to be spent in killing "ripa" or catching fish, and the other half in eating them; and I take it—as we used to say with the coach-horses in England—that their belly is their measure; for however much fish or game they took in one day, it seemed all to be cleared off by night, and nothing left for the next. Except when a stranger comes into the country, and requires a guide or assistance, I could not see that they had any means of earning money; for there is no sale for their game or fish, and every man is able to do all the work he requires at his own home. It is true they don't much want money, for every one has his house and little patch of arable land, a cow or two, a horse, and as much grass for hay from the sides of the rivers and lakes as he requires. But all they grow, and all the fish and game which they get, is required for home consumption. They can turn none of their products into money; and those who possess a few reindeer eat them up all but the bones and skin, which they sell for a few shillings. Some of these settlers have as many as 300 or 400 reindeer, many have none. These wander on the hills under the charge of a Lap, to whom they pay yearly 3d. for looking after each reindeer. Every one has his own mark—certain mysterious nicks in the ear, in some as many as six or eight; and I may add, that in Wermland they disfigure the sheep in the same fashion. They really and truly appear to live from hand to mouth. Each one has a small patch of cultivated land, on which, if the season permits him, he can grow a little barley and potatoes, and each one owns a few cows. Except just in the hay season the men appear to have very little to do, save to fish and to shoot. Every boy of ten years old can shoot, and every man's heart here may be truly said to be "in the forest or on the fell." All the "small chares" are done by the women, who, like all the women in Sweden, are most industrious, and never seem to know rest; and considering they all have large families to bring up—for they are all very prolific—they must have plenty to do. But certainly the men take it remarkably easy. I never saw better smokers in my life. I used to think that we blew a pretty good cloud in Australia; but we did take the pipe out of our mouths while at work. Here the pipe follows a man like his shadow, and, except when they sleep, appears to be continually in their mouths. But rough as it is, each one seems contented with his lot, and nearest to every one's heart appears to be—

"The wish which ages have not yet subdued,
Of man to have no master save his mood."

As may be easily imagined, the cure of the souls in a parish consisting of four families was not a

very onerous duty; and most of the good priest's time in the summer appeared to be occupied in fishing; in the winter, making nets. It is true, once every Sunday he preached in the little village church—generally to a very scant congregation. I have counted seven in the church; and to do him justice, I will say his sermons were befitting a far better audience. On certain anniversaries the Laps would come down, and then the service was in Lap, and of course I did not understand a word of it. He was a kind of missionary among the Laps, and he had six little Lap children to bring up in the ways of Christianity. Not that this troubled him much, as he kept an usher or schoolmaster under him. His wife was a most industrious woman, and, although bred a lady, worked like a servant. But this priest was a man of good standing, and nephew to the celebrated Læstadius, the Lap botanist. He had for some years been located in Piteä, and was, in fact, in point of acquirements and education on a par with any northern priest I have ever met with. Acerbi, in his usual quaint style, describes a priest he met with some sixty years ago, up at Munio, and his description is so rich, that I give it in his own words:—
"The parish of Munio is 200 miles in extent, and the parson is, to all appearance, a peasant like any of his flock, having nothing visible about him

that refers to his clerical dignity except a pair of *black breeches.*

" This poor man had the misfortune of being ruined by a fire, which consumed all his household furniture with his library, from which he could not even save his Bible. This loss was not, however, what he seemed to have felt most severely, as he observed, that after this disaster he found himself eased of the burden of reading Latin. The honest parson was of great use to us during our stay at Munio. He was the most clownish parson I ever saw in my various travels; but sometimes he would discourse on the abuses of birth and hereditary succession, in a manner which I was astonished to hear from a man who had nothing in the world but a shirt, a pair of breeches, and the shoes on his feet.

" He was the better pleased to see travellers, because they never could be any inconvenience to him, since, being very ill lodged himself, it could not be expected he should find them accommodation; and besides, by their arrival, he was sure of some glasses of brandy, with which we used to regale him as often as he came to see us. He declared our brandy was delicious, and with each glass he swallowed pronounced its eulogium in a manner equally energetic and sincere.

" He told us with the most pathetic accents,

that there was not a glass of brandy to be had within the whole 200 square miles of his parish. He told us, likewise, that drunkenness was regarded by his parishioners as the most scandalous vice to which man can be subject, and we could not help suspecting that this was one of the causes of his being so little revered and esteemed by his flock."

Old Acerbi's priest certainly formed a great contrast to our Quickiock priest, who, besides being a rigid disciplinarian, was a strict teetotaller.

As to the true Laps, their reindeer are their only care; and this "all-useful partner of a world of snows" supplies their every want. Their whole life is spent in wandering from one spot to another in search of pasture. And I should say the life of an Australian savage is far preferable, for he can get his kangaroo and opossum without the trouble of tending them, and he lives as it were in one perpetual summer. During the summer the life of the Laplander may be all very well; but in the winter, when the whole country is buried deep in snow, it must be dreadful. It is true they build up little huts, and here, as they are all huddled together (men, women, children, and dogs) in one common room with a fire in the middle, they are warm enough indoors. Their wanderings are entirely guided by their reindeer, whose instinct leads them in winter to seek the forests and lower grounds where the snow is not so deep, and in summer the highest fells, to escape the mosquitoes which then swarm in the forests. There are several grades among these Laps, and, unlike other wild men, who have everything in common, there are rich and poor among them, and their riches are computed by the number of reindeer each one owns. Some will probably own several hundred, and the value of a reindeer is not a little. To say nothing of the general utility of the animal while living, in autumn thousands are slaughtered. The skins they can sell for from 3s. to 5s. each, and the dried flesh is worth about 4s. for 20lb. (a good reindeer will weigh about 120lb. to 150lb.), and the horns are boiled down for glue. Many, however, possess no reindeer, and these are called "Fisk Lappar," generally miserably poor, living by fishing or shooting, or serving their richer brethren—and I should say of all servitude, Lap servitude was the lowest. Many of the richer Laps appear fond of finery, and I have seen some, both men and women, decorated with much silver about their caps and girdles. But the generality of them are dirty in the extreme; they never take their clothes off when they sleep, nor do I believe they cast away their mangy old skin coat until it drops off. That "cleanliness is next to godliness" is a golden motto; but I cannot help thinking that there must be a great deal of humbug in all our sanitary reforms, wash-houses for the million, etc., when I look at these dirty little fellows. I do not suppose one of them ever washes his face, or changes his clothes till they rot off; and yet we see tough old Laps who have never had a day's illness in their lives, and, although "verging on threescore," can still do their thirty English miles a-day over the fells, with 40lb. on their backs, without "turning a hair." Certainly I never saw in Lapland what we used in the colony to call a "clean old man;" and of all dirty old men, a "Lap Gubbe" beats all. Truly, as old Acerbi quaintly observes, "a certain unsavoury smell attends on every Laplander," and what with their blear eyes, dirty faces, *unkempt* hair, and old skin clothes, I don't wonder at it. He, however, seems to have fallen among a very bad lot, according to the following description:—" laziness and stupidity were prominent in all the Laplanders did, in all that appertained to them. The only things that they were able actually to perform were to keep up an everlasting chatter, to smoke their pipes, to chew tobacco, and to drink brandy." Sickness is almost unknown among them. When their time is up, notice to quit comes without any warning; and when a Lap falls upon a bed of sickness, it is usually the bed of death. Doubtless this has been so ordained by a kind Providence, who " tempers the wind to the shorn lamb;" for were sickness as rife in this wild land as in more civilized districts, I do not know what they would do, for no medical assistance is at hand here. Now and then, however, they get a terrible mauling from a bear, and I used to see an old cripple who occasionally stumped down to Quickiock, with a straight leg. He was caught one cold December night in a wolf-trap, which broke the bone of his leg, and he had to lie through the bitter, cheerless, long winter night (unable to extricate himself) till the next afternoon, when the owner of the trap came to see what he had caught. Yet with a broken leg he managed to crawl to the hut (three English miles distant), where they set it; and the best proof of their skill in surgery is, that he was left a cripple for life. Poor as they are, and seldom as they see money, I do not believe any men can be more greedy after it; and yet they never seem to make any use of it—they never part with it. What few luxuries, such as coffee, sugar, tobacco, they may require, they obtain by barter for their reindeer skins. The reindeer cheese they seldom part with, for they eat it with their coffee, of which, as well as spirits and tobacco, they are passionately fond. These cheeses are very dear. I paid 2s. 6d. for one weighing 2lb.; and if I had not known that it was reindeer cheese, I should scarcely have distinguished it from a very white cream cheese. If they can only get hold of a bit of silver, they value it as their heart's blood; and like the unworthy servant in the parable, they never invest their money to bring in any return, but if they possess more than they can carry about with them, they hide it in the crevice of a rock, and often forget where it lies.

Many of the Laps are certainly ridiculously small, and look more like large apes than men; but I have seen some very fair-sized ones among them. They appear to grow smaller as they grow older. Although in general the women are ugly enough, you sometimes see a very pretty face, and a figure as light as that of an opera dancer. That royalty itself has been smitten by their charms is proved by the fact that at Gellivare was (and I believe he lives now) a settler who, to use the language of the stud-book, was a cross between Louis Philippe (who was for some time in Lapland when a wanderer from his native land) and a Lap girl. I never saw him, but have been told that he was a fine-looking man, not unlike his reputed royal father; and they tell of another Lap girl who was taken back to France by a refugee (who came over here during the French Revolution) as his mistress.

She lived in France some years, was educated and clothed as a lady, but the love of her native fells was too deeply rooted in her breast to be ever extinguished, and after a lapse of some years she left the gaieties of Paris and returned to her wild mountain home—so strongly is the love of home implanted in the breasts of these rude mountaineers. It would doubtless be interesting to trace the origin of the Laplander. I can hardly fancy that they are a type of the original Scandinavian race, for they were all mighty warriors, and these little Laps are the most harmless creatures under the sun. It is very probable, however, that in earlier ages, when the country was in a different state to what it is at the present day, they were not confined solely to these northern tracts, but probably wandered over the whole face of the land. I fancy, however, they must be of Asiatic origin, and have travelled eastward through Russian Finmark. Their language is unlike any I ever heard, and I could only catch one word, "porisk" (good day), which is their usual greeting. Although the Lap settlers are very little better than the Laps themselves, and speak their language well, they all appear to be of Lap-Swedish origin, and I could never hear of a *real* Lap who had ever settled down as a farmer. Now, however, as Christianity is yearly spreading more and more among them, and their children receive education from the priest, it is reasonable to suppose that at a future day they will become settled; but as to the present generation, you might as well try to wean the wolf from his bloodthirsty habits as to change the wandering nature of the true Lap. Nevertheless, for savages they certainly are a most harmless, inoffensive race, and even in the stronghold of their native fells a stranger has little to fear from them.

I was much amused lately by two things. The first was the perusal of a little journey through Lapland, in which the writer dwells long and eloquently on the great benefits which might accrue to Sweden by bringing the Lap mosses or morasses into cultivation; and the other was an advertisement for working-men for the Great Gellivare iron mines (which lie perhaps 120 miles N.E. of Quickiock), in which, as an inducement, a little patch of land was offered to each man who would settle and bring it into cultivation. And, as a further incitement to settle, it was stated that the potato disease was unknown in this district. No more is the grouse disease, but I hardly fancy that would be any inducement for an English sportsman to come and settle so far up as this for the sake of grouse shooting alone. And as to the potatoes, I can only say, if the Gellivare potatoes are no better than those which we occasionally (but very seldom) got at Quickiock, it would matter little whether they were diseased or not. I take it the Gellivare district is about as well adapted for agriculture as Quickiock, and although certainly they can *grow* excellent barley (but it is a great question whether it ever ripens), and I have even seen rye up here, it does not make it an agricultural country; it only excites wonder in the mind of the stranger that any cereals can be got to grow in so rude a spot and in such a climate. It is, not, however, the fault of the land, for I have seen as good land on the lower fells around the lakes as ever I would wish to see; and the meadow land round Quickiock is excellent—a deep, rich, black loam, the accumulation of centuries. But man cannot alter the climate, and, clever as he is, there are certain laws laid down by old Dame Nature which he never can get over. They certainly do plough their lands, and I should fancy, to look at their ploughs, they must be after the same fashion as in the old Mosaic days. Their mode of farming up here is primitive in the extreme. They just scratch in their barley early in June, and set the potatoes about the same time. No fear of both coming to a good head, for everything grows like magic here in the summer; but it ripens scarcely one year in three. Two things, however, I remarked in Lap agriculture, which struck me as curious. Every one has more dung than he can use on his arable land, so he casts it on his meadow; and, although I fancied that wherever a man could live a pig could, I found at length that I had come to a land where "pigs *won't* pay for feeding." We had a bit of a garden at the priest's, and when the summer was not too cold, they manage to grow radishes, peas, turnips, and other garden-stuff, just as good as in Wermland. But in the year 1862 nothing ripened. In fact, I fancy things all grew too quick to be ever of much good. I was, however, struck, when I came up, at the good cows which I observed in every cow-byre—quite as good as in Wermland (but quite as dear), and yielding as much milk; but my wonder ceased in the summer, when I saw the crops of natural grass which these meadows and lowlands produce. I have seen many worse crops in the valley of the Nene; and this proves that Providence has not forgotten any of his creatures, for, as long as they can feed cows up here, they can always manage to live. Rye can be brought up from Luleå (certainly at a cost of one rixdaler per Swedish mile for the four bushels, or about £3 10*s.* for an English quarter); whereas, if they had no cows, they could not bring up milk, and as milk and porridge forms the principal diet of the Northern peasantry, the cow is even more necessary to their welfare here than in England. Each settler has a few sheep, and poor ragged-looking things they were.

In the winter, the horses are worked to skeletons in bringing home hay from the meadows and wood from the forest; but in the summer they have a jolly time of it, when they are turned out to grass into the forests and on the fells, and are not fetched home till autumn. They stack the hay where they cut it—not in stacks, as we do, but on a smaller kind of gate than that which I have before described for the linseed. They pile it over this when nearly green, and here it dries, I believe, without ever heating, and, as the top is made slanting, they say no rain can injure it. I had no opportunity of proving whether it retained its virtue as well in this way as in a stack or barn, but I should say not; and I consider the method only as a bit of lazy-bed farming, although I can hardly see what other plan they could adopt here. Anyhow, it stands a very good chance of being all blown away and lost in the snow when the autumnal gales set in, and this often happens. They began to cut their grass early in July, and, although I left before the corn was ripe, I fear if I had stayed till November I should have seen it green. They told me if they could not get it fit to cut by the first week in September, they would lose their harvest. The barley certainly looked heavier in the head and larger in the straw than I have ever seen it in England, and it was not sown until early in June. I have since heard that the harvest in 1862 was a total failure, and had it not been for an unusual quantity of game in the forest in the winter, the poor inhabitants would have fared badly.

As to the idea of bringing the Lap mosses into cultivation by draining, it is too absurd to be entertained for a moment, and could never have entered the head of any one but an "armchair humbug." Where are they to get hands to do it? and how many years would it take to drain an 100-acre moss, when they could only work three months out of the twelve, and in a country where labour is so scarce? Besides, when they were drained, what would be the good of them in a country peopled as this is—where there are no roads, and no means of transport? I often hear the same tale preached in the middle of Sweden, as if there was not good land enough already neglected; and I never hear the same without hinting to the farmer, that it would perhaps be cheaper and better for him if he would first turn his attention to the land which he already has under the plough; and in nine cases out of ten, if that was better done by, he could grow double crops without going to the expense of draining new land. Every year proves the fact, that there are few countries under the sun which cannot be brought to minister to the wants of man, and few places where an energetic, practical settler cannot thrive. But I really believe Lapland was made only for the Laplander and his reindeer; and I fear the Lap settler must be content to live upon the fish and game with which Nature has so liberally supplied him; and if he wants the luxuries of civilized life, he must come and live among his civilized brethren. I have, perhaps, dwelt too long upon this subject, as it is not very probable that any of my readers will come up to Lapland either to cultivate the mosses or work at the Gellivare mines, but still may like to know what will grow so far north; and before I visited Lapland I heard and read such marvellous tales respecting the fertility of this wild land, that I was most anxious to judge for myself how far it was adapted to agriculture, and I have now given the reader my exact opinion on the matter.

The season of 1862 was wretchedly cold, and the wind, which seemed always to blow from north and north-west, would come howling down from the fells through the gully in which Quickiock stood, "like a funnel." Whenever it rained in the valleys it appeared to snow on the fells; but so sheltered is the village that they say neither the corn nor potatoes ever freeze away; and, strange to say, I have plucked both wild raspberries and strawberries here!

As I said before, the situation of Quickiock is romantic in the extreme, and in the summer it would be hard to find a place in Lapland to beat it for wild, natural scenery. Surrounded on all sides by fells and forests, yet, lying as the village does in a sheltered valley, every kind of ground is met with here, and the naturalist could hardly choose a better station. A large river—the Tarra Elf—flows down from the fells close by the village; the proximity of the village to the fells themselves renders it peculiarly interesting to the collector; while meadows and swamps, choked with grass and every species of aquatic plants, intersected with numerous small natural channels and inland lakes, afford shelter for many species of ducks; but, strange to say, there are fewer waders in this district than in any I know. A boat here is as necessary in the summer as skiddor in the winter, for there is only one direction in which you can go a mile out of Quickiock without a boat. The forests just round the village are small, the trees blighted and stunted, and covered with a loose hairy kind of moss. In fact, the Lap forests in general present a strange contrast to the deep forests of Wermland and Dalecarlia. The branches of the fir trees all grow in a slanting direction downward, and as they are for the most part dead and jagged—although the trees are small—it is no easy matter to climb them. The meadows and lower grounds are covered with thick plantations of a species of willow, through which, in many places, it is impossible to force one's way, and immediately above them the forests are composed of fir. We see very little pine here, and what few pines we do see are generally blighted and bare. The higher we ascend the fell sides the smaller become the forests, till at length we miss the fir altogether, and reach the birch district. On leaving this we come to the fell birch, which, exposed as the trees are to the cutting wind in all directions, assumes every fantastic shape. At first the fell birch grows to a height of about four feet, but when we come higher up the fells it dwindles to a mere bush, and at length becomes nothing more than a creeper, matted and tangled on the ground. But the dwarf willow (*Salix Herbacea*), the smallest shrub in the world, grows on some of the fells as high as the dwarf birch. Above this the fells assume their true character, and are covered with lichens or mosses, and, in many places, with perennial snows. It is curious and interesting to stand on a fell top and mark how clearly each line of vegetation is defined below. To describe the fells themselves would be a waste of time and space. Any one can imagine huge masses of ironstone and shingle of all shapes and sizes, the one towering above the other, the summits of the higher ones covered with snow which never melts. "Waldi Spiket" is the highest fell close to Quickiock, and I suppose its summit is about 4,000 feet above the river, and from the bottom to the very top (for it rises gradually) is just $1\frac{1}{2}$ English miles. It is a peculiar-shaped fell. On the one side it rises with a gentle slope, and, though the ascent is very difficult on account of a large bed of boulders and shingle which one has to cross, there is no danger; but on reaching the top and looking down on the other side, it rises as plumb as a wall, and a slip of the foot would hurl the traveller into an abyss some thousand feet deep. No one, however, who has not seen it, can picture to himself the beauty of the valleys that lie between and at the foot of the fells themselves. Nowhere have I seen so rich a vegetation, or such a profusion of wild flowers as bloom in this so-called wilderness; and nowhere do the wild flowers appear so beautiful as when we see them in a spot where we least expect to meet with them. Never did I regret so much that I knew nothing of botany, as when wandering in this wild but beautiful region. To stand in one of these fell valleys on a carpet of grass and moss as soft as the richest that Turkey can yield, variegated with wild flowers of every hue, from one to the other of which rare and beautiful butterflies are continually flitting—to see the rugged fells themselves frowning down in severe majesty upon one, excites a feeling of awe, perhaps, rather than admiration; and though we know that not a human being is within miles of us, we cannot call it solitude:—

" 'Tis but to hold
Converse with Nature's charms, and view her stores unroll'd."

I had, of course, many opportunities now of seeing that most singular Lapland phenomenon—the midsummer sun above the horizon at midnight, for just at this time was our best egg season, and three nights out of the six we were camped on or near to the fells, and for about a month at midsummer we could always see the rays of the setting sun reflected on the northerly fells at midnight—in fact, for above two months the nights were as light as day, and, strange to say, I hardly ever could get a real refreshing night's sleep. We could now see to shoot as well at midnight as at twelve o'clock by day—in fact, most of the game is shot in the night by the settlers here. I shall never forget the night of June 24, when we lay out on the fells in search of the nest of the Lapland bunting. The sky was remarkably clear, and, as I much wished to have a better view of the sun himself, we climbed up to the top of "Porti Fellen," the highest mountain in this fell range, the summit of which is covered with snow throughout the year; and the sublime grandeur of the scene which then met my view I shall never forget. I meant to have been up on the top by midnight, but the road was more difficult than we had expected, and it was half-past twelve before we reached its summit. There are some things, as the Clockmaker says, "too big to lift, some too big to carry after they are lifted, and some too grand for the tongue to describe," and this was one. When we had reached the highest peak of the fells we stood, perhaps, 5,000 feet above the level of Quickiock. Far as the eye could reach, nothing was to be seen but a wide expanse of fells of different shapes and sizes shelving out on all sides, the snow-fells towering like immense glaciers above the others, their silvery peaks, gilded with the rays of the midnight sun, contrasting prettily with the dark, sombre appearance of those that were bare. "Lakes and rivers beneath me gleamed misty and wide" in the deep valleys between the fells themselves, while the lower landscape was covered with forests of boundless extent, presenting to the eye every shade of green—from the dark foliage of the fir, to the lighter and more silvery tint of the birch and the willow. Every object could be distinguished as clearly as by day; but—

> "The scene was more beautiful far to the eye
>   Than if day in its pride had arrayed it;
> The night wind blew soft, and the azure-arched sky
>   Looked pure as the Spirit that made it.
> I stood, and I gazed from the fell's rugged slope,
>   Forgot was the world's rude commotion;
> And methought that the prospect looked lovely as hope—
>   That star on life's tremulous ocean."

Here was a landscape fresh from the Maker's hands. No encroachments of man had marred the rugged, natural beauty of this wild scene, which was probably but little changed since that day when some mighty convulsion of nature raised these huge ironstone blocks into the position which they now occupy. A solemn feeling crept over me as I gazed upon the vast, the grand panorama which lay outstretched around me; and as the night-breeze swept by in fitful gusts, it seemed truly as if I then stood face to face with the Almighty One in the wilderness. A dead silence reigned over all, such as I once remember during an eclipse of the sun, and for a short time all nature seemed buried in a deep repose. But there was something almost unnatural in the solemn stillness of that hour. It was as the silence of the grave. How well I remember Eliza Cook's beautiful lines, but never till this night did I feel their full force :—

> "To hear our very breath intrude
> Upon the boundless solitude,
> Where mingled tidings never come
> With busy feet or human hum;
> All hushed above, beneath, around,
> No stirring form, no whispered sound—
> This is a loneliness that falls
> Upon the spirit, and appals
> More than the mingled rude alarms
> Arising from a world of arms."

It is in vain to endeavour to do justice to such a scene by the pen; for "the description of such natural and varied grandeur can be limited only by each individual's power of graphic portraiture; all, however, far below the truth, and weak to the imagination of the poetic reader." In the north-east, where the fells were lower, the sun shone out of an unclouded sky, apparently about a foot from the horizon's edge—an angry, sullen, lurid, globe of fire, without appearing to emit a single ray of heat, for we could stare him in the face without winking. He appeared to me to go down about due north, and, without rising or sinking, for nearly an hour to travel eastward, when he gradually rose and assumed his wonted splendour. A large herd of reindeer, accompanied by a troop of Laps with their hounds, were crossing the valley below us, and this completed the wild character of a scene such as Teniers might have loved to paint.

Never did I feel my own insignificance so much as when I descended the fell, and left this grand scene behind me. Place man in cities, among his finest works of art, among his manufactories and machinery; bid him jostle his way through the human crowd among whom he lives, and his lip may curl with pride and self-satisfaction as he gazes triumphantly on some master-stroke of ingenuity, or chuckles at the success of some mighty speculation. It is then that he rises, as it were, in his own estimation, superior to his fellow man, and for the moment seems almost to forget that he is mortal. But place such a one in a scene like this, at the hour of midnight, and let him see if his self-pride will not receive a check! He will now be able to compare the most stupendous works of his hands with the works of nature, and then let him strike a balance. His choicest work of art can scarcely vie in beauty with the meanest wild flower he heedlessly crushes under foot; and as for his boasted superiority over his fellow-man, why in this rude spot the little untaught Laplander is worth a dozen of him.

By the time we reached our camping-place, all nature seemed to have awakened. Although little more than 2 A.M., the sun was shining fiercely and hot, while the hoarse laugh of the ptarmigan, as he rose from his bed of crags on the opposite fell, the loud, unceasing pipe of the golden plover, the soft, monotonous single call-note of the Lapland bunting, and the shrill, clear morning song of the blue-throated robin (our earliest and loudest fell warbler), all welcomed the break of another day :—

> "Birds, flowers, song, and beauty,
>   Seemed this rugged realm to fill;
> And what was my soul's entrancing,
> Was the music and the glancing
>   Of a rugged, rock-born rill."

During the time we were on the fell a sharp frost had set in, and when I went down to the little mountain-stream, by the side of which we had camped, to wash, I found it covered with ice a quarter of an inch thick, and this on Midsummer night! Truly—

> "There is a freshness in the morning air
>   Which ease and bloated wealth
>   Can never hope to share;"

and as I kicked the ashes of our wood-fire together to get ready for breakfast, I thought, as I have many a time before done in the Australian forests, that one hour in such a spot and at such a time, was worth a whole year spent in cities.

This evening I left my lad on the fells, and set off home by myself. We were then about fifteen miles from Quickiock, and although most of my road lay through a pathless forest, still, with the sun clear in the heavens, and a perfect knowledge in which direction the village lay, it seemed next to impossible for me to go wrong; but so easy is it for us in this world to stray from the right path, that I did manage to lose my way, and midnight found me wandering in a dense forest at the foot of the fells, without a landmark to guide me which way I should steer. And here I may add, that it is almost impossible for a man to lose himself on a clear day for long in this neighbourhood. He may, perhaps, wander a few hours in the forest, perhaps even a day, but the fells round the village are so well defined, and such sure landmarks, that they must bring him up sooner or later. We used to adopt a very good plan when camping out on the fells, which was to hoist a white flag upon a long pole on the top of a fell, at the bottom of which we camped, and when the day was clear we could see this landmark an astonishing way. Far different is it on the fells in a mist, or when a snow storm sets in. On the road up I was amused at the eagerness with which my two mates purchased pocket compasses, as if they were of the most vital importance, although neither of them had the slightest idea how to steer by them. And this reminds me of a circumstance which happened to me in Australia. I was coming home to my tent one evening from kangarooing, when I encountered a stranger who had lost his way. He was evidently a " new chum," and looked about as much like a tailor as anything else. I wondered what could have taken him so far from the town, but it seemed that he had a friend down somewhere near Western Port, and he had been out to see him. He got down very well, for he stuck to the coast and the main road; but on coming back he tried a short cut through the forest. As Mr. Richard Bragg would say, " this was another pair of shoes altogether," and the consequence was he soon got " bushed." The sun was fast sinking, and he had nothing to eat, and no matches. I took him home to the tent, and on the road he expressed his surprise to me that he should have lost himself, as he had a pocket compass with him; upon which he pulled out a complicated sort of machine, which united a compass and sundial on one face—a most useful bush companion to any one knowing how to use it.

The needle pointed right enough; but when I asked him in what direction he fancied Melbourne now lay, he knew no more than the compass itself. He had no bearings, nor had he the slightest idea as to the use of the compass, but seemed to think that, like the hands of a watch, which point to the hour, the pointer of the compass would show him the road home. As to our two compasses— gingerbread, German things—they were out of repair long before we reached Quickiock, and were just as well broken as whole, in the hands of men who had no idea how to use them.

But to return to my tale. I was not much troubled at my disaster, for I knew it could be but one night out, and I had my gun, plenty of matches, salt and tobacco, lots of ripa in the forest, and water in all the brooks; so as I was rather tired I made up my mind to camp up at once; and while looking about for a likely place I chanced to stumble on the real landlord of this wild domain, in the shape of an old brown bear, who, from his immense size, and grisly, venerable appearance, must have been the very patriarch of the forest. It was the first time I had ever seen old Bruin at home; and, unprepared as I was, without a bullet to give him a proper welcome, I can't say that I much relished the meeting. It was in a deep but by no means thick forest, and my attention was first aroused by the cackle of a lot of willow grouse about 200 yards from me. I immediately supposed that some owl or large bird of prey was making an attack upon the brood, and although my gun was only loaded with No. 7, I thought it possible that I might creep up within shot. I could see nothing as yet; but a cracking of dry branches soon told me that it was no bird, but some beast of prey, that was raising this commotion among the ripa family. I stood still close to a large dead pine, when I indistinctly saw something grey through the trees, which I at first thought must be a reindeer. A few seconds, however, soon showed me that it was no reindeer, but the real "old gentleman in the fur cloak," upon whose privacy I had thus intruded. He came walking into an open space right in front of me—in fact, was within 100 yards of me, and appeared to be coming straight up. I felt at this moment much as I did upon one occasion in Australia, when creeping cautiously down a narrow track through the tea-tree scrub to a favourite waterhole for duck, I suddenly found myself face to face with a half-wild bull, who was leisurely returning from drinking, through a track too narrow for us to pass each other, the scrub on each side nearly as solid as a wall. But to return to my bear. He evidently neither saw nor smelt me, but went rooting about with his nose close to the ground, just like a pig searching for acorns. Here was I in a "pretty tarnation fix," as the Yankees would say. My gun was loaded only with small shot, and my case-knife would be of little use to me, even in a death-struggle; and if it should come to this I well knew who would get the best of it. No use trying to run away—he could beat me at that game; so remembering Tom Spring's advice to his pupils, that "the best way to stop a knock-down blow is to keep a civil tongue in your head," I made up my mind to stand stock-still, and certainly not to molest him if he let me alone, but, if he did charge me, to endeavour to get the muzzle of my barrels into his mouth, and give him such a pill as even a bear would have a little difficulty in swallowing.

Strange to say, as soon as I found that there was no escape, I did not feel in the least frightened —only a little anxious as to the result, in case it did come to a tussle; and as this seemed now more than probable, I did not care how soon it took place. The old bear, however, was in no hurry; he did not appear to take the least notice of me, but went grubbing round and round, as if he had some very interesting botanical investigation in hand, and would wait on me as soon as it was finished. Anything is better than suspense, and I could not stand this *sang froid* much longer. It is now many years since I heard a rattling view-halloa, but I have not quite forgotten the cheery old sound, so I thought I would try the effect of one on Bruin, and I gave a screech, the like of which (if it would not have passed muster at " Finedon poplars" or " Denford old ash") was never, I'll be bound to say, heard before in this wild Lap forest. It was now pretty plain that the bear had no idea that I was so near him, for I shall never forget the start he gave on hearing my voice. I have often been amused in watching the gambols of a litter of young pigs in a farm-yard, when they toss up their heads, spring a short distance, and then suddenly stop and turn round and face you with a sniff and a snort. This was just how my bear behaved. Tossing up his head, he gave a deep kind of grunt, and off he set at a pace which I never could have supposed such a heavy-sterned, unwieldy, lumbering, short-legged monster was capable of. He never looked round until he was about fifty yards from me, when he suddenly stopped short, gave a sulky, half-sidelong look at me out of his little wicked pig eye, and then dashing off into the deep forest, I saw him no more. I now thought, however, that it was hardly prudent to camp out in this neighbourhood, so I made the best of my way out of the wood. After, perhaps, an hour's ramble, I came into a part of the forest which I knew, and reached home about four in the morning. Of course I was well laughed at by all the old bear-hunters round when I related my adventure. One would have done this, another would have done that; in fact, it is hard to say what they would not have done, or could not have done, except coming home, as I did, without leaving the bear dead in the forest. But I was well enough pleased as it was, for it now convinced me that there is little to fear in meeting a bear, provided you don't molest him; and considering that I was liable any day to fall in with one in my solitary forest rambles, to use the words of old Dr. Valpy, the venerable preceptor of my youth, this was to me " a very consolatory reflection."

By all accounts, the Swedish bear is a very well-behaved animal, and, I believe, is never known to attack man unless he is first molested. But when wounded he is an awkward customer. He rarely takes cattle, except at the end of autumn, and, in fact, appears to be far more herbivorous than carnivorous in his habit. Little fear of his even taking a horse in the forest, for they all keep together, as if they felt the truth of the old adage, that unity is strength. That the chase of the bear is attended with very little danger in these forests, is proved by the fact, that there is scarcely an old settler here but has killed his score of bears, and with weapons of the most primitive description. The gun in use here is called a "Lod Bossa"—a small pea rifle, often not more than a foot long in the barrel, fitted up with a very original kind of flint-lock, the mainspring outside, and carrying a ball perhaps forty to the pound. Armed with such a rifle and his spear (to my mind a much more formidable weapon), a little Lap will follow the bear by his spor in the snow in spring or autumn, with the untiring energy of a sleuth-hound, till he is brought to bay, when the Laplander attacks him, often single-handed, and in nine cases out of ten will kill him, without receiving any injury. It is when the bears leave the ice in early spring, and they can follow them in the soft snow, that the principal slaughter takes place. A bear is a great prize to a Laplander, for, independent of the meat, the skin, when properly dressed, is worth from £2 10s. to £4. The black ones are the best. There were lots of bears round Quickiock, and two were killed in the vicinity while I was up, but I saw neither. Formerly the Laps never molested the bear, but looked upon him with a sort of veneration. Now, however, they have learnt the art of killing him from the more civilized settlers, and, next to the wolf, the bear is the principal quarry of the Lap hunter.

Every man has his hobby, from which, if once mounted, it is hard to shake him off; and the hobby of these settlers is bear-hunting. I have sat by the hour and listened to hairbreadth escapes and incidents of the chase—no doubt half of them lies, but still with some truth at the bottom—and I could not help feeling that there is something manly in the way that they attack such an animal single-handed. But if any of my readers wish to know more of the habits and chase of Bruin, I will refer them to Lloyd's "Northern Field Sports"—a book written by one who has killed more bears than any man in Sweden, and a book, moreover, which tells "the truth, the whole truth, and nothing but the truth," rather an unusual thing in a book on sporting.

CHAPTER V.

NOTES FROM MY DIARY KEPT AT QUICKIOCK.

I WILL now proceed to lay before my readers a few extracts from my diary as to how we passed our time; a few hints to the sportsman respecting the shooting and fishing in the district; and shortly notice every quadruped and bird which we met with around Quickiock. From what I could learn from men who had been settled up here many years, it would seem that in general the winter begins in October, and lasts full seven months, or till April; the spring is short, and the summer commences about the middle of June and lasts three months; autumn begins in September and lasts till the middle of October.

The greatest cold is in January, and the greatest heat in the end of July. The greatest cold here has been about 45° Celsius, and the greatest heat, 35° Celsius.

The mean temperature of the four seasons may be taken at :—

    Winter - - - - 9° cold.
    Spring - - - - 6° warm.

Summer - - - - 15° warm.
Autumn - - - - 6° warm.

But the average temperature of the whole year, if we except the periods when the seasons exert their peculiar influence, is about the freezing point of the thermometer, or in other words, constant winter.

Instances have been known of corn being sown and ripening in forty days. In usual seasons—

About March 5th, the melting ice and snow begin to trickle from the roofs.
,, April 10th, the snow bunting appears.
,, ,, 25th, wild geese and swans arrive. The Papilio urticæ is seen. Larks are seen, and patches of bare ground appear.
,, May 6th, the white wagtail arrives.
,, ,, 24th, the marsh marigold flowers.
,, ,, 28th, the birch has leaves.
,, June 6th, summer warmth 10°.
,, Aug. 1st, night frosts begin.
,, May 10th to 25th, the rivers usually open. The ice is fast melting, and they begin to plant the kitchen gardens.
,, Aug. 20th, harvest begins, winter rye is sown.
,, Sept. 20th, the birch shed their leaves.
,, Nov. 20th, the ice bears, and the ground is covered with snow.

They generally reckon here that the sun disappears below the horizon about November 20th, and about January 20th half his disk is seen again above the horizon.

During the whole of April the snow lay two feet deep in the forest, in many places much more, and on the fells no one could tell its depth; it was impossible to get out of doors without "skiddor." As I had never practised upon such a skate, and it is not easy to "teach an old dog new tricks," I was a close prisoner to the house for a great part of the month. However, there was just now very little to do in my line. It is true my lad brought me in many good specimens of hawk owl, Siberian jay, pine grosbeak; but none of the spring migrants had yet arrived, and the first nest we took was that of the Siberian jay, on April 21st. The ptarmigan and willow grouse were as yet in their pure white winter dress. In the middle of April the sun rose at half-past four and set at half-past seven. A good deal of snow occasionally fell, and it was impossible to give any idea of the temperature, for on April 20 the mercury was 18° below zero (Celsius), and on the 21st we had 10° warm (from zero to 50° Fahrenheit). But every one prophesied an early spring. The Laps were fast hurrying back to the fells, and drove after drove of reindeer passed through the village. About the 22nd I began to see open water lie by the sides of the streams, although there was still good sledging on all the rivers and lakes, and the waterfall in a large stream that runs down from the northern fells into the Quickiock river was still frozen over as hard as a rock.

By the end of the month the thaw seemed to set in, and we now began to see many bare places in the snow. For about a fortnight it was next to impossible to get into the forests at all, except just in the morning, when the frost was on the snow. The new snow, however, which melted as it fell, had the same effect on the old snow as the spring rain in Wermland. On April 30th the sun rose at half-past three and set at half-past eight. On the 28th we got our bow nets in order, and set them in the ice at the mouth of a small backwater leading out of a large shallow lake. The fish did not run well at first—and no wonder, for the river in some places, where it was only four feet deep, was frozen to the very bottom. Every prospect this of an early spring! But we now began to hear the roar of the waterfall in the fell river close to the house more distinctly every day, which proved that the ice was gradually melting at the bottom.

Early in May many of the smaller migrants arrived, and large flocks of snow buntings, shore larks, and bramblings covered all the bare patches which the snow had left.

The thermometer varied in the day now from 4° to 10° warm of Celsius (about 40° to 50° Fahrenheit), but at midnight was often as low as 10°

below zero (14° Fahr.). The weather on the night of April 24th, according to the calculation of these Lap settlers, regulates that of the ensuing spring, and as this was mild and warm they prophesied a mild and warm spring. The thaw was now going on rapidly but imperceptibly, for the sun began to have great power, and the snow was now so rotten that we could scarcely get into the woods even on "skiddor;" and if we went any distance from home in the morning (the only time of the day when the snow would bear), it was a great chance if we could get back again till the night frost set in. I once saw a horse standing in the forest up to his belly in the snow. They had taken him out at night to fetch home wood, but as soon as the sun had power the snow melted and would not bear, so they were obliged to leave him there till the night frost again crusted the snow. We could now see how deep the snow lay in the forests, for we often sank in up to our very arm-pits while trying to struggle through it. However, spring was near at hand. By the middle of the month most of the spring migrants had arrived, and the clear, loud, wild, desultory carol of the redwing might be heard throughout the whole night, which was now as light as day. We had at this time a migration of fell lemming, which lasted about three weeks. We began to see "spor" of bear and glutton in the snow, and a wolf took two reindeer in one night close to the village. The nights now were always frosty, however warm it might be in the day. The only nests we got in April were those of the Siberian jay and hawk-owl; early in May Tengmalm's owl, the great black woodpecker, the rough-legged buzzard, and the great grey shrike. By the end of the month all the hole-breeding birds were laying, as well as the fieldfare, willow-grouse, capercailzie, hazel-hen, and mealy redpole. On May 6th we had the last regular snow-storm. It snowed without intermission throughout the whole day, with 4° warm Celsius, but in the evening it turned to rain. On this day we caught the first fish in the bow-nets, 75 lb. of perch, many of them 3 lb. each. An odd teal or two appeared, for there were already a few open places by the shallow sides of the rivers, and a flock of fell geese flew over on the 8th. On May 4th, the last drove of reindeer came up to the fells, and the Laps said the river was no longer safe for sledging. It soon now began to be full of holes, and for a fortnight or so the communication was closed between this and Lulea. I shot the first wader (a golden-plover) on the 15th; saw the first swallow on the 16th. On the 18th, at night, I shot a widgeon and a teal, and in the early morning two capercailzie (which had just now begun to "lek" or play), at least three weeks later than in Wermland; and three willow grouse. Up to the 23rd the spring migrants kept arriving. The ice and snow now went very fast; the waterfall had burst through its icy covering, and the river just at Quickiock was open. But the travelling was now dangerous and troublesome, although the post did manage to row down on the 25th. Spring, however, had now fairly set in, many of the birds were building, and on the 22nd we had 30° Celsius (86° Fahr.) in the sun. But the meadows looked as brown as a turnpike road, and not a tree was yet in leaf. We had now occasional warm showers, and the heavy mist that hung over the fells, entirely obscuring their snow-clad summits, betokened that the melting, or action of the snow, was fast going on. I plucked the first wild flower, a little kind of yellow dandelion, in the snow on the 17th. They began ploughing on the 18th, and by the end of the month the barley was all in. The grayling now began to run into the bow-nets, and they were full of spawn, although I fancied their season over. On the 23rd we could very well get up on to the fells and into the forests, and our egg season had now fairly commenced. On the 27th I bathed for the first time, the water icy cold. On the 31st the birches were just beginning to look green; by June 3rd they had burst out into full leaf, and the whole country suddenly wore a different aspect, as if it had been touched by the wand of an enchanter. Never could I have believed that so sudden a change could take place. A week since, and every birch and willow were as bare as at Christmas, and now the Quickiock valley looked like a beautiful shrubbery in England. On May 29th some Laps came over the fells, from Norway, to receive the sacrament in our little church, and on the road they found the dead body of a man lying on the fells, who had doubtless lost his way in the autumn snow-drift and been frozen to death. They were obliged to leave the body where they found it, and probably ere this the bones have been cleared by the hill-fox and the raven, and now lie bleaching in the wind and sun, a melancholy warning to any traveller who may chance to wander by this lonely spot. I never was lost in the snow in Lapland, for I never was out of sight of home while the snow lay in the forests, but I had one night's experience in Wermland, in March, 1862, when the heaviest fall of snow occurred that had been heard of in the middle of Sweden for very many years. As it is not every one who has passed through such a night, the following account which appeared in the *Field* newspaper at the time, may, perhaps, be interesting to some of my readers:—

A NIGHT IN THE SNOW.

"Like a dead man gone to his shroud,
 The sun has sunk in a leaden cloud,
 And the wind is rising bleak and loud,
  With many a stormy token,
 Playing a wild funereal air,
 Through the branches bleak, bereaved, and bare;
  In fact, if the truth were spoken,
 It's an ugly night for anywhere,
  But an awful one for the Brocken."—Hood.

If the night of the 4th March was only half as bad in England as in Sweden, I can well fancy that paterfamilias, comfortably seated by a blazing fire in a well-curtained, well-carpeted parlour, over his wine and walnuts, would draw himself closer into the hearth as the wild wind and drifting snow rattled against the casement, and remarking to the family circle, "That it was a dreadful night, God help those poor travellers who are out in such a storm!" would ring the bell for John to throw another log on the fire, quietly compose himself for a doze, and give the matter no further thought. Doubtless there were many men out on this wild night to whom one glimpse of that cheery fire shining through his window would have seemed almost as a ray of heavenly light; and as I myself was among the number, I will relate the experiences of one of the longest and worst nights I ever spent in my life, the very remembrance of which even now makes me shudder.

I had left home on the 27th of February on a little charr-fishing trip, and more beautiful winter weather I never remember. Lots of snow had fallen, but it was well set; and as the roads are all cleared with snow-ploughs, etc., at such a time we can travel in a bee-line over forest and lake, and I reached my friend's house in about fifteen miles instead of twenty-four, the usual distance. The weather was clear and bright, and I never enjoyed a walk more in my life. I took one of my lads with me, for I had two objects in view; the first to catch some good specimens of charr, the other to see if I could find the crossbills building in the woods we were about to visit. We had some capital fishing, but although the weather still kept bright and clear, I did not like the appearance of the heaven when the sun went down on the 1st of March; and, on looking out of my window the next morning, was not at all surprised to see that a heavy snow-storm had set in. My lad, with the characteristic prudence of these foresters, immediately went home, for he prophesied three days of snow; and it would have been well had I followed him, but my friend over-persuaded me to stay (no very difficult matter, by the way, when I contrasted the inward comforts of his house with the desolate prospect that reigned over all outside). It snowed heavily without five minutes' intermission, till the morning of the 4th, when, as there was a little break in the sky to windward, I was determined to try and get home, notwithstanding all the assurances of my friend that I should never reach home that night.

At noon it cleared, and the sun peeped out of a leaden sky, but about four withdrew his angry face behind as heavy a bank of snow-clouds as ever I saw. I took a peasant's cart, for the roads were not cleared for sledging, and though we could only travel at a foot-pace (the snow up to our axles), still I could have got home had I stuck to the wheels and the high road; but in two stages I came to a ferry, and, by crossing the river there, I should save more than six English miles. The ferry-boat was frozen in, and although the ice would not bear a cart, I had no difficulty in walking over; and as I fancied I now knew my way, I guessed I should reach home with some little trouble. As long as my path lay on the high road I got on pretty well; for, although the way was so blocked with snow that I could not make much more than one English mile in the hour, still I knew where I was, and if I was obliged to camp up for the night, there were plenty of cottages by the roadside. At last I came to a farmhouse, beyond which lay a lake about one and a half English miles in length, and if I could cross this I should reach a village from which a high road would take me home; but the country between this farmhouse and the village was about the very worst I could have chosen to cross on such a night. It was a wild, bleak, cheerless track by day, and as there was no forest, only here and there scattered clumps of trees, there was no shelter, and nothing to stop the drifting snow, which, in many places, now lay four feet deep. The farmer pressed me to stay all night, declaring it was impossible to cross the lake; but finding me determined, he said, as he dare not send a horse out with me, I could take one of his servants, who knew the lay of the country, to put me into a track which led to the village by the side of the lake. I may add that at sunset the snowstorm set in again as bad as ever, and, although the wind was boisterous enough, it came in wild gusts all round the compass, so that it was impossible to steer with any certainty by that. Thus, as there were no stars visible, and as we could not see a landmark for one hundred yards before us, I had not the least guide, and if I once lost the track it was all up with me. On leaving, my friend the farmer shook his head forebodingly, and, declaring he should scour the country next morning to see if he could find my body lying buried in a snow-drift, we parted. A wilful man will have his way, and for about the fiftieth time in my life I proved the folly of running counter to the advice of the inhabitants of a strange country, who must know their own land better than a foreigner.

With the help of my guide I managed to make a pretty good fight through the snow (for the road was quite blocked up, although his instinct found it), and if I had only kept him till I came to the village, I should have been all right; not that I should have tried to get home then, for it was nearly eight when I left the farmhouse, and I was already getting faint and tired. But after he had followed me about an English mile, he told me if I kept down a long fence till I came to the bottom, and then turned to the right, I must make the village; so I sent him back. I followed his directions, as I fancied, to the letter, and after I had wandered alone for perhaps an hour, I saw what I took to be a house looming in the distance; but when I reached it (after a goodish deal of trouble) it proved to be a clump of trees. Although much disappointed, I did not despair, for I was as yet tolerably fresh and strong. The worst of it was, the snow was blinding me, the air was so thick that I could not see a hundred yards before me, and all the fences were now buried in the snow-drift. I fired off my gun, I shouted, but no answer; so on I floundered, without the slightest idea where I was steering, for I was fairly lost; and if I had even tried now to make " back tracks," the darkness of the night and the heavy falling snow prevented me seeing my spor. I had, therefore, nothing for it but to take a straight line, and keep it, trusting to luck to bring me at last to some familiar object. On I floundered, sometimes the snow-drifts in the hollows four feet deep, always above my knees; and so great was the exertion, that in about an hour more I was fairly beaten; and although I should reckon there was then at least 13° cold Celsius, the perspiration poured off me in streams. Again I fired off my gun, and shouted, but no welcome answer. No one was likely to be out round here on such a night, and even if a cottage window had been blazing within two hundred yards of me, I should certainly have never seen it through the murky waste. I could keep no note of time, but I fancy it must have been near midnight when I reached another clump of trees, and, being now fairly beat, I sat down at the foot of one with my back to the wind, but as soon as I had sat down, a complete revulsion came over me. My blood seemed all at once to stagnate, my head reeled, my eyes appeared to be starting from their sockets, and a drowsiness, the like of which I had never felt before, crept upon me. The horrid thought suddenly flashed across my mind, that if I gave way to this sensation for five minutes I should soon sink into that sleep from which there is no waking in this world. There was now nothing to do but to keep moving, for I knew that my life depended on it. If I could struggle on till the morning, I had no fear; but I was nearly beaten, and I reckoned it still wanted eight hours to sunrise; so I roused myself up, and again struck out—which way I knew not, nor did I care. It would be a miracle if I reached the village, and as to holding out till morning in my present weak state, I fancied to be impossible. When I fell benumbed with cold, the snow would soon bury me; all traces of me would be lost, and there I should lie till the thaw came on. But as long as there was life there was hope. To push on was now my only alternative, and again I struck out into the waste of snow. The cold had caught one of my hands, and I had lost the use of it, and my ears and nose felt just as if I could have snapped them off like icicles. I could feel the cold, as it were, gradually paralyzing me, so I took a good roll in the snow like a dog, and it is wonderful how that refreshed me. I luckily had lots of tobacco for chewing, but no matches. I did not feel hungry, and a handful of snow every now and then slaked my thirst; so I had no fear on this account. My whole life, as I thought, depended upon whether or not I could hold on till morning, and keep myself from being frozen; for now I dare not rest for five minutes, or I would have scraped a large hole in the snow and crept in; but every time I rested I felt that queer drowsiness coming over me, which I knew was the precursor of sleep.

Galton, in his "Art of Travel," I see, expresses his decided opinion that men may live many days buried in a snowdrift. Had I known this, I should have suffered no more anxiety on the night in question than I had ever done when bushed in Australia; but I never referred to Galton till I came home. If such is really the case, all my fine tale of anxiety and sufferings is nothing but a romance; however, it was my firm idea that if I once rested in the snow I should soon become benumbed, and gradually pass off into an unawaking slumber. So, as I dare not try the remedy, it was the same to me as if it had never existed. It is strange up here that *mine* is the general opinion, and every peasant to whom I have spoken on the subject, says that your only chance of saving life is to keep going. I know black grouse often bury themselves in the snow, and remain there for days, as we can see by their droppings when disturbed, and so do bears; men are, however, neither bears nor blackcock. But to my tale.

On I struggled, gradually becoming weaker and weaker, till my foot struck against some obstacle, which soon brought me up. It was a sunken fence (the snowdrift here just reached my waistcoat-pocket), and I am sure that it took me a quarter of an hour to clear it. I was fairly beaten, and as I sunk on the snow I thought, as old Dick Christian says in one of his lectures, "I wor dun now." My gloves had frozen as stiff as icicles. The cold seemed eating into my very marrow. My feet, notwithstanding all the exertions I was making, were completely paralyzed, and appeared to hang on my legs like two lumps of lead; moreover, they felt as if they had swelled to double their natural size; my boots, which had frozen as hard as iron, held them like two vices, and the pain was dreadful. My senses seemed going; I was becoming light-headed, and when I rose again (for I dare not lie long) I reeled like a drunken man. A kind of languid indifference was now stealing over me; I seemed to care little for life, and, although I was determined not to sink as long as I could flounder on, all probability of my now holding out till morning seemed so hopeless that I almost longed for the moment to come when I should fall exhausted in the snow, and bury the agony I was then suffering in sleep, although it might be the sleep of death. The sensations of that night I shall never forget. In the early evening I had felt frightened, but this feeling soon passed away. Hope then vanished, and a kind of desperate and savage courage to fight against fate as long as I could stand up had usurped its place, and I dashed on through the blinding snow with feelings of reckless exultation. Every time that a wild gust of wind swept by me, I fancied I heard the laugh of the "Spirit of the Storm," as if mocking me, and on every such occasion I felt fresh nerve and courage. Such curious thoughts came into my head; trifling incidents of the past, long since forgotten, crowded on my mind, and the whole history of a life seemed to be condensed in the few hours of that dreadful night. We read of the horrid sensations of sailors cast away at sea upon a raft, when all hope has left them, and, maddened by hunger and despair, murder and cannibalism glare in the eyes of men who till then had been as sworn comrades and brothers. I can well now believe all I have read on this horrid theme. I had no incitement to cannibalism, for I was alone, and, moreover, was not hungry. But quite as dreadful a thought flashed across my brain—that of *suicide!* I had long given up all hopes of escape. Why, then, prolong sufferings which now I fancied must inevitably end in death? I had my loaded gun, and one moment's pain would save the agony of a lingering death, which now seemed inevitable. Thus whispered the fiend in my ear, and the horrid thought gradually took such hold on me, that fearing that in a moment of desperation the temptation might prove too strong for me, I dashed my gun in the snow to render it useless, and at that moment felt like another man. No blame could attach to me that even for a moment I entertained such a dreadful and sinful thought. I was no longer master of myself; my whole disposition seemed changed. How long I now wandered on I had no means of guessing. I moved mechanically, as if in a trance. My clothes were all frozen, and every time my foot sank into the snow it seemed to take me five minutes to get it up again. Every sinew in my leg was cracking, and my hands hung down like useless and dead weights at my sides. At length I saw something indistinctly looming through the fog before me. I was close to it. I struggled on, and found that it was an empty shed by the side of the lake, used for keeping nets and fishing gear in. I staggered in, sank down upon a heap of old netting, and lay for some time in a kind of swoon. However, I was now safe, for I was sheltered from the snow, and I could at least keep my blood in motion by walking backwards and forwards round the hut. The reader will possibly imagine that I was overpowered with feelings of joy at such a deliverance. Not a bit of it. I had looked imaginary death in the face so long, that it seemed to have lost all its terrors, and a sullen indifference had settled on me. A savage desire came over me to set the place on fire, and have a glorious warm; and had I possessed any means of getting a light, in five minutes the old shanty would assuredly have been in a blaze. Strange! One would have thought that, after all the trouble I had taken in reaching this haven, I should have been content to remain there till daylight. But not so; I now knew where I was, and after I had rested awhile I set out for the cottage, which I knew was not far distant. I soon reached it. All the inmates were asleep, but the door was unbolted, and I walked in. I soon had the peasant up; and when we got a light I saw by the clock that it was just five, so I had been wandering in the snow for about nine hours; and as my thermometer, when I reached home, stood at 18° cold, Celsius, I calculated that in the night it must have been as low as 25° (about 13° below zero, Fahrenheit)—and, mind, I had no pea-jacket! I durst not take my boots off till I got fairly home; but the blazing fire, and a cup of hot coffee with which the peasant provided me, quickly brought me round; and as soon as I was a little refreshed I hobbled home. I had to cut off my boots. When I pulled my stockings off and bathed my feet in *cold* water, they looked just like raw meat; and any one who knows what it is to ride hunting in a pair of tight tops can to some extent fancy what I felt. However, beyond great pain in my feet, I suffered no serious inconvenience, and twelve hours in the blankets set me all right again.

Twice before in my life have I spent as long and dismal a night as this—once lying out on the bowsprit of a Swedish schooner, when we were caught in the race of Alderney, and, drifting along the east coast of that island, with breakers on our starboard, we expected to strike every hour; and another time, when bushed in an Australian forest during a storm of thunder and lightning, which raged the whole night with such violence as only a thunder-storm can rage south of the equator. But on neither occasion did I experience the feelings of this night in the snow.

And now, if any of my readers should fancy I have made "much ado about nothing," and spun a fine yarn out of a trifling thread, I can only assure him that I have faithfully described what I felt; and if he fancies I have exaggerated in the least, I only hope that it may be his luck, just for once, to be out himself on such a night, and he will then see how he likes it.

Since that night I have had a deal of conversation on the subject with many of our fell men and foresters, and all agreed that I could have scarcely been bushed in a worse night. In general, when the snow is falling, the wind is still and the air dull and warm; but on this night the cold, piercing wind turned the soft snow-flakes into sleet, and the thermometer was many degrees below zero. So heavy a snowstorm has not been known in Wermland for twenty years. In the last such storm it was computed that 105 lives were lost in the north. They all agreed that I was perfectly right in keeping going; and said that if I had once sunk exhausted in the snow, I should never have risen again. On the Lapland fells, where it is not unusual to be lost in a snow-drift, the plan they adopt is this: They push on for awhile, and when they find their track is fairly lost, and they must be snowed-in, they scrape a deep hole in the snow, lay their "skiddors," or long snow-skates, across the top of the hole, which prevents the falling snow quite blocking them in, and leaves a little air-hole. They creep in, and lie pretty warm and snug till they begin to feel drowsy, when they must at once rouse themselves, go on again, and dig another hole; and so they go on till they find their track. The great thing is to avoid becoming exhausted; for in that case, if sleep comes on a man, it will be the sleep of death; but it is not so dangerous if sleep should overtake a man while he is fresh, for he might then possibly live for days in the snow, and be taken out alive, in which case he might recover, and live even for a few years; but he will never be the same man again afterwards, and in all probability will soon die of consumption. This is what I have since been told by practical men, and they all agreed that, considering the deep, loose state of the snow, and the coldness of the night, I had a very narrow escape.

But to return to my Lapland diary. The potatoes were planted by June 3rd, and in about a week's time the country was indeed beautiful to behold. All the lowlands were covered with the light silvery foliage of the willow, and wild flowers of every hue (many of them strangers to me) met the eye at every step. But I missed many of my little home favourites, for the daisy, the cowslip, the violet, and the lily of the valley appeared to be strangers here. A little rain fell in the beginning of June, but for the rest of the month the weather was beautiful, and we were not kept in-doors for one day by bad weather; and this was lucky, for June is by far the most important month to the Lap collector. Throughout the whole month our occupation was the same, collecting every day. As I had little time myself to go and seek for nests, the plan I adopted was this: whenever any of my boys found a nest in the neighbourhood of Quickiock, they never took it, but marked the place (and these peasant lads never forget a place which they have once marked, even in the deepest forests). Two days in every week I used to go round and take the nests myself, and, if it was necessary, shot the old bird. By this plan I was certain not to be deceived; and as I much wanted type specimens well authenticated for my own collection, it was worth a little trouble to obtain them. Towards the middle and end of the month I had two or three most interesting trips up on to the fells, where we camped out each time for two or three nights, in search of the eggs of Buffon's skua, which birds literally swarmed on our fells this summer—a most unusual occurrence; and I had the pleasure both of watching the habits of this rare bird in a state of nature, and of obtaining a good collection of both birds and eggs. I was also now much engaged with the ptarmigan and pine grosbeak in summer dress. On June 15th the sun rose 40 minutes after 12 at night, and set at 22 minutes after 11, and by my Lap almanac, seems never to set again till the 28th.

By the beginning of July the egg season was over—in fact, most of the birds had young, and it was only the very early breeding birds which we shot; as it is an act of the greatest cruelty now, to shoot an old bird when there is a chance that the unfledged young are dependent upon her for their food. Although perhaps no collector, let his pursuit be what it may, can be altogether free from the imputation of cruelty, there are many needless acts of cruelty which he can avoid; and if he can content himself only with taking the eggs from a nest, and makes it a rule never to shoot a bird unless he really wants it, his pursuit is far more harmless and innocent than many others which man indulges in only to gratify his love of sport.

For about six weeks in June and July the rays of the setting sun might be seen gilding the fell tops during the whole night. The hottest weather was in July, and often at midday I saw the thermometer in the sun as high as 35° Celsius (95° Fahr.) The priest told me that in winter he has seen the glass as low as 45° below zero Celsius (49° below zero Fahr.) But the nights were always cold, and I believe every night there was a frost on the fells.

By what I could hear, this was an early season, for frequently the ice does not go from the river till the middle of June, and the fell lakes are not clear until the end of the month. They generally expect the first snow-storm in autumn, about Michaelmas (but the river is often not frozen up till the middle of November). The ground is then usually covered with snow, the sun disappears below the horizon, and is never seen again until the 20th of January. It came on to rain about the first week in July, and for about six weeks I don't think we had above six days in which no rain fell; and my lad, who lay out on the fells generally two nights every week without a tent, used to complain bitterly of the cold. To work these fells properly a man requires a small tent, and three or four of these half-civilized Laps to help him. By the second week in July the young willow-grouse were three-parts grown, and strong flyers (and I may here remark that I never did see young birds grow so fast as these), but it was not until the first week in August that I could find any young ptarmigan fit to shoot. By the middle of July some few ducks had brought their young broods down to the water holes and lowland swamps, but it was not until August that we had any real sport with the flappers—for I cannot call it sport, as they do here, to murder the old females and the young brood in the grass before the latter can fly, and shoot the old males when they are moulting and have lost their pinion feathers. I was, I must say, rather disappointed with the duck-shooting here, for, owing to the want of bulrushes, reeds, and other high covert, the young birds so soon become wild and take to the open water that they generally rise out of shot; I could, however, manage to bag ten or twelve strong flyers any evening early in August. This was a very bad season for butterfly collecting, owing to the high wind and cold dull days on the fells; and the rarest fell butterfly, the *Colias Boothii* (which they call here the "verdandi," and which appears to be confined to only one fell range in this neighbourhood), did not show. I remarked, however, that most of the butterflies had disappeared by August 1st. I only heard thunder once up here—in fact, they say that a thunder storm is of rare occurrence. About August 13th they were in the middle of the hay harvest. The cows and horses were turned out into the forest about the middle of June, and would probably remain there till early in September. The barley was quite green when we left, and it appeared very doubtful to me whether it would ever ripen. About the second week in August the weather cleared, and on August 21st we left Quickiock, improved in "limb, wind, and sinew," after spending four very interesting and pleasant months in this "land of forest and fell." I made a very good collection both of birds and eggs. I added about thirty new authentic eggs to my own private collection; I obtained many birds in a state of plumage in which we never see them but in Lapland; and what was better, I had an opportunity of studying the habits of many of our rarer British birds at that most interesting time of all, the breeding season (and the few observations which I made will be faithfully chronicled hereafter); but, what was best of all, I left Quickiock with the good wishes of all the village, for the little money that I had spent among its poor inhabitants in the summer would help them to obtain many little comforts for the next long and dreary winter which they must have gone without had I not come up.

When we left Quickiock the highest fells were still covered with snow, which never melts, and, in many of the chasms between the fells, I have no doubt lies 100 feet deep, the accumulation of ages.

CHAPTER VI.

HINTS TO SPORTSMEN AND NATURALISTS IN LAPLAND.

NEVER did I see in any country so much game as in Lapland. Immediately around Quickiock, where every one shoots and snares just as he pleases, the game is, of course, as a natural consequence kept down; but the shooter need only wander a few miles from the village, and I am certain that on any day he will be able to shoot more game than he can well carry home. It is hardly likely that any one will travel up here solely for the sake of sport; but as an Englishman seldom leaves home without his gun and fishing-rod, it will probably interest many to know what sort of sport is to be obtained in this wild land. I will, therefore, devote a page or two to their especial benefit, and, although I know nothing of any other part of Lapland, my remarks will doubtless apply pretty well to the whole country.

For capercailzie, hazel grouse, and willow grouse, the shooter can hardly go wrong, let him pitch his tent where he will south of Kanto Keino.

Black game is not nearly so abundant in any part of Lapland as further south, and appears to be very local—for at Quickiock we rarely saw a blackcock, while at Iockmock, eighty miles south, they are very plentiful. Every fell literally swarms with ptarmigan, dotterel, golden plover, and mountain hare. A curious feature in the habits of the game birds up here, is their uncertain migrations from one tract to another. I don't know whether the ptarmigan and willow grouse wander much; this particularly applies to the capercailzie, and black grouse.

For flapper-shooting in July, Lapland would be hard to beat, for half the lowlands consist of rivers, rushy swamps, and inland lakes; and this country is the great breeding resort of half the wild-fowl in Europe. The common wild duck is rare in Lapland, but scoter, velvet duck, scaup, golden eye, pintail, and widgeon, wild swan, bean, and white-fronted geese, flock in hundreds, as soon as the ice breaks up, to these northern waters, where they can breed in undisturbed security far away from the haunts of man.

Although Lapland itself may lie almost beyond his range, the day may not be so very far distant when the English grouse-shooter will have to turn his attention to the Swedish and Norwegian fells, where shooting is to be had for the asking, and neither grouse disease nor heather-burning has as yet swept off the game. There are many places on these fells, within the pale of civilization, where a party could pitch their tent and live quite as comfortably as on the Scotch moors. In the matter of £ s. d. they would most probably be gainers; and if they only chose a good district, I am certain that they would find as good sport both for the gun and the rod as in any part of North Britain. There would not be half the trouble in the journey that they might anticipate; in fact, we can reach the Dovre-fell from Christiania by rail and steamer; and I should say that any of the fells a little north of Sneehatten would be good shooting ground. The worst part of it is, their game would be little or no use to them; and there is something repugnant to the feelings of the fair sportsman in shooting game merely for the sake of slaughter. But as we read of men paying about £90 per year for a Scottish moor, and getting in return fifty brace of grouse, I fancy these shootings would be quite on a par with that; for out of fifty brace, a man, if he treated himself to grouse for his dinner when on the moors, would have very little left to send to his friends, while the shooter here would at least be able to supply his own table and have much better sport, without paying any rent. The English salmon fishers have already taken the

Norwegian rivers by storm, and, although we may not live to see it, the day will assuredly come when the British shooter, disgusted with exorbitant rents, scarcity of game, and expenses of preserving at home, will have to look out for a fresh field, and that field will be the great dividing fell-range between Sweden and Norway. The red grouse has, however, now been lately introduced into Sweden, and if they only thrive, which I fancy they will, the day perhaps will soon come when a new field, and one very easy of access, will be opened to the British shooter.

But although the country around us swarmed with game, I troubled myself very little about it; I had other work in hand. My time was fully occupied, and, moreover, ammunition was scarce, and it was rarely we shot a bird which we did not want for the collection. I never, therefore, tried how much game I could kill in any one day; but I am certain that in August I could have easily bagged twenty brace of willow grouse on any afternoon; and ten or twelve brace of ptarmigan, on the fells, would have been an easy day's work. I have often killed six brace of willow grouse, just to keep my hand in, without losing sight of the village; and, as the English sergeant said in the Crimean rifle-pits, on one or two occasions I have had "some very pretty shooting indeed." I did here what I never before did in my life. I bagged seven full-grown capercailzie in one afternoon, killing two fine cocks right and left. The country round here would have swarmed with wildfowl, if they would only spare the breeding birds; but whenever a pair of ducks drop in the water in spring, within sight of a settler's house, their death-warrant is sealed. "Holkar," or little wooden tubs, are set up against the trees by the river side, in which the golden-eye and merganser breed; but the birds are so much disturbed that very few stay to breed just round the village, but go back into the forest and the scrub under the fells.

To the naturalist visiting Lapland I will offer the following advice: Neglect not to bring up plenty of fine, tough ladies' curling-paper and pins to wrap up the specimens in, for you can't get any here; and skins never travel so well as when they are separately wrapped up. I had nearly 1,000 skins to bring down, many of them large; and as I was anxious to stow them away as closely as possible to save expense of carriage, I took out all the tow from the inside of the birds, and packed them close. This plan answers very well with some birds, such as ducks, divers, etc.; but with most other skins it is far better to stuff them out in shape at first, and let them remain so.

Arsenical soap, on the whole, is the best preservative for the traveller, as a little goes in a small compass, and in a tin canister there is no fear of breakage. But he should also take up a pound of alum and saltpetre, finely powdered, and mixed in equal parts, to fall back upon; in fact, I like this preservative nearly as well as any other. A few *coloured* engravings of the birds he most wants he will find useful. I have often wasted half an hour in trying to describe any particular bird to a northern peasant, without avail; but when I showed the coloured figure of the bird, he has recognized it immediately. Boxes for packing he can procure anywhere—at least very good substitutes, made by the Laps and settlers of birch bark; these will do to transport his things down to the coast, when he can get proper ones made. A dozen egg-drills and tin blow-pipes will not be too many for the egg collector. Above all things, he should bring up with him a few yards of light oil-skin; it will be useful on the fells to rig up a temporary tent, and will preserve his specimens from wet in a boat. Tow and cotton wool he can procure at any seaport town here, but he must take all he wants up into Lapland. Whether he be an insect hunter or not, he may as well bring up a net, a few collecting boxes, and pins, for he will meet with many rare butterflies, and they take little room. If he wishes to preserve specimens of fish, he has but two plans: he must either skin them and stretch them on cardboard or wood, or he must dry them in *dry salt*, in a box, which will preserve them perfectly fresh for a little time. The moisture, however, runs out of a *wooden* box. Before putting them into the salt, let him wrap each specimen separately in paper or fine linen; for without this precaution the fin-rays will become so brittle that they will break off. Pound the salt fine, as, if it is in lumps, it will leave dents in the fishes; and lay the fishes in layers, with a good bed of salt between each. The entrails should be taken out, or they will rot and spoil the specimen; but preserve the stomach with the food in. He can get no spirits after he leaves the towns; and if he has to carry his baggage any distance, a keg of spirits will be a very expensive article. Still, if his real object be ichthyology, there is no way of bringing home really good specimens except in spirits; although, since I came from Lapland, I have seen specimens of fish preserved wholly in zinc canisters, with common salt, keep very well for months; and this plan I shall certainly adopt another year. Cover over the aperture with wet bladder, which will effectually keep the air from the specimens. Salt can be got up in Lapland, and all the collector needs in this case is to take up a zinc box to put his fish in.

However, I will waste no more time on this subject. The collector knows what is really necessary; and although he should never burthen himself with a *single unnecessary* article, he should take care not to *leave a single really necessary* article at home. If he is a sportsman, he can depend upon getting shot either in Stockholm or Gefle—*nothing else*. If he is a fisherman, he must bring with him *all his tackle*—in fact, if a man really means work, he must leave nothing to chance. He can procure assistance and meat everywhere; but let him depend upon nothing else.

The telescope I have used for the last year has been Steward's rifle telescope; it is the handiest glass I know for the collector, and answers every purpose, without being cumbersome. I have since obtained his " Lord Bury telescope," which is certainly, for its size, the most splendid glass I ever looked through.

The collector will do well to bring up a spare extra cheap gun, for wherever he goes he will always find some one willing to shoot for him; but they all use small pea-rifles up here, which injure the specimens too much. He can always get rid of a cheap gun when he leaves, and receive its full worth in money or specimens.

I never was in a worse district than this for snipe, and I never could account for the absence of this bird from a country so well suited to its habits; but there are so many little secrets in nature hidden from us, that the more we study the habits and economy of the animal creation, the more are we puzzled at the various anomalies which we meet with. I saw only three snipe all the time I was up—one double and two full birds. This circumstance strikes me as most singular, for I know the jack-snipe breed further north, at Munioniska, and the double snipe, I am told, is tolerably common up near the Alten.

The woodcock appears to be unknown here, and I don't believe they come so far north.

A high-couraged setter is the best dog for these fells, where there is never want of water in the summer; and a heavy retrieving close-hunting spaniel, that will face water, is indispensable for the woods and lowlands. English powder, and, above all, English caps, should be brought up, for the foreign rubbish won't fit an English nipple; and it is a good plan for the sportsman, before leaving England, to have a couple of small nipples fitted into his gun, in case from necessity he should have to turn to foreign caps. Never keep your English caps mixed with the foreigners. If you do, the foreign caps will creep inside the

English ones, and can't be got out without a deal of bother.

As to dress, every sportsman has his own ideas on that head, so I will say no more, except that it cannot be too strong ; and if a man really means work, he cannot do better on the fells than to adopt the Lap costume as far as skin breeches and shoes go. Above all things avoid hobnailed shoes on the fells; they are both dangerous and troublesome. A pair of good light water-boots will often prove a real comfort in wading these fell streams, in which the water is always icy cold; and in the summer the forests are always wet. No fear of the shooting dress being too thick or too warm, especially if a man camps out much on the fells, for I have seen these fell lakes coated with ice on a midsummer night, and on a windy day my fingers have been so numbed that I could scarcely load my gun. The weather may be warm enough down in the Quickiock valley, but it will be very different on the tops of the highest fells, especially when the north wind comes howling over the dreary waste of perennial snows lying between this and the Arctic Ocean.

I need not remind the naturalist and collector that, in a trip like this, the identification of his specimens is of the utmost importance. To every bird's leg he should, of course, attach a label noting sex (♀ for female, ♂ for male), date of capture, and locality; and for eggs the best and simplest plan, is this: his egg will of course be blown with a blow-pipe from one hole in the side; above this hole let him write his initials, and under it a number:— All the eggs in any one nest will bear the same number. Thus I take my first nest of the Siberian jay on April 16th, with three eggs. I mark all the three eggs with No. 8. I have a small note book ruled thus:—

Date.	Name.	No. on Egg.	Remarks.
1862.			
Ap.16	Garrulus Infaustus 3 eggs ..	8	Taken by myself (as the case may be) at Quickiock, out of a small fir, 6 feet from the ground; old bird shot. Eggs a little sat on. Nest (describe nest, and add as many particulars as you choose).
„ 18	Tengmalm's Owl 4 eggs ..	9	Taken, etc.

If he chooses, he can paste a neat printed label over the whole, with the name of the bird. This plan I have adopted for years, and I know none so good. With small birds I always, if possible, preserve the nest with the full number of eggs, for I consider the nest quite as valuable and interesting as the eggs themselves. As all the eggs belonging to the same nest are numbered with the same figure, by a reference to his little note book, the identification of any egg (even if his eggs get mixed) is very easy.

No matter how hard an egg is sat on I can always clean out the embryo by the following process, which beats all others:—Make a largish hole in the side, by cutting a square piece of the shell out with a scalpel or scissors; pick out as much of the young bird as you safely can, and then blow water into the egg with the blow-pipe; let it stand for some days in a dark drawer or box, and keep repeating this process about every third day, gradually blowing more water into the shell, and picking a little out till the whole of the embryo has rotted away. This is by far the safest and surest plan with a valuable egg.

CHAPTER VII.

ON THE FISH PECULIAR TO THESE WATERS, THE REPTILES, AND THE INSECTS OF LAPLAND.

To the angler and ichthyologist I will now say a few words, although, while staying in this locality, I had but little time to devote to the "gentle art." I had some tackle with me, but notwithstanding I now and then took a cast, *I never killed a single fish*, for I had no fly tackle; and the fish in the Quickiock rivers would not look at the artificial bait, although I tried one of Alfred Gould's most life-like imitations, which never yet failed in the Wermland waters. I attribute this much to the clearness and shallowness of the water in the Tarra river, and there being no real good streams or eddies. There was certainly a magnificent trout stream running down from the fells to the Quickiock river, which came dashing and tumbling over the rocky bottom, full of streams and pools; and doubtless the fly would answer here; and I have seen the little fell lakes literally alive with the fish rising at the evening flies. To fish these little lakes properly, I should say that one of

Cording's India-rubber boats would be just the thing, for it would be so easily transported. I think, however, that for Lapland the fly is better than the bait; but from what I could hear, the few·English fishermen who have visited Quickiock all agreed that it is one of the worst stations for the angler in Lapland. Iockmock seems much better, for the river there is full of good streams. Sea-salmon come up to Iockmock waterfall, and there are more species of fish than in the Quickiock waters; but I question if they have the charr there. The fly that I used to see on the fell waters in the end of June was, I fancy, the common stone-fly—at least, if not, it was a very good imitation. The May-fly appeared to be scarce, and came on the water late. It struck me as being smaller than our drake. The fly in use here for grayling was a fancy fly—black ostrich body, white wings. I think, however, the fish are not particular in these waters, and will rise at a fly which a pampered Thames trout would turn away from in disgust. The two flies which I have mentioned, a green drake and lake-trout fly, dressed thus—body red, with silver twist; wing, golden pheasant; shoulder, blue jay—and a few red and brown palmers, would be standard flies for any part of Lapland. The tackle must be strong, and everything of the best, for a grayling of 5 lb. or a trout of 10 lb. in these rapids will give some play. I have seen charr rising here at the stone-fly as well as trout.

According to Mr. Lloyd, the salmon neither take bait or fly well in any of the Bothnian rivers. He adds :—"It is a curious fact that these salmon will not rise at the fly, and one worthy the attention of naturalists. The only attempted solution I ever heard is that these fish may not be the genuine *Salmo salar*, but a huge trout resembling it in appearance."

In journeying up from Stockholm to Tornea, I counted upwards of one hundred rivers. Many of them, as the Dal, the Umea, the Calis, the Tornea, of great magnitude, and some navigable to a considerable distance into the interior. This deluge of waters, considering that the country whence they take their rise is of no great extent, always puzzles the Scandinavian adventurer.

I have always heard that the best salmon rivers are on the north and west coasts of Norway, but for trout, grayling, and charr I fancy almost any Lap stream or fell lake is as good as another.

The Quickiock waters contain fewer varieties of fish than any which I know, and, strange to say, not one single species of the genus *Cyprinus* is met with here. This I attribute to the clearness of the water, and the total absence of all grass and water weeds from the sides and bottoms of the rivers and lakes. The water is as clear as crystal, and we could see to the bottom at almost any depth; and it is curious to stand on a high fell and look down to the very bottom of a lake which lies at the base. The *only* species of fish peculiar to the Quickiock waters are pike, perch, trout (certainly two distinct species), charr, grayling, gwynniad, vendace, and burbot; at Iockmock, I believe they take roach. But although the number of species may be few, the name of the individuals is legion; and for sweetness of flesh, fatness, and good condition, I will back the Quickiock fish against any in the world. Such charr! and trout as red as blood. Even the old pike tasted here quite a different fish from those we take in the sluggish British waters.

The trout in the lake and small streams here are undoubtedly the common trout (*Salmo fario*), varying, however, much in colour and appearance according to the water from which they are taken. They run to a good size, 3 lb. to 5 lb. not being uncommon. But we used to take another trout in the river Tarra (never up in the lakes or smaller streams), which I fancied was altogether a different trout from any I have hitherto seen in Sweden. The fishermen here called it "borting," and said they could distinguish it at any age from the common trout by the total absence of red spots from all parts of the body, and by its bright silvery appearance when first killed. It struck me as different from either of our Wenern lake trout, and appeared more to resemble the salmon trout (*Sal. Trutta, L.*) than any other species, and I fancy that it is the real *Salmo Trutta*, Lin., acclimatized in fresh water. However, whether or not it was distinct from our Wenern lake trout, one thing is pretty clear that it was certainly distinct from the common trout; but as I shall probably at a future day, when I am more at home with the Swedish salmon, make a few more remarks on the subject, I shall dismiss it for the present, merely remarking that we used to take those borting from 2 lb. (I rarely saw them under) up to 12 lb. I never saw a red spot on one, although the common trout in the same water (but they were rare there) were spotted precisely like the common British trout. The flesh was always paler than in the common trout. The borting was a shorter, plumper fish than our Wenern lake trout, and altogether resembled in appearance the salmon trout (*S. Trutta*).

Mr. Lloyd in his Scandinavian adventures gives the following useful advice to the northern angler:—"In conclusion, a knowledge of the waters which experience and practice alone can give is needful to ensure success in the northern waters, otherwise days are lost in fishing places where no fish are to be found. Early in the season the deep pools below the falls and rapids are the best; as the summer advances, the fish get strength and take to, the strongest streams; and as autumn comes on, the heaviest fish lie just above the largest falls and rapids. It requires some nerve as well as skill to fish in these places. Two men, with a pair of sculls each, is requisite, and great care must be taken not to get drawn too near the falls, as in that case nothing can save one."

The charr which we usually took in the fell lakes was just the common charr (*S. alpinus*, Lin.), but they vary much in colour, and we have two distinct varieties, in the one of which the flesh was pale, and in the other red. The red ones are found in the higher fell lakes, and the higher the lake the redder and handsomer are the charr. But they say that the charr are never found on the very fells themselves, nor higher up than the birch region, which has its highest range 2000 feet under the limits of perpetual snow. The common trout (at least that variety which is called the *S. punctatus*, Cuv.), however, has a higher range—in fact, goes further up into the fell waters than any European fish. I never saw the charr here (except in one lake) exceed 3 lb. in weight. But in a lake at the foot of a high fell, about six miles from Quickiock, there was a large variety or species of charr which, I take it, must have been identical with Nilsson's "Wetterns roding." The largest specimen which I preserved was 28 inches long, and weighed 6¾ lb. They are, however, often taken up to 8 lb., and now and then as heavy as 12 lb. The specimen which I caught in a net was a splendid fish; it was in fine condition—belly and flesh as red as blood. It was a male fish, and had a small crook (it was taken on June 20), a thing I never recollect seeing before in a charr. On comparing it with three common charr of about 3 lb. weight, which were sent me in from another lake the same morning, I could observe no specific differences. They appeared to be precisely the same, both in shape, colour, number of scales, and finrays, and the only difference appeared to be in the size. It was, however, the largest charr I have seen, and certainly a magnificent fish both to eat and look at.

The grayling run here to a large size, but they are not plentiful. I saw several specimens about 3 lb. in weight, and one which I preserved was nearly 5 lb.; but they all said up here that this was the largest grayling they had ever seen. This was 19 inches long to the root of the tail. Mr.

Lloyd mentions killing in one day, 50 brace of grayling in a tributary of the Kemi river, 69° north lat., weighing upwards of 100 lb.

The burbot were neither large nor numerous, and the season for them closed just after we came up.

The perch were remarkably fine and large in these waters. We often took 60 lb. or 70 lb. in one large bow-net in a night. I observed that we seldom saw one under ½ lb., and 3 lb. was not an uncommon size. Some years since a kind of epidemic raged among the perch here, and nearly all were swept off, but they are now recovering their numbers again.

We had certainly two species of gwynniad here. The *Coregonus oxyrhinchus*, Nilss. (Näbb-sik, Swed.), and the *Coregonus Lavaretus* (or Löf-sik, Swed.). We used to take both in the same haul of the net, but the *C. Lavaretus* was by far the rarest. It is said they are often taken up to 8 lb. I never, however, saw one above 5 lb. There is a smaller species here, at least they used to consider it a distinct species, which they called the "asp," a name, however, which we use in the middle of Sweden for a very different fish, the *Cyprinus Aspius*, Lin. They always ran small, and I never saw a specimen over 8 inches; but they were always full of roe or milt, in June and July, whereas I never then saw any roe or milt in a small gwynniad. I fancied they must have been the vendace; but the fishermen here said not, for they never take any vendace till the end of September; we took these little fish all through the summer.

According to Professor Widegren, who has just brought out a Treatise on the Scandinavian *Salmo*, we have five distinct species of sik, or gwynniad, in Sweden, besides the vendace, four of which are common in the Lapland waters, viz.:—

    Coregonus oxyrhinchus, Lin.
    C. Fera, Jur.
    C. Lavaretus, Lin.

In all of which, according to Widegren, the upper jaw projects beyond the under; but their differences are constant at all ages, and although they frequent the same waters, they are nevertheless very different in their habits, and the localities which they frequent; and he also mentions two more, in which the jaws are even.

The same author appears to doubt the identity of this Lap "asp" with the vendace (*C. albula*), and probably the Quickiock fishermen were correct in saying it was another species. However, much confusion still exists respecting the different members of this family, and it would be very interesting if a man like Dr. Gunther would turn his attention to this subject, as he has already done to the charr.

Should this Lapland "asp" prove to be a distinct species of *Coregonus*, I believe it is as yet undescribed by any Swedish naturalist, unless it is the *Coregonus Nilssonii*, Val., which Widegren says is met with in the Lap waters. I never identified the vendace up at Quickiock, but they told me there that they do not begin to take them until September.

The largest pike I saw was 16 lb. The pike season here is short, and only lasts just during the spawning time, for I rarely saw a pike taken in a drag-net, but only in a large species of stake bow-net, which is set in the ice, at the mouth of any good spawning-ground. These we began to set in the end of April. At first we took nothing but perch, and after that pike, and then wound up with grayling. I never saw either trout or gwyniad taken in a bow-net, but occasionally a burbot finds his way in; there appears to be no way of taking gwynniad but in drag-nets. The quantity of pike sometimes caught in one night is astonishing. I once recollect seeing two men come home in the morning with as many pike as they could bear suspended from a long pole, which they carried between them on their shoulders. They must have had above 2 cwt. Three weighed above 12 lb. each. But, as with the game, so with the fish, they must gradually decrease when such a war of extermination is being continually waged against them, for the principal catch of all the fish is in the spawning season, and drag-nets are used, the meshes of which are so fine that no fish three inches long can escape. I observed here that after the middle of July very few fish were taken in the drag-net. I fancied they had then gone back to the deeps. This is a very bad river for leistering, a successful mode of poaching (and of which I must admit I am very fond), much in vogue in our Wermland waters.

They say there are no reptiles in Lapland. I only wish any one who fancies so had been with me one fine spring day when I turned over a heap of dry grass in a meadow in search of a field mouse. I am certain if there was one lizard under it, there must have been a thousand. They were just the little common viviparous lizard, and I saw no other up here. I never remember seeing a toad in Lapland; but as for frogs, I thought that one of the plagues of Egypt had descended upon us, when one fine day in spring, just as the snow went, every lowland seemed alive with frogs, leisurely hopping down from their winter quarters to the water holes and ponds which the ice had left. This was on May 15th, and I saw none before. I certainly never observed such large or handsome-coloured frogs. I never saw a newt in Lapland, nor do I ever remember noticing a common land snail, although there were many little water snails in some of the waters here. I saw only one snake all the time I was up. This was a female adder about 18 inches long, early in June.

In a small river near Iockmock they find a species of pearl, and the shells of this Lapland pearl mussel appear to be exactly identical with those we pick up in some of our Wermland brooks. I bought some on my way down, which I sent to England, where, however, they were little valued.

The Quickiock district was very rich in insects, and a wide field is open to the entomologist, for many rare and beautiful butterflies abound on these fells, among them I may mention—

Chionalias Norna.
Erebia Medusa.
,, Embla—peculiar I believe to Sweden.
,, Disa.
,, Manto.
Melitæa Iduna—peculiar to Sweden.
Argynnis Freja.
,, Polaris.
,, Dia.
,, Frigga.
,, Thore.
Colias Boothii.
,, Nastes.
Lycæna Aquila—which has only yet been taken at Quickiock, by Walberg, and considered the rarest butterfly in Sweden.
Lyrichlus Centaurus, and some others.

This sort of collecting was a new game to me, but I bought a largish collection, which, however, turned out scarcely worth sending to England. Being nothing of an entomologist myself, it is very probable that the legs and antennæ might have been wanting to some of my specimens; but still one would have thought that a collection of insects from a fell tract would have been interesting in England; but no one seemed to care anything for it.

It seems that an old German had been up here collecting, and every man and boy in the parish had acquired a taste for entomology.

I used often to laugh at the little lads here. They had all caught up a smattering of the Latin names from this old German professor, and they used to come into my room, their caps covered with beetles and butterflies impaled upon pins, for every one of which they had a Latin name, such as I am certain could be found in no work on entomology now extant. However, "Keitel" (this was the old German) called it so, and their scale of prices seemed to be completely regulated by what "Keitel" paid them. In fact "Keitel" was the authority in this little village regarding insects, as doubtless I shall be for the future as regards birds and eggs.

But *the* Lap insect of which everyone has heard

is the mosquito, and it is a pity that this is not worth collecting, or a man might make his fortune in a week. I had heard such fearful accounts of the swarms of mosquitoes which we should encounter up here, and so many different remedies as preventives against their bites were recommended to me, that I really began to fancy in the summer we should not be able to get on at all. Some recommended smearing the face with train oil and tar, but as it seems that if any of this mixture happens to get into your eyes or nose you stand a very good chance of being blinded or suffocated, I was inclined to think that the remedy would be worse than the disease. One botanist assured me that it was quite impossible to collect flowers in Lapland during July, because you can't well collect in gloves (I should fancy not), and it was impossible to have the hands bare on account of these plagues. But he was a very fine gentleman, and when I looked at his delicate lady-like hands I thought it very probable that the mosquitoes would prefer his blood to that of a smoke-dried Lap. One recommended great green specs; another a green veil, such as "gents" wear on the Derby day. I wonder no one recommended a patent respirator. Mr. Buckland, in a letter to the *Field* of Aug. 29, 1863, recommends spirits of turpentine as an infallible remedy against the attacks of mosquitoes. He says that any chemist could, as the doctors have it, make up the turpentine into an elegant formula in the shape of an ointment, which could be easily spread over the face and hands. I shall certainly give this a trial next year. However, as I have ever during my wanderings consoled myself with this reflection, that where one man can live another can; and, moreover, as I had already stood the attacks of the mosquitoes for a few years in the Australian swamps, I made up my mind to chance it; and all I can say is, that although just before rain I have been much annoyed by them, I never was once prevented from shooting, and I used neither gloves, veil, tar, or any other preventive. It was true that the summer of 1862 was cold and windy, and all said that there were fewer mosquitoes than usual; and another thing,—although very rapacious, I fancy your mosquito is a dainty feeder, and all flesh does not suit its taste, for they seldom trouble me much; whereas my lad, who was a juicy young red-faced peasant, used to complain dreadfully, and as he was out much more than myself he had far more experience. The worst is at night. It is not so much their bite as their horrid buzz which annoys me, and I never can tell from what quarter it is coming. You must be very careful never to leave windows or doors open here in the summer, and must even stop up the chimney, for they will find their way into a room through the smallest aperture. But the mosquito is not entirely confined to Lapland, for I recollect this very summer sleeping in a house by the banks of the Venern, in South Wermland, Sweden. I had been hard wading for ducks all day, and being very tired, turned in early, while it was yet light. When I went into my room there were, I am sure, more than a thousand mosquitoes flying up and down the window panes, and their music was so loud that, tired as I was, there was no chance of sleeping. I could not open the window, so I lit my pipe and crept quietly to bed, and for about an hour lay in a constant state of anxiety watching them, dreading that one might find me out and bring the whole mob down upon me. They evidently partly "winded" me, for occasionally one would come piping half way across the room in the direction of my bed. However, they never seemed quite to be able to get on the scent, and as soon as it was dark they all became quiet. Mosquitoes are certainly not pleasant companions, either out of doors or in bed; but I take it that a good deal of exaggeration has been used as regards their numbers and annoyance. And I do not believe that any one need be frightened to visit Lapland on their account.

CHAPTER VIII.

A CHAPTER ON THE MAMMALIA BELONGING TO THIS DISTRICT.

The different quadrupeds met with in the district around Quickiock I shall just slightly notice, without going into their natural history or habits, for I can state nothing new with respect to any one of them.

I have already noticed the reindeer; but I cannot help here contradicting the statement I met with in "Wood's Natural History," quoted from the *Field* newspaper, where the writer says: "There is nothing of the antlered monarch about the reindeer, but a careworn, nervous expression, which I do not wonder at, considering how they are bullied. There are creatures which sting them all over, and creatures which lay their eggs in their ears and nostrils, and make themselves comfortable under their skin; and wolves, and gluttons, and dogs, and Laps; in short, I know of no animal so persecuted, barring a rat (and he has his revenge, and lives on the fat of the land), and nothing in return except snow and moss, which tastes like sponge." Whatever the reindeer moss tastes like I cannot say, but that the reindeer thrive on it is proved by the fact that no park-fed deer in England can look fatter and sleeker than the reindeer when they come down from the fells at the end of summer; in fact, " fat as a reindeer" is a common saying here. It is true they have their enemies, and so has every other living creature: not even man himself, the monarch of all. But the reindeer has plenty of cunning and ability to evade his persecutors. It is very rarely that a bear attacks the reindeer, and, though both the wolf and the glutton occasionally make havoc among the herd, it is not half so often as one might suppose. They escape the attacks of the insects in the summer by moving on to the very highest fells. Certainly, the reindeer that are used for draught are bullied enough; but, for all this, like the donkey at home, they do pretty well as they please, and it does not seem to affect their constitutions much. But a man must not look at a herd of draught reindeer, tethered round a Laplander's encampment, and take them as a sample. He must go on to the fells in the middle of summer, and watch a herd wandering free, and if he does not see quite such magnificent animals as the real " antlered monarch of the forest," he will at least see very different creatures from what he would be led to expect, after perusing the above exaggerated description. I recollect the last day I was on the fells; we had a large brown setter with us, which doubtless the reindeer took for a wolf; and one magnificent old white reindeer bull, with the finest pair of antlers I ever saw, followed us and kept our company for hours, stopping when we stopped, and never leaving us till we came upon the herd of about 600, feeding in a fell valley, when he trotted off and joined them. I thought I never in my life saw a much finer animal for its size; and there was an elasticity and freedom in his steps as he trod the heather which showed that he, instead of us, was the true monarch of this rude fell tract.

It was strange that there were no wild reindeer in this district, although I believe about Gellivare, and further north in Lapland, they are to be met with.

The elk (*Cervus alces*, Lin.) is not met with so far north. But, thanks to the care with which they are now preserved, this noble animal is yearly more and more spreading in Wermland; and as, through the kindness of a friend, in whose forest they are now tolerably numerous, I have had more than one opportunity of joining in the chase of the elk, I trust that the following description of an elk skall, in 1861, although not strictly referring to Lapland, may not be deemed out of place here:—

THE ELK SKALL.

"Tell —— that if he does not come soon, the elk and trout season will all be over." Such was the message I received from a friend when I came down from the fells in the middle of October, 1861. As I knew there was no time to lose, for the elk season closes here on the 1st of November, I proceeded without delay to get my tackle together, and, two days after, with a peasant for my guide and baggage-carrier, I set off, in anticipation of a pleasant and interesting visit, in which hope I was not disappointed. The invitation came from a friend, about twenty-five miles north of us, a thorough sportsman, and the owner of an immense tract of forest land, which (for Sweden) was tolerably well stocked with game. He has of late years been strictly preserving the elk in his woods; and, at a rough guess, I should say his herds now number some twenty or thirty head of deer. There is excellent trout-fishing in the little mountain streams, which intersect his forests in all directions; and two lakes, situate on the top of the highest mountains, are filled with charr *(Sal. alpinus)*—probably the southern limit of this fish in Sweden. I never yet had the good luck to kill elk, and the charr was a fish I much wanted to study in its native waters. Moreover, I was sure that I should receive a hearty welcome in "Bachelor's Hall," and that the longer I stayed the better would my host be pleased.

I left home early on one of those lovely mild mornings which we occasionally enjoy, even in these northern climes, in the fall of the year. Our way lay partly through the forests, partly by boat, for about ten miles up a large stream, the "Bye Elfven," which runs from the little northern town of Arvika down to the Lake Wenern. Of course I took my trolling tackle with me, although our fishing season, especially for pike, was nearly over. A walk of about six miles through the forest brought us to the river-side, where I hired a boat of a jolly cobbler, who, being himself a bit of a fisherman, volunteered to accompany us. It is true he had lots of work, which must stand still during his absence; but the love of sport was strong within him; and as he knew every inch of the stream, I gladly accepted his offer, gave him a couple of shillings for his loss of time, and off we started.

The morning was all that an angler could wish, mild as spring, with just breeze enough up the stream to raise a slight ripple on the water. But the bright yellow leaves of the birch which fringed the banks of the river, and that peculiar stillness which reigns throughout the autumnal landscape, unbroken save by the chattering of the fieldfares and redwings passing southward, and the occasional hoarse croak of the raven or hooded crow—all plainly spoke to us in mute and eloquent language of the "dying year's decay."

We had some very fair sport with the rod, and I reached my friend's house by sundown; and, before turning in, we agreed to start early next morning, fish the little mountain-streams up into the forest, and find out, if possible, the most likely ground to look for elk.

The situation of this estate is peculiar. The house, saw-mills, iron-forges, and cultivated land, are situate at the bottom of the mountains, by the river-side, and the water that works the machinery is supplied from the mountain-lakes. These lakes lie, as it were, in a chain one above the other, connected by streams which, in many places, form pretty cascades over the bed of rocks, in which are dams here and there for the purpose of stopping and letting on the water, and long shoots, or sluices, for carrying down the timber from the high mountains to the saw-mills below, which is an immense saving of land carriage. When the water is well on, I never saw better streams for trout—here and there a still, deep hole, but most of the water full of small eddies, formed by the rugged character of the bottom. There is, however, but little good to be done in these streams, except when a flush of water is on; consequently, spring and autumn are the only seasons when any sport can be had, and the only bait that can be well used is the worm. The higher lakes are, of course, the reservoir of the trout; and these streams also abound in crawfish and minnows, certainly the finest, both in colour and size, that I ever saw, for I took many of the latter nearly six inches long. The highest lake lies on a mountain top, some thousand feet above the level of the river, surrounded by as wild a tract of forest as I ever saw in my life. Every kind of ground—forest, swamp, and morass—is met with here. Many of the trees are of immense growth. Some of the old pines, scathed and branchless, stand like spectres among their living brethren; while others, borne down by old age, lie rotting in the wind and sun—the whole giving one a very fair idea of the primæval forests of the north. Hill and dale, gully and range, for miles and miles; the mountains clothed with forest, the lower gullies interspersed with morasses and lakes, on many of which a boat has never floated, and in whose waters a line has never been wetted. Such is, more or less, the character of the whole of this country from hence up to the North Cape, save that a little further north we shall reach the true fells, on whose rocky crests no vegetation, save the moss and the lichen, can thrive. The two lakes which hold the charr are situate on the highest mountains, and appear like basins cut out of the solid rock. In one, the rocky banks tower perpendicularly above the water, which is, perhaps, fifty fathoms deep at their base, the water as clear as crystal, and even in summer icy cold. I could not see a single weed or aquatic plant in either. These lakes may, perhaps, cover 150 acres each. In one, no fish are met with but charr; in the other there are charr, trout, and minnows. I may here mention that the trout peculiar to these lakes is the common trout *(Salmo fario)*, but they run to a large size, 6 lb. or even 8 lb. not being uncommon. All that we took were very dark-coloured, some nearly black.

We started at day-break with two days' provisions, and, rowing over two of the largest lakes, one of which was nearly a mile long, we came to our first stream. There was hardly flush of water enough for first-rate sport, but the day was beautiful, and we (three of us) managed to land about 100 trout of all sizes, from 4 oz. to 2 lb. Our forester, who fished with a string line, a hazel twig, and a hook and worm double the size I ever saw used for trout, beat my fine tackle hollow.

Altogether we had a delightful day. We camped at night in a forester's cottage, and, after a hearty supper of fried trout, new milk, and some of the very best potatoes I ever ate in my life, we threw ourselves down on a bed of new hay spread for us on the floor. In a few minutes I was dreaming of "flood and fell."

We set out next morning on the track of the elk, and it was not long before we came on fresh "spoor." This we followed up in a body, instead of making a bend on each side, as we should have done, and thus trying to head the elk. The consequence was that they went on; and, after a tiring walk of about twelve miles through the forest, every now and then rising game which we could not fire at, we had the disappointment of finding that the elk had doubled back and returned to their old quarters from whence we had driven them in the morning. The herd consisted of a bull and cow. I did not see them, but they passed within shot of one of the wood-watchers who had no gun. The day was now far spent, and, as we were six miles from home, we left the forest at sundown. I never remember so beautiful a night, for, as we rowed across the large lake, the moon was just rising over the top of the forest, and the northern heaven was in a blaze with flashes of the aurora borealis. I think I never saw so splendid a sky before. Although disappointed, we were gratified with the reflection that we knew where to look for the elk when we wanted them.

The next was a bye-day, and I took a stroll in the forest with one of the watchers. It was, perhaps, just then the very dullest of all seasons for a forest ramble in the north. All the summer migrants had left, the winter ones had hardly yet come down, and not a single song-bird was heard. Save the loud wild laugh of the great black woodpecker, the shrill chirp of the crested tit, the chattering of the crossbills, flitting from tree to tree in search of fir cones, or the heavy measured fall of the distant woodman's axe, scarce a sound broke the solemn silence that reigned over all. No woodland scene that I have witnessed can equal the melancholy gloom of a northern forest late in autumn, increased as it is by the damp aguish appearance of the whole landscape at this season.

I picked up a blackcock and a hare, and at night went out leistering for pike before the moon rose. We had fairish sport, and in about two hours I got 35 lb. weight, but nothing large. It is always a mystery to me where the big fish get to in these waters. It is very rarely that ever we kill a 14 lb. fish; and a pike of 10 lb. I consider a large fish up in Wermland.

Another beautiful morning, mild as spring—in fact, such an autumn as this up to November, I never recollect in the north. We went up again into the forest about 2 P.M., to try fishing again. It seems, however, that the weather did not just suit the trout, for we had hard work in about two miles of water to catch enough for our dinner. We dined by the side of the lake, and then proceeded to lay out the long line, and this took us till night. Our baits were dew-worms on large perch-hooks. We also set four standing flews, a species of net I never recollect seeing in England.

By the time we had finished our work, evening was closing in; and, as we had a keeper's cottage within two miles, thither we repaired to wait anxiously for the morning. In the night we were joined by two friends, the one a regular "bushman," one of the best bear and elk hunters in the north; the other a townsman, in a frock-coat and Wellingtons, of whom a grim old wood-watcher observed, *en passant*, "They should not send such a fellow as that out into the forest without a collar on him." However, he was the only one of the party who was fated to get a shot at an elk next day.

We were out as soon as day dawned, and it was the very morning of all others for elk-shooting. A little rain had fallen in the night, and a heavy mist hung over the forest like a dreary pall; the wind blew gently from the south, and, as I loaded my gun outside the cottage door, reminiscences of many a hunting morning in the days of "auld lang syne" rushed across my mind, and many an early breakfast by the cheerful kitchen fire in the old house at home (for the housemaid has not yet got the parlour in order), and ride to covert on such a morning, seemed like the visions of yesterday. It was indeed a beautiful hunting morning; but how different our meet to those of the days of yore. No merry chat, no jovial laugh—all was silent as the grave, and we looked more like a band of conspirators in the grey twilight than a parcel of jovial hunters. We had the elk in a gully between us and the lake, in which our long line lay; we did not know how near they might be to us, and the least noise might disturb them. Our only chance of a shot was for the shooters to walk silently through the forest for about two miles, plant ourselves on a rise (over which the elk were sure to come when the drivers roused them), and wait quietly for the driven deer. We had four guns and four drivers; and, issuing strict orders for the drivers to give us time enough, we picked our way in silence through the wood, speaking only in whispers, and soon reached our post. All our caution, however, was not superfluous, for so keen is the sense of hearing in the elk that they will start at any unwonted sound, which they can hear at a surprising distance; and once afoot, there is no saying where they will stop. As I was leaving the house I chanced to cough, when an old weather-beaten forester, seizing me by the arm, implored me, as if it were a matter of life and death, to clap my cap tightly before my mouth to deaden the sound in case I coughed again. By all accounts it seems, as the Scotch would say, that these elk are indeed "kittle cattle to shoe."

Never could we have a better chance of a shot, for if the elk were only once started it was certain that they would make for this rise, which was bounded on one side by the charr lake, on the other by a long open gully. This rise terminated in a long tongue heavily timbered; and it was here that two guns were planted, the other two going on. I had the post to the extreme left, and commanded the gully and the forest in front. My next neighbour was "the Cockney," at about 400 yards distance. I had scarcely been on my post a quarter of an hour before I heard a crashing through the timber and the falling of loose stones behind me; and on looking round I saw a magnificent cow elk quietly walking up the mountain-side within about 300 yards of me. Instead of coming up the gully, as I fancied would have been the case, and ascending the gentle slope before me, she had crossed the swamp behind us and chose the most precipitous part of the mountain for her ascent. But what mattered this to such an animal? It proved, however, how keen must have been her sense of hearing; for the drivers were at least a mile distant, and yet she had heard them and left her lair, in company with an old bull which crossed the gully some hundred yards higher up. I had nothing but a single smooth-bore, loaded with an ounce ball; and, as the distance was too far for a certain shot, I would not fire, for there was a chance of her coming nearer, and it was even on the cards that there might be more behind her. I therefore kept my gun down and stood motionless, watching the movements of one of our finest forest game in the freedom of its native home; and this alone was worth a trifle. Although the elk is a fine animal, there is something very ungainly and repulsive in its appearance, and nothing of that graceful airy bearing which characterises the red deer. The large head, thick overhanging upper lip, small pig eye, immense ears, and bearded throat, give this animal a singular and ferocious appearance; and certainly a bull elk is an awkward customer when brought to bay. The movements of this cow were conducted in a very leisurely manner; she would walk a few yards, then stand still snuffing up the air on all sides, her large ears moving to and fro the whole time. It was evident that she was totally unconscious of the hidden danger that so closely surrounded her, but appeared to be anxiously listening for the beaters. What surprised me most was that she did not smell me, for she had a side wind. I had my gun on her three or four times, for she presented a fair broadside, but the distance was too great. She kept in sight of me for nearly five minutes, when she moved slowly on, right up to the next gun. She was soon lost to my view, and I anxiously waited for the report; nor did I wait long. "Bang!" "ping" whistled the bullet close by me, from which I made a fair guess that my friend had missed; but what puzzled me most was that there was no shouting, nor did I hear the elk go away. Of course I could not move from my stand till I heard a challenge, and the few minutes that intervened between the first and second shots seemed to me an hour; at length it came, and a crashing through the timber told me that the elk was not down. She was evidently coming right up to me, and I stood like a statue, with my gun cocked to give her the *coup de grace*. But again I was doomed to disappointment. She came in sight in an open space about 600 yards below me, evidently hard hit. She stood still for a few seconds, rocking to and fro, with her head turned to me; when at length recovering herself, she struggled into the deep forest, and I saw her no more. It appears that she came within thirty yards of the stand next to me, and gave a fair broadside to my friend with the double. He was rather near-sighted, and at first could not make out whether it was a cow or an elk, and, when he had made out, was too excited to take a steady aim; and this accounts for his ball whistling so close past me. But the most singular part of the affair is, after he fired, the elk stood stock still; and, according to his own account, forgetting that he had a double gun, he proceeded to load again, but, finding out his mistake, he fired his second shot, when the elk made off. It was evident, however, she was hard hit, for we soon found blood on her "spoor," and when the beaters came up we commenced a trail hunt. But "a stern chase is a long chase;" and so it proved in our case. We started on the trail about nine in the morning, and followed it till six in the evening, when we lost it in a swamp intersected with fresh footmarks in every direction. It was beautiful to watch the foresters follow this trail. It reminded me exactly of a lot of hounds picking up a dead scent on a grassy fallow. We could hit it off pretty well at first; but the swamps beat us, for there the tracts became so mixed. Although hard hit (for we came upon many places in the swamps where she had lain down to cool herself, and left great patches of blood behind her), she was clearly not mortally wounded; and when we came to a fallen tree about four feet high, which lay across the track, and saw where she had scrambled over, one of the old watchers remarked to me, " this won't be an hour's job;" and he was right. Tired and disappointed, when we lost the trail we made for a neighbouring cottage. I am certain we all would have gladly bivouacked under the nearest pine and waited till the first light of morning to try and recover the lost trail; but we had no provisions, as we had fully depended upon breakfasting at the keeper's house after the first drive, on fried charr and probably an elk's liver. None of us had tasted a mouthful since 5 A.M.—we were, therefore, glad enough to reach the cottage; and although we got nothing but herrings and potatoes for supper, I don't think I ever relished a meal more in my life.

There was but one room in the house, and this not a very large one. I was, therefore, anxious to see how they would manage to bed us all up; for the household consisted of man and wife, two children, two men servants, two maids, an itinerant shoemaker, and a taciturn old gentlemen farmed on the peasant at so much rye per year. Eight of our party just filled up the floor. Our bed, as usual, was dry hay, and we turned in like troopers' horses, all standing, so closely packed together that we could hardly turn ourselves, but must sleep as we pitched. As I lay on my back I curiously watched the household preparing for bed. The man and wife occupied a niche in the wall, and the two men servants another on the same side. The children filled a small cot, and the two girls crept into a box (it could hardly be called a bed) in size and shape much resembling a coffin. I could not exactly make out where the shoemaker got to. However, all seemed comfortable enough, except the old gentleman, who sat on a bench smoking his pipe, and refused to move for any one till we were all down. Whether or not he had been turned out of his bed, or where he would pitch, was a mystery to me. At first I thought he meant creeping into the oven; however, as soon as we were quiet, he just curled himself up like a dog on the hearthstone, close into the burning ashes, and seemed to sleep as well as any of us. There were thus eighteen of us stowed away in a cabin about ten yards long by six wide.

Tired as I was, it was impossible to sleep, for every sleeper seemed to snore in a different key; so, as the moon had risen and the night was calm,

I roused up one of the youngest of the foresters, and we started out for the other charr lake that lay near to the cottage, to fish by moonlight. I had a line and hooks with me; we made a fairish rod out of a long sapling, and in about half an hour were seated on a rock by the lake enjoying the pure night air, now rendered doubly refreshing by the contrast with the heated atmosphere we had just quitted. I do not care where I sleep, or how hard my bed is, if I have but air. A bivouac in the forest, if the night is only clear, suits me quite as well as the best furnished bedroom; and I can sleep just as sound with the grass for my mattress, a log for pillow, and the sky for my canopy, as in the best four-poster. But I cannot stand a close bedroom. These peasants, however, doubtless for the sake of the warmth, cannot lie too close; and certainly there is no mock modesty about the peasant women. How they escape being burnt in these close cottages I cannot imagine. The fire burns all night, and instead of candles they use splinters of turpentine fir, which they carry in their hands, the sparks dropping about all over the floor; and I observed that each man who brought in a bundle of hay for our beds, carried a lighted fire-stick in his mouth.

I fished in water about ten fathoms deep, without a float, my baits lob-worms, and a small white grub which we picked out of the rotten fir bark (a favourite bait for charr). My guide every now and then kept throwing in handfuls of dead yellow birch leaves on to the top of the water, to attract the fish. They bit capitally, and I would have fished on till daylight, but the wind rose, the moon became obscured, and, as dirty weather seemed brewing, we went back to the cottage. Early to bed and early to rise, is the motto here; and although it wanted nearly three hours of daybreak, the household were astir. The hunters were up, the hay cleared off the floor, and breakfast was preparing. The charr I had caught proved no bad addition, and we luckily got some coffee.

It was about as nasty a morning for the forest as we could well have; a drizzling rain was falling, and the fog was so thick that we could not distinguish an object at fifty yards' distance. But this did not seem to make much impression on the foresters. The elk must have fallen, and determined they were to have it. However, they reckoned without their host, for they never could hit upon the lost trail again.

As soon as I could see, I started back to the lake with one of the watchers, to take up the long line. The rest of the party went on in search of the lost elk, and we agreed to meet by the side of the lake, and dine off what charr we could catch, aided by whatever contributions we could levy from a peasant's house in the neighbourhood. It took us nearly four hours to get up the line. The fish had evidently been well on the feed, for nearly every worm was gone; but owing to our having left the line in the water a day too long, we lost a great many fish. As it was, we caught about seventy charr in all; and a more splendid lot of fish, when we laid them out on the grass, I never beheld. Seven or eight weighed about 3 lb. each, and I remarked that these were all male fish, and in splendid condition. The rest were of all sizes, but the majority of them about 1 lb. They were all ready for spawning, and full of roe or milt. The colours of the male fish, when just taken out of the water, were brilliant in the extreme: nearly black on the back, the belly and fins vermillion red, the sides yellow spotted. But the colour quickly fades after the fish dies. I did not observe in a single specimen the crook in the under jaw peculiar to the male salmon or trout in the spawning season.

I do not believe the charr spawn in the same manner as the salmon, for, a few nights after, when fishing by torchlight, I took up by the side of the lake many branches covered with their spawn. On referring to Thompson's "Natural History of Ireland," as good a description as I know of the charr will be found, and I can corroborate many of his remarks. As he says, they vary so much in colour in different waters, that it is hard to distinguish the male from the female. In both these lakes there was no difficulty at all in the matter. Bloch's figure of the *Salmo salvelinus* is not bad, but his spots are too dark. This is clearly a male fish; and his figure of the *S. alpinus* well represents our female fish. And we took some quite grey, without spots, exactly like his figure of the *S. limata*. Not a single one of the large fish that we caught exhibited in the slightest degree any transverse markings along the sides, like the parr; but in every young fish from four to six ounces they were very conspicuous. It seems, according to Thompson, that in some of the Irish lakes the charr only appear about the middle of October, and are then seen but for ten days or so. I fancy, by his account, they are then supposed to leave the lake; but, in my opinion, this is just the time they come on the shallows to spawn, and directly that is over they draw back again to the deeps; at least such is the case in our lakes. And they never leave the lake; for although trout are always taken in the tributary streams when there is a fresh of water, never has a single charr been taken, except in the lake. The charr spawn here in the end of October, and the best fishing is from the time the birch leaves begin to fall, throughout the whole winter. They will also bite till June. The best fishing is certainly, however, in the winter, in the deep water, through a hole cut in the ice. The hook in use is covered on the shank with bright lead, in the form of a small fish, and although sometimes no bait is used, a little piece of fat pork stuck on the point of the hook is a very good bait. I do not believe a fly was ever cast or a bait spun in these waters; but I should say both would answer, if you could only hit on the right pattern. The charr in these lakes are not unfrequently taken up to 5lb.; seldom larger.

About two we were joined by the rest of our party; and camping on a beautiful rise by the side of a small trout-stream, we "spread our table-cloth." Butter, bread, milk, and potatoes we procured from a neighbouring peasant, and we made a splendid dinner off fried charr and "chambertin;" for our host (who is not above enjoying the good things of this life) keeps a small cellar, and of a good vintage, too, at one of his keepers' houses. Thus we enjoyed two luxuries in the forest which many a *bon vivant* might envy. I never tasted such fish as these charr—far richer than salmon, and the flesh blood-red. We went home that night; and none of us were sorry to turn in between clean sheets.

The next day messengers were despatched to some neighbouring friends to help to form a "skall," on a large scale, the day after; and in the evening we again camped in the forest. The worst of these amateur skalls or battues is, that they are sure to bring together so many of the "Mr. Briggs" class of sportsmen; and ours was no exception to the general rule. We mustered strong (about a dozen guns), two or three good men and true, but the rest in far too blooming a condition to live the pace over so severe a line of country as this. One thing, however, was certain, they were determined not to depend for their dinner upon the elk we might shoot; and it was, indeed (as the Yankees would say), "a caution" to see the knapsacks unpacked whenever a halt was called. As the bottle went merrily round, each one was loud in his own individual praise; and it was hard to say, from their own showing, which was the keenest sportsman of the lot: but for all this I was much inclined to think that—

> "Save at the flagon,
> And prog in the waggon,
> They did nought that the muse
> Ever heard of to brag on."

This day's proceedings are easily described. It was a succession of picnics from beginning to end. We had scarcely finished breakfast before

"Where shall we lunch?" was the cry; and the same with dinner. The very beaters seemed to have caught the infection; and I could plainly see at starting that on this day, at least, they were determined not to lose us, for, believe me, we did not trust them with the knapsacks. It was indeed a jovial day; but it is needless to say we never saw an elk; and the only shots that we fired were at an empty bottle on a tree stump after dinner, and very harmless shooting we made of it.

So much for our second "skall;" two blank days, and not much more than a week left of the season.

The next day I walked home for another gun, and on the 27th came back again; for we had made up our minds to give the woods a good dusting the last three days of the season, and see if our luck would not change. We had fixed the 28th for the skall, and I arrived about five o'clock in the evening of the 27th, when I found the party had started, but left word for me to follow them, directly I came up, to one of the keepers' houses in the forest, about six miles distant. This was pleasant; I had already walked twenty-four miles, and I reckoned on a good supper and night's rest to freshen me up for the morning. Moreover, the moon would not rise till two, and to grope my way through these thick woods by twilight was no joke. However, there was no help for it; so, taking a fellow with me who said he knew the way, we started. Night set in before we had got half way. So far we had a little daylight, and all went well; but darkness came on, and found us in a thick forest, when it turned out that my guide knew the way no better than myself. I knew very little of the lay of the country, but I have found from old experience that, when once bushed in the dark, it is little good wandering about to try to hit off the lost path; the best plan is either to camp up at once, or strike out one certain direction and keep it, for sooner or later it must bring you up somewhere; whereas if you keep wandering round and about, you tire yourself without making the least headway. An old trapper once remarked to me, that when you are lost at night in a forest, nine cases out of ten, your tent is sure to lie directly in the opposite direction from which you fancy it does, and this I have found correct. The night was thick and cloudy, or the stars might have guided us; a drizzly rain was coming on, and the prospect of camping out on such a night was annoying. I heard a waterfall in the distance, and this I was determined to make for. I fancied if I got to the side of a stream I should know better where I was. The fellow I had with me was moreover an arrant cur; so I struck out my path, and kept it. The waterfall could not have been more than a mile and a half distant, but the wood was so thick, and the ground so covered with fallen timber, over which we kept tumbling about every five minutes, that we were nearly two hours before we reached it. However, when we got there my guide knew that if we followed it down for about two miles we should reach one of the keepers' houses; and right glad was I to see a light at last in his cottage window. After wandering for about six hours, we were nearly as far from the meet as when we left home. The keeper was getting ready to start, but, like an old soldier, would wait till the moon rose, for he said that even he, who was bred in the forest, would hardly venture out on such a night. A cup of coffee and four hours on the floor (after the old fashion, five women and two men in the same room) was anyhow better than a night in the forest, for it was indeed a wild night, and the old pine-trees fairly groaned and cracked " 'neath the howling blast." However, when the moon rose the weather cleared, and at four we started. No fear now of losing my way with such a bloodhound for my guide. He was in great hopes this time; for although, as he said, our party was small, they were all good men. Each man had to bear his own provisions for three days. At six we reached the keeper's cottage, and found all in a bustle; and I could plainly see now that mischief was meant, and that—

> "Still the best horse was reserved for the day
> When Pilton was named as the meet."

After the hearty greetings usual on such occasions had been exchanged, we got our breakfast, and then commenced preparations for the "skall." We were all marshalled in front of the house, and one of the oldest wood-watchers and my friend the bushman were masters of the ceremonies. We mustered in all about seventeen. The seven best men were picked out for shooters, the rest for drivers. Each man had a number chalked upon his breast or cap; and the old forester laid down the plan of the day. And now I had time to give a glance over the ranks, and a hardier, more weather-beaten crew I think I never saw in my life; and formidable opponents would such men prove in a guerilla war against any enemy who dared to attack them in the fastnesses of their native forests. All were armed to the teeth, and each had the Swedish bushman's never-failing friend, the axe, stuck in the girdle of his leather apron. But if space only allowed me to describe the guns which were brought out for this occasion! I have certainly seen some marvellous "spouts" at a day's rook or rabbit shooting in England, but never anything like the extraordinary machines I saw on this morning. I would have given a trifle to have picked out six of the most antediluvian, and placed them for exhibition in the *Field* window. The process of loading commenced; and when I saw misfitting bullets hammered down upon charges of blasting powder which would try the best English barrel, and examined the locks, half of which would not stand at half-cock, and many at hardly any cock at all, while some triggers were without any guards — I really considered that it would be indeed a miracle if no serious accident happened this day. One old backwoodsman begged me to examine his lock, upon the construction of which he much prided himself. It seemed to be altogether destitute of a scear, but with a famous mainspring. Of course, a trigger was useless in such a piece of machinery; and he explained to me, that when he fired he had nothing to do but draw up the cock sharply, and let it fall again on the cap. I was well pleased when the examination concluded, for I expected every moment, as he was fiddling with the lock, that the gun would go off in his hand. These peasants are in the highest degree inquisitive, and my gun and appointments were all critically examined, even down to the very buttons of my shooting-coat. I was armed with a small double gun, and unfortunately left my spare single behind. Moreover, I had only six conical balls, for I considered it was 100 to 1 if I got so many shots at elk in one skall. But the sequel will prove the truth of the old adage, that "store is no sore."

The first drive was precisely over the same ground as on the previous occasion, and I took my old stand. Three guns were left on this tongue of land, and four were sent over the lake to watch a winter way through the forest, where it was probable the elk might break. The arrangements were beautifully carried out. We had an hour allowed us to plant ourselves before the beaters started, and I felt confident now, that if elk were only in the drive, one or other of us would surely get a shot. When the heavy mist had cleared away, the sun broke out in all its splendour, and even in England I never remember a more glorious autumnal day. This was lucky for us sentries, for the drive was a long one, and it was nearly two hours before I heard the cries of the beaters. They came nearer and nearer, but, passing by us in the forest below, I gave up this drive as a bad job, for, had elk been in, I naturally fancied we should have seen or heard them before this. I was, therefore, just preparing to leave my post, when a heavy shot to my right boomed over the lake, which was in about five minutes answered by another, and all was still. After waiting for perhaps ten minutes, in case any elk might head back to us, we rowed over the lake, and, making for the smoke of the bivouac fire curling over the tops of the trees, found the whole party assembled. It was very plain to read in their countenances that they had got no elk. It seems that a magnificent bull-elk came up singly within twenty yards of the oldest wood-watcher, who fired, when the elk dashed on apparently unhurt, and some minutes after another flying shot was fired at him with no better luck. No one was more disappointed than the old watcher himself, who fired the first shot; and as he was regarded as one upon whom some dependence ought to have been placed, he was not a little "chaffed" at missing what appeared to the others who saw it a very easy shot. I saw the old boy was annoyed, and I therefore proposed a stroll together to the spot where he had stood, partly to see if we could find any indications of the elk being wounded, and partly to avoid the "chaff," which was now becoming personal.

We strolled on in the forest, following the spoor of the elk, when, suddenly coming to a burn with steepish banks, we could plainly see that the elk had fallen when crossing it, and marks of blood were evident on the other side where he had struggled up. This was cheering. We now separated, for the spoor became confused, and I had not left him many minutes before the Swedish "who-whoop" rang through the forest, and on running up I had the satisfaction of seeing the noble brute lying dead on his side, the keeper's ball, which was easily recognized by its size, as his gun was nearly the calibre of a small blunderbuss, having passed clean through it. The elk had, however, gone perhaps two English miles before he fell. "They laugh best who laugh last," is an old Swedish proverb, and it was now the old boy's turn. I could see he had been "fairly riled," for his skill in woodcraft had been called in question. Our shouts soon brought up the rest of the party, and great was the rejoicing over the fallen beast. I had never seen a dead elk before, and the bulk of this huge animal as he lay on the ground struck me indeed with astonishment.

He was about six years old by his horns, which were magnificent. His length as he lay, from nose to tail, was about 9 feet; the height over his withers more than 6 feet; and his carcass, when dressed, was guessed by the old hands to weigh nearly 1000lb. Whether this was correct or not, however, I could have no means of judging, but I daresay it was not far from the mark. His throat was immediately cut (although he had been dead some time) for the sake of making some blood-cakes with flour. The blood of every animal is eaten here with great avidity. I can bring myself pretty well to every kind of diet, and, as may be supposed, in a wandering life like mine, I have eaten many curious kinds of dishes; but these blood-cakes I cannot stand. Another fire was soon kindled close to where the elk lay, and after he was "grulloched" we left him, intending to sledge him home next day. We did not forget, however, to cut away a good supply of beef for our supper; and in high glee we all set off for another drive. This, however, was unsuccessful, and lasted till sundown, when we all made for the cottage where we had slept on the previous occasion. I was the only one who fired a shot in the second drive, for just as it was ending, and we were certain that no elk were on foot, a fine male capercailzie, disturbed by the beaters, perched on a fir about 100 yards from me, and I cut him out very prettily with a single ball. I was rather pleased, as I had never yet tried the range of my gun.

Our party, on returning to the cottage, was too large for all to obtain a shake-down indoors; so it was agreed that we "swells" should have the floor, and the mob light a large fire and bivouac outside. The evening was spent in listening to adventures of forest and fell, each man endeavouring to outvie the other. It has often been a question in my mind whether the lies which one generally hears when a parcel of "falconers, fishermen, and hunters are wont to congregate," are spontaneous and hatched on the spot, or whether there is a glimmering of truth at the bottom. Harmless as this practice of drawing the long-bow may be when confined only to a man's own exploits, it is attended with this serious disadvantage, one never knows how much to believe, and doubtless many a true tale is set down as false. For my part, I dare scarcely ever make a note of what I hear out here, and probably lose much valuable information from the fact of doubting its truth.

The night was chilly, and the blue faces of those who had camped out (their beards and whiskers powdered with the white hoar-frost) looked grim enough in the grey twilight of morning. However, no one complained. We had a rare line of country for the day's drive, where we were certain to find elk, and all were impatient to be "up and at them." We had nearly six miles to walk to our posts, and the drivers had to make a wide circuit, commencing at the very boundary of the estate, to drive the elk back into the home forests. It was therefore nearly four hours before we heard anything of them again. My post on this occasion was beautifully chosen. At my back a deep forest rose for several hundred feet, in front was a swampy meadow (perhaps 600 yards across, and two English miles long), through which ran as sweet a little trout stream as I have ever seen in this country or anywhere else. Beyond this rose another deep forest, and as it was pretty certain that the driven elk would cross this meadow and stream to reach the forest at the back of us, the guns were planted, but at wide intervals (for we had to command a long line), along the little stream. I lay at the foot of an old pine, lazily watching the trout rising in the little stream at my feet. The air was warm as spring; the sun shone clear in an unclouded sky, over as fair a panorama of nature as the eye ever gazed upon.

> "Beetling crags hung high above me,
> Ever looking grandly rude;
> Still there was some trace of mildness
> In this scene so weird. Its wildness
> Might be sought for solitude."

All at once the distant cry of the beaters broke upon my ear, and at the same moment I heard a crashing in the forest before me. Starting up from my reverie, I saw a bull elk walking leisurely down to the meadow, as if he apparently meant to cross right opposite to where I sat. He had evidently heard the beaters, for he would every now and then stand still and listen, his long ears all the while moving backwards and forwards, but he was quite unconscious of the danger which menaced him in front. He seemed all at once to change his mind, and instead of coming into the open, kept on in the forest, and I soon lost sight of him. The meadow made a bend beyond me, and I could only just see the shooter next to me, at about 400 yards' distance. I now felt certain that the elk, if he crossed the meadow, would do so at the extreme point to my right, where a double gun was planted, and it was with no little anxiety that I waited for its report. The elk, however, seemed in no hurry, and a quarter of an hour elapsed before a double shot, quickly followed by a single one, and a loud shout to "Pass up" (look out), told me that he had turned and was coming down the meadow back again upon us. He was soon in sight, and came on at a shambling trot, evidently wounded. He dashed at the brook above, in the very face of the next gun; but the fellow was far too excited to take a steady aim, and missed him. He now turned straight down to me. The track in which I was standing (for I had moved a little way up into the wood) was so narrow that the elk had to force his way through it; but in far less time than I can take to write it, he was down upon me, maddened with pain and rage, in a headlong, desperate charge. I never should have believed that he could come at such a pace. I took as steady an aim as the circumstances and hurry allowed, and fired point-blank at his chest. It was a snap-shot, and I missed him clean. I had but a moment to struggle backwards into the bushes (for the underwood was very thick) when he was close on me, and in a few seconds would have reached me. My second shot, however, told, and he fell within a foot of me. I could just indistinctly see a huge dark mass roll over at my feet with a thundering crash; but, such was the excitement of the moment, that I saw nothing more. It was clear that I had had, indeed, a very narrow escape. But even now he was not quite dead, and there was something awful to witness in his death-struggles. I soon, however, "picked myself together," and, quickly loading, put a bullet through his ear, thus ending his agony and his life. I was not the only one who had a narrowish escape on this occasion, for the next man to me, as soon as he missed and turned the elk, instead of standing at his post, ran on after him, shouting all the while to me to look out. The consequence was, he was right in the line of my fire, and my first ball, which missed the elk, glanced off a rock (as we could see afterwards), and cut the bark off a fir-tree a few inches from his head. However, this appeared to be regarded by the foresters as a very trivial circumstance; and had I killed the man I am confident that if a jury had been impanelled on the spot, the verdict would have been "served him right." Upon examining the dead elk, it seemed that two balls from the first shots had entered his loins, without, however, touching a vital part, and but for my second shot, he would probably have gone away as strong as ever. By his horns he seemed about five years old, but smaller than the one we had already killed.

Now the elk was down, the next question was, how to get him out of the forest, for it was impossible for a sledge with horses to reach the spot where he lay. We were just one mile from the nearest lake into which the little trout-stream ran, and it was decided that he must be carried there and rowed across in a boat. This certainly did not appear an easy task, looking at the huge carcase that lay on the ground; nothing, however, is too hot or too heavy for these peasants, if you only give them time. Two young fir-trees were soon cut down, and trimmed up for bearing-poles; while the beaters cut a lot of long willow twigs, and, twisting them round and round till they were as pliant as cord, a sort of net-work palanquin was formed, strong enough, as was observed, to carry a house. The ponderous burden was soon hoisted on the shoulders of eight powerful men, who marched off with it in triumph.

An hour's rest had enabled us to enjoy our dinner and our pipes, and as soon as the beaters returned, we arranged the last drive for a fresh tract, and a certain one. This was the widest drive of all, but the beaters had not to go so far as ourselves. We walked through the forest for about four miles, till we came to a large swamp, at the end of which was a forest lake. Several wooded rises ran out into the swamp in tongues, and had the trees only been different I should have fancied myself again in Australia—for it gave me a very fair idea of an Australian bush scene, and was precisely the sort of ground we should have drawn for kangaroo in that country. From the tracks it was evident that the elk were continually coming down these tongues of forest to save the swamp, and on each of these rises we left one or two guns. My post was at the extreme end of the swamp, to guard a favourite pass by the side of the lake. It was certainly the surest stand, and was assigned to me out of compliment, as a stranger, on account of the nature of the ground. Our line stretched, I should say, a mile and a half, and I was at least half a mile from the gun below me. I had certainly a beautiful stand. On my right was the lake, within fifty yards; and by its side a well-worn run proved that the elk often came that way. The swamp here terminated in a point, and was not 100 yards over. A clump of fir-trees, covering a stony rise of perhaps 100 acres, was at my back; and fronting me just over the swamp, the forest rose on a rocky mountain some hundred feet high, so perpendicular and steep that it seemed almost impossible for any creature to keep his legs coming down it. Directly in front of me, however, was a clear run from the mountain-top, and if the elk were started it was next to certain they would come down this run, and either cross the little hill on which I was stationed, or pass to my right, and, skirting the lake, make for the deep forest which lay behind me. Such at least were the calculations of my old friend the wood-watcher, and they were borne out to the letter. I had not forgotten my old bush experience as a kangaroo hunter, and sitting down in front of a large pine close to the edge of the swamp, and cutting some fir-branches I made a little screen before me, behind which I ensconced myself, like a jolly old spider in his web, on the look-out for any unfortunate fly that might chance to come within his toils. I lighted my pipe, and was very comfortably reading an old number of the *Field* which I happened to have in my pocket (for I always like if possible to have something readable with me whenever I leave home), when suddenly I heard such a crashing and rolling of loose stones down the mountain side in front of me that I fancied a whole mob of elk must be coming right down upon me. The pipe was soon out of my mouth, and the paper in my pocket, and with my gun cocked I peered anxiously through my leafy bower up the hill in front of me. But my suspense was short, for right opposite to me I saw an immense old cow elk and calf come trotting down the hill with as much ease and action as a high-stepping cab horse over the London stones. The loose stones flew in all directions, but neither stopped to look back till they reached the bottom, when they both pulled up, appeared to listen for the distant beaters, and then commenced walking leisurely across the swamp right up to me. To say that I was not nervous would be to tell an untruth, for depend upon it, let the man be who he may, if he has but one ounce of flurry in his composition, such a moment will bring it out. Here I had them all to myself, and if I made a lucky double-shot I should be by long chalks the king of the day. Thus whispered ambition. But then prudence, or perhaps cowardice, stept in. I had only two balls left, having fired one at the capercalizie and three at the last bull, and no weapon besides my gun save a butcher's common case-knife. I well knew, from what I had read, that a wounded elk was a roughish kind of plaything, and moreover—lies or no lies—I had not quite forgotten the hairbreadth escapes, and other little incidents attendant upon the chase of the elk, which had been poured into my ear by the foresters on the night previous. Moreover, all the pines near me were branchless within twenty feet of the ground; it was impossible "to tree" in case the wounded cow rushed at me. The reader may possibly say, "What fear of an old cow without horns?" But gently; it is not the horns so much as the dreadful long fore-feet that are the offensive weapons in the elk; and as I look on this very cow's hoofs, now dried and lying on my table, I feel very little inclination to shake hands with such a monster. However, they came marching very leisurely across the swamp. I had my gun at my shoulder, when I was rather puzzled which to take first. The calf was probably the easiest and surest shot; but then I fancied if I shot it down I stood a poor chance against the infuriated mother, unless I luckily killed her dead with one bullet, which was far from probable. I thought it best, therefore, to fire first at the cow;

for if I did luckily bring her down with the first ball the calf was mine, and anyhow I had then a spare ball left. Had I been an old elk-hunter, I should have waited till they came right up to the muzzle of my gun, for it was plain now that they neither saw nor smelt me, but evidently meant crossing the rise close to me; and I made another mistake, excusable in a green hand, for, instead of sending a bullet right into the chest, which might have brought her down at once, I aimed at her forehead. We all know that the curl in the forehead is a vital part in a bullock's head. An elk, however, carries its head not like an ox, but in a horizontal position, the nose nearly in a line with the withers, thus presenting little or no front to aim at. She was exactly twenty-five yards from me when I pulled the trigger—for I measured it afterwards—and my bullet instead of crashing into her forehead, struck just "a leetle bit" too high, and glanced off. It, however, brought her up pretty quick; she looked about for a few seconds, wondering what the deuce was up (but she did not see me), and turning leisurely round, headed up the swamp. I had now a fair broadside, and sent my second bullet right through her shoulder. She fell on her knees, but instantly recovering herself, started up, and for a few seconds stood still, fiercely looking round her. All at once her eye caught sight of me, for I had now sprung up, and never shall I forget the look of wild reproach which she cast upon me. She was then evidently debating whether she should charge me or not. I was behind the tree in an instant, and got the gun-barrels out of the stock, as the best weapon I had at hand. She, however, thought better of it, and after standing for perhaps half a minute " backing and filling like a ship in stays " —to use a nautical phrase—she walked quietly down the swamp, with her calf at her side, allowing me lots of time to have loaded both barrels and fire again if I had had more bullets. In these skalls it is a very good plan to have a couple of bullets, properly patched, sewed on the outside of your shooting jacket, as they are ready at hand and torn off in an instant. I could see that she was dreadfully wounded, for she could hardly get along, and stopped three or four times on her road, and I fancied on each occasion would drop. She, however, reached the next rise, her calf keeping pace with her, and I lost sight of them for the time.

It is not easy to express the mortification which I felt at losing so splendid a prize as a cow elk and calf, and all for want of a couple more bullets; and as soon as the excitement was over I must say—I trust without being accused of maudlin sentiment—that a feeling of remorse and pity rose uppermost in my mind. From my little experience I could see that the elk is a tame unsuspecting animal, and there was something very cowardly in the way I had assaulted these two. Perhaps, had I been lucky enough to kill the cow and calf, a feeling of triumph would have outweighed any other; but as it was I had sent her away probably to die a lingering death in the forest where no one would find her, and I grieved for the fate of the poor calf, which, if it escaped the other guns, would wander alone and unprotected through the deep forest, or probably stand through the chilly autumn night moaning over the dead body of its mother. But I had little time for such reflections. Three more bangs to my left told me that they had reached the other guns, which soon commenced a dropping fire, for I had counted seven more shots—and all was still. The beaters were now close up, and I left my stand to join the other guns and see how the *battue* had ended. I soon found when I came up that some of the shots had taken effect, for there lay the calf riddled with three balls. I was glad of this, for the loss of its mother would now matter nothing. "But there were two," I exclaimed; upon which one of the foresters, with a grin of exultation in his face, led me away three or four hundred yards into the wood, and there lay the body of the cow. "Who killed this?"

was my next question. "I did," he said, "with my rifle." She lay on her right side, and he pointed to a bullet-hole in the left shoulder. That was just where I shot, and, as the wound was evidently old, for the blood had crusted round it, I felt certain this was my bullet-mark, and if there was no other the elk was mine. But it would soon be proved upon examination whose bullet had brought her down, for I was the only party who used a conical ball, and, moreover, my bullet was much too large to fit his rifle. When we turned her over we could find only one bullet-hole, although four shots had been fired at her after mine; and when we skinned her I took my ball out of the body, which had passed through the shoulder and lungs, breaking two ribs, and lodging in the skin on the opposite side. She had thus carried my ball nearly two English miles, and, after escaping all the other shots, had at length fallen from internal hæmorrhage. The man who fired the rifle shot owned that it was a long snap-shot, and the elk went on; and had not one of the beaters chanced to stumble over the body which lay in his path, we should have lost her. I think it almost an act of cruelty to shoot at an elk with less than a 2-oz. ball, for they hardly ever appear to drop at the first shot; and to prove how easily they will carry away a small ball, I may mention that when we skinned the elk, we took two slugs out of the hind quarters of one of the bulls, and in the flank of the cow was the scar of a bullet which had passed clean through her, perhaps a year before. I am certain, as I always used to be when kangarooing, that a charge of light shot thrown well in behind the ear at a close distance, beats any bullet, if a man is only collected enough to let the animal come close to him. I don't mean to say that loose shot would be of any use to such an animal as an elk except at very close quarters; but in close quarters I would depend upon it more than on a bullet.

We had now made a glorious wind-up—four elks in two days; and as we thought we could not mend it, and every one seemed to have had enough, we agreed to knock off, especially as we had to get the elk home next day and dress them. We were now far away in the forest, and it was near midnight before we arrived at home, all pretty well knocked up. I was not sorry for a rest on the next day, and in the evening the four elk were brought home in triumph on sledges. The whole village joined the cavalcade, and as the punch and brandy was handed round pretty freely, our "skall" was brought to a right jovial conclusion. I must say it was a sight which has not fallen to the lot of many, and one which probably

I may never again witness, to see four such splendid animals lying side by side at one time on the grass-plot in front of a house; and considering that I was as it were a novice at this work, I deemed myself lucky in falling in with such a share of the sport. The next day we were fully occupied in skinning and dressing the carcases, and I must say that had the butchers on this occasion practised but a little of the skill and neatness of our English park-keepers, the venison would have looked all the better. But, like the Yankee's singed cat, it ate a great deal better than it looked. At a rough guess, I should say the meat on the four elk would pull down 3000 lb. No bad stock of beef this for the ensuing winter. The largest was the bull we first shot; but the cow was very little less, and the calf, which to my astonishment all the foresters declared to have been dropped in July (and the dugs of the cow were full of milk), was exactly 6 ft long and 4 ft. high. Pretty well this for a four months' calf. The skins are worth little or nothing except for leather, which, however, must be everlasting, for a pair of elk-skin breeches is an heir-loom in the families of these foresters, and are handed down from father to son for several generations. Pleasant wearing, I should say, in hot weather, after about a score of years' service! The hair all came off the skins of these elk, and I noticed one peculiarity in the coarse hair of the elk which 'I never recollect seeing in any other animal, viz., that it is quite brittle, and can be snapped in half like a carrot; it appears as it were rotten. This is also the case with the hair of the reindeer, at least many of them, and the Lap settlers say it is owing to the quantity of dry moss they eat. Can this be so? But the reindeer skins make capital rugs for sledges, and I never saw the elk skin used for this purpose. The skin of a large elk is worth about 20s. here, and the meat in a town perhaps 6d. per pound. I claimed the head and horns of the bull, and the two forefeet of the cow, as my share of the booty. I may mention that we found in the forest an immense bull elk lying dead, probably shot last winter, for it was little more than a skeleton. I secured the horns, which were the largest I ever saw. It seems that the horns of the elk are full grown in length at five years old, but that afterwards they yearly increase in breadth and number of tips up to eighteen or twenty. I observed, however, in all the horns which I saw that there is always one more spike on one side than on the other. I shall not weary the reader's patience with entering here into the natural history of the elk further than to say that from what I could see and learn, they are very domestic for a wild animal, and seem rather to court than shun the society of man if he comes as a friend. Their habits much resemble the kangaroo. They seem always to keep to one spot, have their favourite camping places and feeding grounds, and are very partial to swampy forests. They have their regular runs, and appear to be as easily driven as tame cattle in any direction that may suit the driver. When they have once fixed upon a certain tract, they never leave it unless driven away; and when once in a forest, the owner may always reckon upon keeping up his breed, provided the wolves (their worst enemies when the snow is deep) do not molest them.

The stomachs of all the elk that we opened were filled with the shoots of the bilberry *(Vaccinium myrtillus)*, but their principal food I take to be grass and the leaves and tender shoots of several species of green trees, especially the aspen. Thanks to the stringent manner in which they are preserved, these noble animals are yearly spreading over our Wermland forests, and in fact a stray elk is now occasionally seen very far south. The season for killing them is limited to two months—September and October; and the penalty for killing one in close-time is heavy, with forfeiture of the animal and the gun. This is about the only clause in the Swedish Game Laws which seems to be at all observed. Considering their wild nature, and the immense developments of their organs of hearing and scent, I was much surprised to see how leisurely and unconsciously in every instance they approached the guns; and on this very account I did not, I must confess, see any very great pleasure in hunting them as we did. No doubt the chase of the elk, single-handed by one man and a dog, which follow on the spor perhaps for days, till the elk is brought to bay, is fraught with much more adventure and vicissitudes, and when pursued on skidder or snow skates, probably possesses much excitement to a keen hand. But there is something tame, butcherly, and cowardly in killing them after our fashion; and when the animal is driven up to be shot in this cool-blooded manner, I look upon it as slaughter, not sport, and care little whether the object to be killed is an elk, a kangaroo, an ox, or a sheep.

A curious circumstance happened here early in September. A small steamer was passing over a lake on its way to the Wenern, when the mate who was on the look-out observed at day-break an elk swimming across the lake. The steamer gave chase, soon came up with the elk, a line was cast over its horns, and it was drawn alongside. There unfortunately happened to be a Justice

Shallow on board, in the shape of a landsman or magistrate, who declared that it was out of season, and in the king's name ordered the captain to cast it loose, which he very reluctantly did.

One more night in the forest, and my visit was at an end. On this night we camped out by the side of the charr lake, to try our luck at angling for them by torchlight. They bit pretty well in the beginning of the night, but afterwards the weather came on windy and boisterous, and we had little sport. Up to this the weather had been beautiful, but this night was winterly and cold. We had a rare camp-fire built on the Dalecarlian system—a large blasted pine cut down into lengths of about twelve foot each, and the sides hacked into splinters with an axe, that they may more readily catch the blaze. These are laid one above the other (kept in their places by slanting posts), and a space of about four inches left between each. Lighted chips are inserted into this space, and the logs catch fire. The advantage of this is that we had a regular heat the whole night, and no trouble to replenish our fire. The season, however, for camping out in these forests was, to my fancy, about at an end; and as I had seen a flock of waxwings a few days previous, I knew that the first snow-storm was not far distant. We spent the next day in fishing and shooting hazel-grouse, and in the evening I bade adieu to the forest.

On the next morning I left my friend's house, after a happy and interesting visit, carrying away a small elk-steak, as he called a large junk of about 70 lb., just to show them at home that I had been in at the death; and as I jogged home on one of those infernal bone-setting machines which the peasants here call carts, I could not help thinking to myself that there are few countries in Europe where a man can enjoy so much sport for so little money as in old Sweden, and few kinder-hearted or more hospitable fellows under the sun than a true Swedish country gentleman.

The bear (*Ursus arctos*, Lin.) is very common around Quickiock; but I have already alluded to him.

The glutton (*Gulo borealis*, Lin.; "jerf," Sw.) appeared to be common on the fells. I never saw one wild; but the Laps, one morning, brought an old female and a young one which they had shot on the fells. The skeleton of the glutton seems to be much sought after here. I bought three very perfect skeletons, and gave a high price for them. The glutton does not seem, however, to be confined to the very north of the country, for wherever the wild reindeer is met with (and these appear to come further south on the Norwegian fells than the tame reindeer) the glutton is also found. No northern beast of prey, for its size, can compare to the glutton in voracity, and nothing appears to come amiss in the way of food —reindeer, goats, hares, lemming, ptarmigan, and offal, and even fish and reptiles; and perhaps no wild animal is more dreaded by the Laps, for it can climb like a cat, and will even steal the provisions which the Laps leave in the autumn on the fells, in a box set on a high pole, for the next spring. The glutton is a handsome animal, and sometimes you see a perfectly black skin, which is very dear. The spor of the glutton in the snow is nearly as large as that of a bear. Of course, like all other northern skins, the winter skin of the glutton is more handsome than that of summer.

The wolf (*Canis lupus*, Lin.; "varg.," Sw.).— I had always fancied that these northern forests and fells were overrun with wolves, and that it would hardly be safe to wander alone in this wild country; but, strange to say, they do not appear to be more numerous here than in Wermland or Dalecarlia. I am at a loss to account for the scarcity of so shy and prolific an animal in a country so well suited to its habits, and one affording so good a supply of food. It is true that "war to the knife" is the Lap's motto, as regards this bloodthirsty, cowardly animal; and truly may we say that every man's hand is against them here. As soon as the track of a wolf is seen in the snow, the Laps hunt him down on skiddor, and never leave the ·spor till the wolf is killed. Those who first start on the trail follow it up till they are tired, when others take up the running, and so on, till the beast is fairly brought to bay. By this means many are killed every winter; but still, considering all things, they are certainly very rare in the vicinity of Quickiock, and they never seem to hunt in flocks. They appear to follow the herd of reindeer singly, or in pairs; and as soon as ever the reindeer came up to the fells in the spring, two large old wolves appeared in our forests. We saw them twice, but we never were within shot. One day in the end of April, my lad, who was out by the side of a frozen lake, saw a wolf coming right up to him over the ice. He hid himself behind a bush, and made sure of a shot. The wolf, however, probably smelt him, and crossed above him, just out of shot. Immediately afterwards, a solitary young reindeer came trotting up to the lad, doubtless for protection, and followed him right down to Quickiock. Probably it was that reindeer that the wolf was after. We never heard the howl but once, and that was one night, when camped out on the fells. Of all dismal howls I think this is the worst, and one's very marrow seems to freeze on hearing it.

The common fox (*Canis vulpes*, Lin.; " skogs räf," Sw.) was not nearly so common around here as the Arctic fox (*Canis lagopus*, Lin.; " fell räf," Sw.); and I never heard of one being killed while I was up. But the Arctic fox was very common on these fells, and we got two old ones and four cubs. The male was what they call the blue fox, and considered rare. It was not, however, blue, but a dingy black-brown; the female was whity-brown. The male weighed about 9 lb., or little more than a good hare. The habits of these fell foxes are curious. They appear to live in holes under boulders of rock, and as soon as a man approaches they just poke their heads out and bark; but such a bark—just like the cough of a wheezy, asthmatic old man. If you go near the hole they withdraw; but as soon as you turn away they come out again directly to have a look; and this curiosity often costs them their life.

The fell hare (*Lepus borealis*, Nilss.).—I never saw more hares in any part of Sweden than here. We used to find them in the small bushes on the fell sides as well as on the fells themselves, and any day we could have killed two or three, if they had been worth the trouble of carrying home. They did not appear to assume the grey summer dress till nearly the end of May. I observed here that the black tip on the point of the ear was much less conspicuous than in our Wermland hare, which is considered by Nilsson as the same species; and I think so too, for the two craniums agree perfectly. Now, this black ear-tip is one of his great specific marks of distinction between the *Lepus borealis* and the *Lepus canescens*, or southern Swedish hare; but if there is no other specific difference in the osteology, I am almost inclined to think that they are the same species, for the tips of the ears are much blacker in our Wermland hares than in those which we killed on the Quickiock fells; and it seems to me that, as we go further north, so does this black tip diminish.

The otter (*Lutra vulgaris*, Erxl.; "utter," Sw.) was by no means rare here. The only specimen that I shot, however, I lost, for the body was carried over a high waterfall, and I could not reach it.

The stone marten (*Martes foina*, Briss.; "Sten märd," Sw.).—This is the only species that I was able to identify in this district, and it was by no means common. They may probably, also, have the common pine marten (*Martes sylvestris*, Ges. "Skogs märd.), but I never saw it. I have heard it doubted whether these two martens are distinct species, or only young and old of the same animal.

I cannot for one moment doubt that they are two very distinct species, their habits are so different; and even allowing that the white spot on the throat may become yellow by age, or *vice versâ*, in the stone marten the soles of the feet are bare, while in the pine marten they are always covered with hair, and this at all ages.

I never saw the weasel (*Mustela vulgaris*, Erxl.) here, although it is occasionally, but very rarely, killed, for I purchased a skin of a weasel killed at Quickiock in the previous winter, and although I know some doubt exists whether the weasel turns white in winter as well as the stoat, I can only say that this skin was pure white.

The stoat (*Mustela Erminea*, Lin.; "hermelin," Sw.) was very common around Quickiock, and in the summer seemed to be confined to the high stony fells. Respecting its change of colour from brown to white in the winter, I have never had opportunities of sufficiently studying them at the season; but I had plenty of specimens through my hands during the spring, both before and after the change from the winter to the summer dress; and from attentive observation, I think Professor Bell is clearly right, and that this change takes place, as he says, "by an actual change in the colour of the existing fur." Be this as it may, however, the change is very rapid and suddenly effected, for on May 8th we killed them in pure winter dress, and by the 17th they were in full summer dress, and after that we never obtained a white specimen.

The squirrel (*Sciurus vulgaris*, Lin.; "ekorre," Sw.).—In certain seasons squirrels abound in the Lapland forests, on others very few are to be seen. They are much sought after, by both settlers and Laps, for the skins, which are sold for lining ladies' cloaks—and a pretty and expensive lining they make. They are shot in autumn and spring, not in the depth of winter, at which season it appears they hybernate, like the dormouse. At this season they are silvery grey. The skins are sold by the forty, the price of forty being this spring about 8*s*. 6*d*. I remarked that the summer dress of the squirrel is much darker and browner in Lapland than I have ever seen it elsewhere.

The lemming (*Lemmus Norwegicus*, Wom.; "fjäll lemmel," Sw.).—We now come to an animal peculiar to these northern tracts, and one whose migrations have given rise to so much conjecture and so many exaggerated statements, that I was most anxious to see how much truth there was in the accounts which I had heard of the countless thousands of these little mice marching straight over the country in a compact body, swimming rivers, never turning from their course, and devastating the whole land as they passed over it. As luck would have it, I had a good opportunity of judging for myself, for in the spring of 1862 we had a large migration right through Quickiock, and for about a month the whole country swarmed with them. Such a migration had not been seen for many years. It is true that for the last two seasons a good many had appeared on the Quickiock fells, and they say that these migrations always last more or less for three years. Few are ignorant of the natural history of this strange little mouse, yet perhaps few have had the opportunity of seeing one in a state of nature, and I shall therefore give a short description of the animal itself, and proceed to make some remarks on its habits, and on that most singular of all phenomena in natural history, its irregular migrations. The lemming is a little animal not unlike the water vole in shape, but much smaller, and with a very short tail, being scarcely in all more than six inches long; the colour above is rusty yellow, with a black streak down the middle and each side of the back, much fainter in some than others; belly and under sides, and throat, pale yellow. The fur is beautifully soft and thick, and although the skin is very thin, might doubtless be put to some use by the furriers. The skins are beautifully red when taken off just in the early spring, but fade very much in the summer. It is considered by our naturalists that, besides this fell lemming, there is another species here, the *Lemmus schisticolor* (Léljeborg), "skögs lemmel," or wood lemming. This is smaller than the last, the colour is more grey, and the spot on the back rusty yellow instead of black. This smaller species was discovered by Prof. Lélljeborg, in the forest near Gullrandsdalen, in Norway, but I cannot say that I ever identified it up at Quickiock; but really, the lemmings which we killed, varied so much in size and colour, that without a careful examination a new species might be easily overlooked. The teeth of the lemming resemble those of the beaver and dormouse, and they are therefore herbivorous, living on leaves, grass, small branches, moss, roots, etc. In the winter they do not lie up in a trance, but dig runs under the snow, and, unlike the little dormouse, lay up no store of winter food. Respecting their uncertain migrations from one tract to another, of which I had read so many marvellous accounts, I will proceed to describe exactly what I saw, and I think the reader will agree with me that there is nothing more wonderful in these irregular migrations than in the more certain migrations of the waxwing, mealy redpole, brambling, and others of our birds of passage. About the end of April, just as the snow was beginning to melt, I was walking by the river side, and saw scores of dead lemming, which had evidently perished in the winter's snow. On May 3rd I got three specimens killed to the south of Quickiock, and after this they began to appear in such numbers that by May 15th I had obtained nearly five hundred skins. These all seemed to come up from the south, and to be heading to the fells. The whole country now swarmed with them. It was my impression that they had been frozen up in the neighbourhood all the winter; that many had perished under the snow, and those which we saw were the survivors making their way back to their native home on the northern fells. This impression was confirmed by seeing, when the snow went, their runs in every direction in the forests and meadows round Quickiock; and large heaps of dung marked their resting-places. They remained in the open for about three weeks, living under tussocks of grass, old logs, heaps of rubbish, cracks in the river bank—in fact, wherever shelter was to be obtained. But by the end of May they had all retired into the forests, and about two weeks after this the lower fells swarmed with them. They did not, however, all leave the forests, for during the whole summer the woods were full of them, and they bred there; for about the first week in July some of the young were more than half-grown, while some females were heavy with young, and I often observed them running about the forests with their mouths full of grass to build their nests with. It is curious that about the middle of May there appeared to be another smaller migration of them *down from* the fells *southward.* Although the lower fells were covered with them in the summer, I do not recollect seeing one upon the very highest snow fells. As to the wonderful stories of their marching in a body like soldiers, surmounting all obstacles, swimming rivers, and devastating the whole country as they passed over it, I can only say I never saw them in a body; all that I saw were scattered here and there over the whole face of the country. If ever by chance I saw one travelling in the day, it was running singly to hide itself, and we rarely saw one on the move unless we had first disturbed it from its lair. I never saw them either enter a house or outhouse, or attempt to climb a wall. They had no occasion to swim much, as there was plenty of ice on the rivers and lakes (but they can swim strongly and well); and as for devastating the country as they passed over it, the bare open patches which were clear of snow when the lemming first came up were already as barren as the deserts of Arabia; and as soon as the spring came on there was keep enough in the forests and on the fells for millions of little creatures like these.

Their habits on the march were just what one might suppose the habits of any small animal would be who knows it is passing through an enemy's territory. There was no order or regularity. They seemed to travel much by night, and by day you might observe them on the move, running from one heap of grass to the other, evidently in a great bustle and trepidation. All seemed heading to the fells, and each one tried to reach this point as well as it was able, but none seemed in a hurry to get there. During their journey, every animal larger than themselves claimed a perfect right to persecute them, as though, instead of being one of the prettiest and most harmless little animals we have in the north, the lemming were to be regarded as a venomous snake; and how so many escaped I think most wonderful. Boys, dogs, birds of prey of every description, ruthlessly pursued them, and as many were killed for sheer wantonness as for the sake of food, for I observed that very few dogs ate them; and although I saw our old cat (and we only had one cat in the village) kill them whenever he had a chance, I never saw him eat one. It is a curious, but I believe a well-substantiated fact, although I never witnessed it, that the reindeer greedily devour them. I certainly never yet saw an animal which combines stupidity with bravery so much as the lemming; they really seem to court destruction; for when you pass by one hidden under a tree, stone, or tuft of grass, instead of lying still and unnoticed, the little lemming immediately sends forth a challenge by uttering a shrill squeaking bark, and, facing its enemy, gives battle even unto death. If the bear had only half the savage pluck of these little creatures there would be no living in the north; and this is not a habit acquired by age, for the young ones do just the same; and if you only point a stick at one, it will seize the end of it with its teeth, and is with difficulty shaken off. But in the summer, when the ground is clearer and places of concealment are more easily reached than in the winter, they appear to become much more timid, and it is not nearly so easy to kill them. I think I never saw an animal that is so easily killed; the least blow from the smallest switch will kill them in an instant. Much conjecture has been hazarded as to where all these lemmings have their native home; and some suppose that one certain high fell range in the north is the matrix of the swarms that occasionally come down. But I cannot see why one particular fell tract more than another is to be assigned as their peculiar home, when we see that there are hundreds of miles of wild unexplored fell tract, from the south of Lapland to the North

Cape, all well suited to their habits. Hundreds of thousands of lemmings might be scattered over its surface, and yet need not live in colonies; but the *cause* of these irregular migrations is and probably always will be, a secret known only to an All-wise Creator, who, we may rest assured, has ordained nothing in vain. In my opinion, much exaggeration and useless mystery have been used by those writers who have described these migrations (to say nothing of the palpable lies gravely uttered by the older writers); and I can see little more wonderful in them (save that their numbers are much greater) than the uncertain migrations, without any apparent cause, of the squirrels in this very country, the opossums in Australia, and of many other animals. They sometimes in these migrations travel very far south, for in 1819 they appeared in the neighbourhood of Carlstad, in Wermland, where none had been seen for a hundred years.

I should much like to know whether the lemming has ever been kept alive in confinement. They have an idea here that this would be impossible, and that if two were put into the same cage, they would inevitably fight till one or both were killed.

I never met with either the common brown rat (*Mus decumanus*, Pall.) or the black rat (*Mus rattus*, Lin.) in Lapland, although the former is found in all the coast towns, even up within the polar circle, and from thence is gradually spreading inland. The black rat appears now to be nearly rooted out of Sweden by the brown rat. In Stockholm, where thirty years since they were said to be plentiful, they are now never met with; and in Carlstad, and other places along the banks of the Wenern, where the black rat was formerly the only species, the brown rat has now quite usurped its place.

I never saw the common house mouse (*Mus musculus*, Lin.) in Lapland, and it seems to be a stranger to the Lapland fauna.

The shrew mouse ("alman nabbmus," Sw.) was certainly rare, although both the common shrew (*Sorex vulgaris*, Lin.; "muluard," Sw.) and the water shrew (*Sorex fodiens*, Pall.) go far up into Lapland. I killed one specimen of the common shrew.

The mole (*Talpa Europea*, Lin.) does not come so far north. Its northerly range in Sweden is not, however, yet clearly defined; but in Norway, according to Nilsson, it is never seen north of Dovre fell.

One very fine fresh-killed specimen of the black water vole (*Arvicola amphibia*, Dem.; "storre iord rähe," Sw.), the largest I ever saw, was brought to me at Iockmock, but it seemed to be very rare, for no one knew what animal it was; and this was the only one I saw in Lapland.

We used to kill both the bank vole (*Arvicola riparia*, Yarr.) and the field vole or short-tailed field mouse (*A. agrestris*, Flem.); and besides these we had another species of field vole (the *Lemmus medius*, Nilss.), which is peculiar to the north, and met with in all the valleys and meadows at the foot of the fells, from Gudbrandsdalen, in Norway, up to the North Cape. I cannot see this species noticed in Clermont's "Mammalia," and fancy that it has been confounded with the *Arvicola terrestris*, De Selys, which it appears much to resemble. It is about 5 inches long, tail 2 inches (7 inches in all); but specimens which I killed varied very much in size and colour. The colour is usually dark bright brown above, under parts pale grey. It rather resembles the water vole in form, but the fur is more silky; and Nilsson argues that, from the absence of the stiff bushy hairs which are strewed over the body of the water vole, its habits are far more terrestrial. Of this I can say nothing. I never saw one in the water, but we used to get them in all the wet meadows, and often in cow-houses and outhouses.

There are also two other smaller species of field vole in Lapland (the *Lemmus rufucanus*,

Sund., and the *L. rutilus*, Pall.) I was only able to identify the former at Quickiock, and there it was considered very rare. It is met with, however, both in Luleä and Torneä Lapmark, principally in the birch regions, but I have killed them pretty high up on the fells. This pretty little species is about $3\frac{1}{2}$ inches long, the tail about 1 inch. The colour is red-brown along the back and crown of the head, sides and under parts ash grey, with a very plain division of colour. It can be easily confounded with the *Lemmus rectilus*, but the colour is rather different, the tail is much shorter, the head appears much larger, the ears are shorter. All these differences are very apparent when two specimens of the different kinds are laid together. But it is very difficult to say decidedly what the species is before a careful examination; and as I had no work on the Swedish mammalia with me, my plan was to preserve all the specimens I could fall in with, and lay them aside for careful examination when I arrived home. This I have now done, and I am very much deceived if we shall not find even another species as yet undescribed; but the size as well as the shades of colouring vary so much in this class, that it is very difficult to decide which is a variety, which a new species; and nothing but great practice and research can effect this object. I am sorry to say that I paid far too little attention this year in Lapland, both to these small field-mice and to insects. I hope, however, at a future day to have another opportunity.

I never saw a bat at Quickiock, but at Iockmock I hear that the *Vesp. borealis*, Nilss., is occasionally, but rarely, killed.

The lynx (*Felis Lynx*, Lin.; "lo," Sw.) does not appear to be met with in any part of Lapland, at least certainly not in the Quickiock district; and it is much to be regretted that the beaver (*Castor fiber*, Lin.; "bafuer," Sw.) should have been quite rooted out of this land. What an interest would be added to a forest ramble in Lapland if we could occasionally come upon a colony of the industrious and interesting animals.

I never heard of either the badger or polecat up here. Strange that the wild cat is an entire stranger to the Scandinavian fauna. I should have fancied even the gloom of "the Trossachs" would be nothing compared to many a wild spot on these secluded fells. Perhaps it could not stand the winter. And although, as I before said, we had one old domestic cat in Quickiock, you never by any chance see one in a Laplander's tent. This kind of wandering life is hardly comfortable enough for pussy.

That all domestic animals will thrive as far north as this, is proved by the fact of the horses, when not overworked, being quite on a par with those in the middle of Sweden. The cows are also as good, and the sheep, could they only have been well fed in winter, would have been very tolerable. No doubt pigs would live in Lapland if they only had enough to eat, but the expense of carriage of corn up here renders it too valuable to be given to the pig.

Although, perhaps, rather out of place, I may add that the carriage of a quarter of rye up from Luleä to Quickiock, even by sledging in winter, which is the only time it can be brought up, is about £3 10s., so that the price of rye in Quickiock, in 1861, which was a dear year in the north, might be quoted at about £7 the quarter. No wonder, therefore, that bread is scarce up here; I do not believe the Laps often see it on the fells. But then their substitute is reindeer cheese with their coffee, and a very lasting and excellent food to work upon is this same reindeer cheese. Like the Australian damper, a little bit goes a long way, and, I suppose on account of its indigestible qualities, sticks by a man a long time.

CHAPTER IX.

ON THE ORNITHOLOGY OF LAPLAND.

THE birds of Lapland now come under consideration; and I will proceed to give a short account of all we met with in the Quickiock district. I shall make a few remarks on their breeding habits, and describe as well as I am able the nest and eggs of some of the rarest, believing that will be as interesting to the collector at home as to any naturalist who may at a future day visit this remote district. Many of my observations will be found to differ a good deal from the accounts which we read of the breeding habits, number of eggs, etc., of some of the birds. I will, therefore, only remark, that *everything which I state as a fact came under my own observation;* and, without saying that another man is wrong, I can safely say that I am right as far as my own observations went.

Golden eagle (*Aquila chrysaëtos*, Cuv.; "kungs örn," Sw.). The white-tailed eagle (*Haliaëtus albicilla*, Sav.; "hafs örn," Sw.). Both the golden and white-tailed eagles bred in the neighbourhood. The Laps call both the eagles "goastern," but we never obtained the nest of either. The golden eagle appeared to remain here throughout the winter, but not the white-tailed. We rarely went out on the fells without seeing an enormous golden eagle, whose eyrie was clearly in the neighbourhood, soaring high above our heads, but we never could find the nest. On our road up, a little old Lap brought me a fine specimen of an eagle, nearly as large as himself, which he had picked up dead in the forest. It struck me as very different to any golden eagle I had before seen. It was very much spotted and dashed on the thigh, and wing covered with light yellow. I fancy, however, that it was nothing more than a young golden eagle, for the upper half of the tail was white.

I may add as a hint to the young naturalist, that he may at a glance determine the difference between the golden and the white-tailed eagle by the leg, which in the golden eagle is feathered down to the toes; in the white-tailed, bare.

The Norwegian jer-falcon (*Falco jer-falco Norwegicus*, Wooley; "rip spenning," Lap.; "jagt falk," Sw.). Of this dark jer-falcon I only succeeded in obtaining one nest with three eggs, which was taken by a Lap on June 8th, from a high cliff on the shore of Lake Wihrigaur, on the Norwegian frontier, about fifty miles west of

Quickiock. The neighbourhood of this lake must possess many attractions for the naturalist. I obtained the nest of the snowy owl not far from here. Buffon's skua, and other rare fell birds, and some of the rarest fell butterflies and plants, are brought from this district. It can be easily reached from Quickiock in three days.

The Lap name of this falcon is "rip spenning." Spenning is the name for every bird of prey, hawks, owls, etc., and the word ripa is added on account of the havoc which this jer-falcon commits among the ptarmigan.

I will now say a few words respecting this northern jer-falcon. And, first, I will refer the reader to Dr. Bree's "Birds of Europe not observed in the British Isles," in which he will find a life-like picture of this bird, be it the same as the Iceland falcon, or a distinct species. I have not had the luck to examine many specimens of this falcon, but all I have seen have been as dark in plumage as Dr. Bree's figure. They all appeared to be smaller than the Iceland falcon; the colour different from the young Iceland falcons which I have seen, and more resembling the peregrine falcon; and although I am hardly competent to give an opinion, in my mind it is clearly a distinct species, entirely confined to the Scandinavian fell (but not only to Lapland, for it is met with as far south as the Dovre fells, in Norway, where it is known by the name of the "blä falk," or blue falcon). The egg coloured by Dr. Bree is from a specimen in the British Museum, and more resembles a light variety of the egg of the *Falco Islandicus* than the eggs of this dark jer-falcon which I obtained. The three eggs which were brought to me with part of the old female were of a uniform dull brick-dust red colour all over, not speckled or patched, and of a more elongated form. This bird is well known to the Laps, who well distinguish it from the peregrine, the only other large falcon that breeds on these fells; and it appears to be not rare; in fact, from what I could gather, more common in this district than even the peregrine. So much confusion has existed, and so many different opinions have been given respecting the identity of this falcon, that any observations which may tend to throw a light on the matter must be acceptable to the naturalist, and I shall, therefore, make no apology for troubling my readers with a few remarks on this subject. Whether or not there be three distinct species of the jer-falcon, as some naturalists contend, one thing appears to be clear, that this dark falcon never became perfectly white, as in the Greenland and Iceland forms. And here let me correct a mistake which seems to have gained ground in England, "that in Scandinavia the forms found in Greenland and Iceland never seem to occur."

Far from this being the case, I never yet heard of this dark variety (unless, indeed, we follow Nilsson, and consider this dark form as nothing more than the Iceland and Greenland bird in a dark state of plumage) being killed off the fells; and certainly *all* the jer-falcons which are killed in the south and middle of Sweden (and I have seen them very white) appear to belong to the Greenland and Iceland forms. Nay, more than this, I bought at Quickiock a skin of a very fine white old Iceland falcon, which was killed up there in 1861. The man who shot it considered it a great rarity, as he had never seen one so white before, and, in his opinion, it was very distinct from the common "rip spenning," and so it clearly was; but I do believe that the only bird which *breeds* on these fells is the dark *Falco jer-falco Norwegicus*. I very much doubt, however, whether we are correct in applying the Linnæan synonym of *Falco lanarius* to this bird, and in this opinion I am borne out by Nilsson; for, in the last edition of his "Birds of Scandinavia" (1858), he describes the *Falco lanarius*, Lin., as quite a different bird, under the Swedish name of "slag falk." And although Linnæus, in his "Systema Naturæ" (at least, in my translation by Turton, of 1800), in describing the *F. lanarius*, does not say anything regarding the colour of the head, Nilsson, in describing the "slag falk" (*F. lanarius*, Lin.), distinctly says, "head white, tinged with rusty yellow;" and except that he gives the length of the old female twenty inches, his general description agrees with Dr. Bree's description of the lanner falcon (*Falco lanarius*, Schleg.) of his admirable work, p. 37. Linnæus' description of the lanner was from a younger bird, killed in Sweden. In Nilsson's description of the *Falco jer-falco* (Lin. and Nils.), he does not use Linnæus' synonym of *Falco lanarius*, but he gives to it the synonym of *Falco rusticolus*, Lin. Faun. p. 19 (older female); and also *Falco jer-falco*, Lin. Faun. p. 22 (young bird).

Neither Nilsson nor Sundeval will allow that there is more than one species of jer-falcon in Sweden, in describing which Nilsson uses all these synonyms:—"Falco gyr-falco Islandicus, candicans; Grœnlandicus rusticolus, fuscus, umbrinus;" and he gives it the Swedish names of jakt-falk, hort-falk, blä-falk (the name by which this dark Falco gyr-falco Norwegicus is known on the Norwegian fells); and he also gives to the same bird the Lapland name of riefsakfalle—thus clearly identifying it with our Lap "rip spenning," which word has precisely the same meaning as the riefsakfalle, only used in another district. He then gives us descriptions and measurements taken by himself from fourteen different specimens, varying in length from 21 in. to 25 in., and presenting every shade of plumage, from the dark young to the old white mature bird. It would have been interesting if I could have inserted a full translation of his descriptions, but I cannot find space. Nilsson's experience in Swedish ornithology is very great, and has extended over many years, and his opinion, with me at least, always carries weight. I may remark that he divides his specimens into two series—the *first* with *oblong*, the *latter* with *transverse* spots.

He winds up his remarks with the following pertinent note, which I translate freely and fully:—"To this latter series probably belongs Schlegel's Falco candicans Islandicus, as he has described it in his 'Révue Critique,' p. 4. It is also undeniable that Linné's Falco rusticolus and gyr-falco belong to this group; but by referring to the above measurements it does not appear that the gyr-falco is so much smaller than Candicans Islandicus. Herr Schlegel, 'Révue,' p. 57, expresses his surprise that the true Norwegian gyr-falco ('den ratta Norska gyr-falco'), which he (Schlegel), nevertheless, supposes to be identical with Linné's Falco lanarius, Faun. Suec., should have been altogether unknown to the Scandinavian naturalists until he (Schlegel) described it. And Degland, in his 'European Ornithology,' reiterates the same. Yes, it would indeed have been very surprising had such been the case; but not only has this Falco gyr-falco been known to us even from Linné's time, but we also know the transitions from this to the Falco candicans Islandicus, Auct.; therefore we do not consider ourselves justified in dividing them into two or more species."

So much for Nilsson. He clearly considers this Falco ger-falco Norwegicus (Wooley), the Falco Grœnlandicus (Hanc.), and Falco Islandicus (Hanc.), as all varieties of one bird—Falco Gyrfalco (Lin.), and not three distinct species; and, presumptuous as it may appear for me to differ from a naturalist of such standing, I cannot help it. Without going into the question as to whether Falco Islandicus (Hanc.) and Falco Grœnlandicus (Hanc.) are anything more than local varieties of the same bird, I consider the dark Norwegian jerfalcon a clearly distinct species from either; and although, perhaps, the young of this may be easily confounded with the young of the Falco Islandicus (Hanc.), there is too marked a difference in my eye between the old birds to admit of their being considered as nothing more than the same bird in a different stage of plumage. But, as I said before, my experience is small, and my opinion carries but little weight.

Kjærholling, the Danish naturalist—of whom I have also a great opinion—distinctly says that this Norwegian jer-falcon, which he calls *Fal. gyr-falco* (Schlegel)—"den Norske jagt falk" (*F. lanarius*, L.), is distinct from both the Iceland and Greenland forms (which, I fancy, he is inclined to consider as two distinct species). In his description, he says of this Norwegian bird:—"It never becomes white. From the young Iceland and Greenland falcon it differs in its smaller size, in the same sex, by the dark spot on the cheek (as in the peregrine), by its yellow-green legs, which appear to be peculiar to this bird at all ages; and further, in that the spots on the under part of thy body and sides have the form of 'transverse bands.'"

The peregrine falcon (*F. peregrinus*, L.; "pelegrim falk," Sw.) was far from common on these fells. I rarely saw a specimen, and never obtained a nest, although they certainly breed here. This is a difficult egg to obtain, well authenticated.

I never met with the hobby (*F. subbuteo*, L.) up here, nor do I believe it comes up so far north, although Löwenhjelm includes it in his list of birds that breed in Luleå-Lapland.

The merlin (*F. lithofalco*, Gm.; "dverg falk," Sw., "tsitsasch falle," Lap.) was the common hawk in this district, and must have been one of the early spring migrants, for I shot a female on April 19. It was impossible to walk on the fells without meeting this bold and pretty little hawk, which I have even seen chasing the ptarmigan. I never found the nest of the merlin here anywhere but on the ground, either on a bare cliff or in the heather, always on tolerably high fells. The first nest which I took was on June 9. When first laid, the eggs of the merlin have a beautiful violet-red tinge, with red-brown spots; this, however, soon fades, and they assume a red-brown ground colour, with dirty brown spots. It is said by the Laps sometimes to build in a tree. The number of eggs appear to vary from four to six; and so much do they resemble those of the kestrel, although, perhaps, in general a very little smaller, that when I have mixed a lot I should never have been able to separate them if each egg had not been numbered. I have often been struck with the great difference in size that there is between many of the old female merlins that we kill.

The kestrel (*F. tinnunculus*, Lin.; "torn falk," Sw.), and the sparrow-hawk (*Accipiter nisus*, Nils.; "sparl hok," Sw.), were both common here, as well as the goshawk (*Astur palumbarius*, Bechst.; "techuon falle," Lap; " duff hok," Sw.), but I was never lucky enough to obtain the nest of this latter bird here—a circumstance, however, which I did not so much regret, as it breeds very commonly in Wermland. It is very remarkable that, although we often kill the young birds, it is exceedingly rare that we ever kill a perfectly mature goshawk, most that we kill being birds of the year. The goshawk does not migrate from Sweden, but remains here throughout the whole year—the old birds, according to Nilsson, in the vicinity of the breeding-place, the birds of the year migrating to other tracts—like the snowy owl and jer-falcon; and this is borne out by the fact that if ever we kill one of these latter birds in the winter in Wermland, it is almost sure to be a bird of the year. All the eggs of the goshawk that I have obtained in Sweden have been dirty-white, save in one instance, when I have seen the egg very faintly, almost indistinctly, dashed with light red-brown—the usual number, five.

The osprey (*F. Haliaëtus*, Lin.; "fisk ljuse," Sw.; "tschiftscha," Lap.) was not uncommon in this district. We took the first nest on June 1. I never saw either the kite (*Milvus regalis*, Briss.; "gläda," Sw.), the common buzzard (*Buteo vulgaris*, Ray; "orm wräk," Sw.), or the honey buzzard (*F. apivorus*, L.; "bi wräk," Sw.) in Lapland, nor do I believe that any of these come up so far north.

The rough-legged buzzard (*Falco lagopus*, Brunn.; "fjösbent wräk," Sw.; "biekkam," Lap.) was by far the commonest of all the birds of prey in the Quickiock district during the summer, probably owing to the quantity of lemming which swarmed on these fells. Of all the hawks, I think that this buzzard varies most in the shading of its colouring, and I have remarked that the female is generally lightest, becoming nearly grey-white with age. But if the birds themselves vary, I am sure we may say the same of the eggs, for I have taken them of every shade, from pure white to a dark-brown blotched egg. It is almost impossible to distinguish these eggs from those of the common buzzard's, except that in general the egg of the rough-legged buzzard is a little larger (but I have seen the egg of the common buzzard as large), and it has a rather finer and bolder character—if I may be allowed the term.

They appeared on these fells as spring migrants. The first I observed was early in May, and the first nest I obtained was on May 21, with three eggs; and although I have obtained the nest with five, and once even with six eggs, I observed that three was the most usual number, and most often sat on, and I have noticed that three eggs is the usual number laid both by the common buzzard and the kite. The nest, a coarse "edifice" of sticks, moss, and grass, loosely put together, was often on a fell-ridge, often in a tree, but never down in the forest; always on the sides of the fells, but always below the snow region, as I often obtain the nest of the honey buzzard in Wermland. I may here observe that we invariably find them breeding not in the deep fir forest, but in smaller plantings, where much birch is mixed with the fir. The nest here, however, is always on a fir, not on a birch. It is nearly as large as that of the common buzzard, built chiefly of thickish sticks; but there is one peculiarity in this nest which I never observed in any other of the buzzards. You will always find some green birch branches interwoven with the dry sticks. They go to nest the latest of the whole tribe. We never take a nest till June; and this year, 1863, I obtained one as late as August 14. The eggs vary much in colour, and are certainly finer and deeper-coloured than any others of this genus. The only egg for which they can be mistaken are those of the peregrine, but they are usually rounder and deeper coloured. Two is in general the full number. I have occasionally seen rough-legged buzzards beating over the lower meadows in the end of July, after the young ducks, but I never by any chance saw one in the forests. The fells appear to be their peculiar summer home, for they breed in no other part of Sweden; and on August 18, the last day that I was on the fells, I counted seventeen on the wing, soaring very high over one fell tract; and the reader may further fancy that they were very common here from the fact that more than fifty nests were destroyed in this district during the spring of 1862. In habits, flight, and appearance, the rough-legged buzzard much resembles its congener, the common buzzard, from which it may be always distinguished when in the air by the white root of the tail. Its cry is a loud "ka haa" (not unlike the melancholy call of the common buzzard), and is in perfect harmony with the wild, lonely fell-tracts which it frequents. The period of breeding must extend over a very long space of time, for I observed downy young ones in a nest on August 6. I do not think this bird is so sluggish in its habits as the common buzzard; and, although doubtless lemming and fell mice form their principal food, I am certain that they destroy many ptarmigan, for I have seen the ground surrounding the nest thickly strewed with the feathers of the ptarmigan.

Of the harriers I am not certain that I saw one in Lapland, although I fancied once I saw a pair of the marsh harriers flying over the riverside at Quickiock.

The snowy owl (*Strix nyctea*; "fall uggla,"

Sw.; "ku ku," "skuolfe," Lap.).—Owing, perhaps, to the lemming migrations, which appear to draw all the birds of prey in the north into one focus, the snowy owl has not been rare on the Quickiock fells during the last three seasons; and in 1861 three nests, all containing young birds, were destroyed by the Laps within sixty miles of Quickiock. In no single instance were the old birds killed; but they did not come back to breed in the same localities in 1862, for we carefully examined every old nest. However, in the beginning of June, I sent two Laps off to the great lake Wihrigaur. The road was bad, and the snow lay deep on the fells; but they returned within the week, bringing with them a nest and six eggs of the snowy owl, as well as the old female, which they had shot. I was much pleased to see the marked difference between this egg and the egg of any other of the large European owls. It is more elongated and not so round or large as the egg of the eagle owl (but of course perfectly white); and it is larger than that of the Lap owl (*Strix Lapponica*). The egg of the snowy owl measures just the same in length as that of the eagle owl ($2\frac{1}{4}$ inches); its breadth is $1\frac{3}{4}$ inches, that of the eagle owl being 2 inches full. The nest was nothing more than a large boll of reindeer moss, placed on the ledge of a bare fell.

The old birds appeared to guard it most jealously; in fact, the Laps often kill them with a stick when they are robbing the nest, which they do upon every occasion that presents itself. The snowy owl will occasionally make its nest on the large turf hillocks in some of the mosses.

Considering the number of eggs that the snowy owl lays, and the wild inaccessible nature of the country in which its nest is usually built, I cannot help wondering that this bird is not more common on these fells; but if we take into consideration the immense fell tract stretching from the Dovre fell, in Norway, right up to the North Cape, and think of the tens of thousand acres whereon human foot never treads, but over which these birds have almost an undisputed range, our wonder ceases. The old birds appear rarely to leave the high fells, and if we want them we must seek them in their wild mountain home. They appear, however, to make periodical migrations after the lemming, and therefore in some seasons are common in districts where they have perhaps not appeared for years. Still, I fancy the snowy owl is more local than erratic. On some years there appears to be a kind of general migration of these birds down from the fells, and I remember in the winter of 1860, they were so numerous in Wermland, that about fourteen specimens (chiefly birds of the year) were shot or trapped in that province.

An opinion is held here that the snowy owl becomes whiter in the winter (and I think this very probable), and that the female is always purer in colour than the male. It is clearly a diurnal bird; for any day when we went out on the fells we could see the white owl perched on a distant rock watching us, or beating over the fells with a stately measured flight—always, however, out of gunshot. Its shriek when on the wing resembles a loud "krau-au," repeated three or four times; but it is seldom heard except when the bird is excited. Some of the movements of this bird are very extraordinary, and I once saw one fall from a considerable height on to the ground, where it lay for some time perfectly motionless, with outstretched wings, as if it were shot. I tried to creep up within gunshot, but it rose out of distance, and sailed away uttering a wild loud cry, "Rick, rick, rick," as if mocking me.

The hawk owl *(Strix funerea,* Lath.; "hŏk uggla," Sw.; " girgelodde," Lap.) was by far the commonest owl in this district, and although, of course, like the rest of the tribe, the lemming forms its principal food when they are "in season," I don't believe this bird migrates much, but remains stationary in the same district throughout the year. It is true, however, that in the winter we occasionally kill an odd example, both old birds and birds of the year, as far south as Wermland, but I do not think, except as stray individuals, that they migrate from their native forests. The range of the hawk owl in the north is precisely that of the Siberian jay—the lower fir forests at the foot and by the sides of the fells; but I fancy that the Siberian jay breed further south than the hawk owl. You never by any chance, however, meet with them out of the fir forests.

The hawk owl is by no means shy, and in the breeding season it is one of the boldest of all birds. Seated on the top of a dead pine, close to the nest where his mate is sitting, the old male bird keeps a constant watch, and as soon as any one appears to be approaching the nest, he raises his tail and head, after the manner of the cuckoo, and uttering a shrill cry, not unlike that of the kestrel hawk, down he comes full on the head of the intruder; dashing by with the speed of lightning, he returns to the charge again and again, till he has either cleared the coast, or has paid the penalty of his rashness with his life. My lad was really frightened at this bird, and always hated to go up to a nest; and well he might, for on one occasion, when taking the eggs out of a dead pine, without a branch to help him, holding on, as the sailors say, "by his eyelids," forty feet from the ground, the old bird made a swoop down on his head, struck off his cap (through the top of which a large slit was cut), and in a moment returned to the charge, tearing off a very fair-sized claw-full of his hair. I was standing below, and knocked the old bird over; and had I not been at the bottom of the tree with my gun, the lad might easily have been beaten off his hazardous perch. There is no trouble in shooting the hawk owl if you have only a dog in the forest; for, whatever time of year it may be, as soon as ever the bird spies a dog below him, it always descends to give battle.

In flight, manners, and appearance, the hawk owl is closely allied to the hawks. It is strictly diurnal in its habits, and to the stealthy quiet flight of the owl adds the spirit and courage of the falcon. Hardly a forest bird is safe from the attacks of these owls. I have seen them strike down the Siberian jay, their closest neighbour, on the wing, and more than once have I disturbed them feeding on the old willow-grouse, a bird half as large again as themselves. Their principal food appears to be birds, lemming, and wood-mice; but I have often taken insects out of their stomachs. There is little difference in the plumage of the male and female, but the latter is rather the larger; and in the breeding season I have observed that the breast and belly of the female is strongly tinged with reddish-brown. The male takes his turn at sitting (as is the case with the woodpecker), for I have shot both as they flew out of the hole from the eggs. The hawk owl moults very early, as do many of the northern birds. Like the Siberian jay, the old birds may be seen in deep moult, without tails, even before the young are flyers; and in both the autumnal moult is complete as soon as the young birds are full feathered. The hawk owl is then in its best plumage, and its clean, pure, shiny dress at that season is very different from the dingy colouring of spring.

The nest is always in a hole in a rotten pine or fir, sometimes at a considerable height from the ground. Morris says the eggs are white (here he is right); but he also says the " nest is *built* in a tree, and composed of sticks, grass, and feathers; the eggs, like those of the owls generally, of the dual number." Now I know of no European owl which, as a rule, lays so few as two eggs. The eagle owl, in every instance that I have seen, lays three; and though I never myself took the nest of the Lap owl (for although it is shot occasionally there, it does not appear to breed in the Quickiock forests), through the kindness of Mr. A. Newton, I possess a genuine specimen of this egg, which was taken from a nest with *seven* eggs near Muniovara in 1861. This egg is rather rounder and not so elongated as that of the snowy owl. Of the breeding habits of the Ural owl *(Strix Uralensis,* Pall.), we know nothing for certain; but of *all* the other European owls I believe five or six to be the full number. On June 13th, I took a clutch of the hawk owl with eight eggs— probably a second clutch from a bird whose first nest had been robbed, for we seldom found fresh eggs after the second week in May, and early in June we shot young flyers. I also took, on May 30, a clutch of Tengmalm's owl, with ten eggs. But these certainly were exceptional cases. As to the nest, I never saw a *nest* of either, the eggs having been always laid, like those of the woodpecker, in a hole, with nothing under them but a few dry splinters and chips of the rotten or fresh wood, as the case might be.

The eggs of the hawk owl very often so much resemble those of the short-eared owl that one might well pass for the other; but they are in general a little smaller, more elongated and pointed at the small end, of a deep dirty white. Usual size—$1\frac{1}{2}$ inch by $1\frac{1}{8}$.

Tengmalm's owl *(Strix Tengmalmi,* Gm.;

"perl uggla," Sw.) was, next to the last, the commonest owl in our forests, but being much more nocturnal in its habits than the hawk owl, it was not so often seen; not that the light appears much to affect its vision, for here the summer nights are as light as day, and we rarely went into the forest on any night without seeing this pretty little owl hawking after its prey. The eggs of this owl vary much in shape, but not so much in size. In the same nest you will see some eggs as round as musket-balls, others oval and elongated. The usual size, however, is about $1\frac{3}{8}$ by 1 inch. This owl has a much more southern range than the last, for we not unfrequently take nests in South Wermland; but, strange to say, they are met with, like those of the crossbills, only about every third year. This owl goes to nest early; after the end of May you rarely find eggs. It has been remarked that whenever this owl has appeared in autumn, in the very south of Sweden, a severe winter has always followed. We found it to occupy in the Quickiock forest precisely the same range as the hawk owl, and we never by any chance saw one on the fell sides higher than the fir region. It is a bold, voracious little bird. One light night I shot a female in full chase after lemming on a frozen lake. In Wermland, on one occasion, having caught an old female on the eggs,

I took her home in a small fishing creel, and casting in a titmouse which I had shot, found it nearly devoured when I arrived home. I had her for a long time in a cage, and a very pretty little pet she was, becoming very tame. The call-note was a very musical soft whistle, which, however, I never heard except in the evening and night. I could never detect the slightest difference in plumage between the male and female. Till I took the nest in Wermland, no Swedish naturalist appeared to be aware of the fact of this little owl breeding so far south. We took our first nest at Quickiock on May 2, and our last on May 30. In Wermland we often take the nest in the end of April.

The lesser European sparrow owl *(Strix passerina,* Lin., " sparf uggla," Sw.).—No Swedish naturalist seemed to be aware that this little owl had so high a northern range as Lapland, nor did I fancy so myself, for I always considered that the midland forests of Sweden and Norway were its proper habitat. As I had not succeeded in finding the eggs at Quickiock, I began to feel convinced that such was the case, but on July 12th one of my lads brought me in a family—an old female and four young birds, which must have just left the nest, for he chased the young birds down. They were evidently bred in this immediate neighbourhood, and I was much pleased at obtaining

them, for it is always gratifying when we can add any new facts, however trifling, to the knowledge we already possess relative to the habits of the feathered race. This female, and one of the young birds, are admirably figured in Dr. Bree's beautiful work on the birds of Europe, and he also quotes the following remarks from my letter to him of March, 1863, on the habits of this little owl:—
"I have lately been in our forests, and found out more about the habits of this little owl. It certainly breeds with us (in South Wermland), and I do hope to get you the eggs this year." (This, however, I failed to do, and strange to say, I know of no egg collector whose cabinet possesses authentic specimens of the egg of this little owl, which is by no means scarce in the middle of Sweden.) "I have a live one now in a cage, and a most amusing pet it is. Although diurnal in its habits, it seems always to sit very still, except in the early morning and evening. As far as I can make out, this is the earliest bird in our forest, for the old poachers who go out before daybreak to shoot the capercailzie on the perch in spring, say that the first call note they hear in the forest is that of this bird. They also say that as soon as ever they hear this in the spring they reckon that the season for the 'lek,' or play of the capercailzie is not far distant.

"The note of this little owl is a whistle, one long loud whe-e-e, like blowing into a key, then a number of fine notes, quickly repeated, 'ti-meet, ti-meet, ti-meet, ti-meet,' not so loud. One night early in March, I slept at the house of a gamekeeper, in a forest which we knew was frequented by these little owls, and about 4 A.M. I heard the first note. The bird was in a fir planting about 800 yards distant from our house, and yet, as the morning was still, we could hear it very distinctly. I had often heard this note before in our forests, but always took it for that of Tengmalm's owl. I stole up quietly, and, to make quite sure, shot a female of this little owl, with the ovary rather forward.

"I do not think that they breed in the south of Sweden, and they are rare or accidental in Denmark. They are bold and voracious for their size, and I have, more than once, known them strike down a titmouse in the forest. In fact, my little owl made very short work with a wounded crossbill which I put into its cage. Although, at present, we appear to know little or nothing for certain of the breeding habits of this owl, we may take it for granted that it lays more than two eggs, as stated by Temminck, for out of the family we saw at Quickiock I obtained four specimens, and I am not certain but that one or more escaped."

This little owl must not be confounded with the little night owl of Britain, to which Nilsson has given the best synonym, that of *Strix nudipes*, nor with the American little owl (*Strix acadeca*, Bon., p. 66, Wilson), which latter bird seems to me to be a kind of link between Tengmalm's owl (which does not appear to be known in America, although Wilson evidently confounds it with the American *Strix acadeca*) and the *Strix passerina*, L. It differs from the little owl of Britain, in that its toes are covered thickly with downy hair like feathers, even to the very claws, and the tail extends nearly an inch and a half beyond the closed wings, whereas in the British bird it is scarcely longer than the wings themselves. Moreover, in the little owl of Britain, the first wing feather is equal in length to the sixth, the second like to the fifth, the third longest. In the little Swedish owl, the first is like the ninth, the second like the sixth, the third and fourth the longest.

I may add that the little British owl can hardly be included in the Scandinavian fauna, only one specimen having been taken, in a church in the south of Sweden; and although, according to Dr. Bree, the lesser European sparrow owl is met with in Switzerland and occasionally in the north of Germany, I fancy Scandinavia is its proper home.

Some confusion still exists in the identification

of the smaller owls, and much yet remains to be proved regarding their habits and geographical range.

The eagle owl (*Strix bubo*, L.; "berg lef," Sw.; "lidno," Lap.).—Although I neither saw the bird or obtained its nest in Lapland, the eagle owl bred on a high mountain just opposite Quickiock, on the other side of the river; and the deep-measured "boo, boo," of the old bird, like the distant bark of a gruff old watch-dog, might be heard on any evening when we were out in the neighbourhood of its eyrie. I not unfrequently take the nest in Wermland, and it breeds commonly both around Gothenburg and in the south of Sweden; but I think its proper home is more in the midland than in the northern districts of the country. The egg of the eagle owl is the largest of all the European owls' eggs. Nearly round, measuring often $2\frac{3}{8}$ by 2 inches.

The short-eared owl (*Strix brachyotus*, Gm.; "igjalodde," Lap.; "kort œraduf," Sw.) was a summer visitant to Lapland, arriving towards the end of May, and during the whole season was very common on all our fells. It frequented exactly the same tracts as the merlin; and although, perhaps, strictly speaking, more nocturnal than diurnal in its habits, was very often to be seen hawking over the fells in broad daylight; its flight much resembling that of the goat-sucker. It is a very bold bird, and I once saw a short-eared owl actually beat off a golden eagle from the vicinity of the nest. I have often been amused, while lying by my camp-fire on the fells at midnight, by watching the curious gyrations of this bird in the air, which much reminded me of the common lapwing. Its loud cry, "wau-au," is like the barking of a dog. We always used to find the nest on the ground, on the lower fells (not on the snow-fells), and the full number of eggs appeared to be six. The egg tolerably round, measuring $1\frac{1}{2}$ by $1\frac{1}{4}$ inches.

Neither the long-eared owl (*Strix otus*, L.), nor the brown owl (*Strix aluco*, Gm.) are met with in Lapland—at least certainly not in this district. Old Acerbi, however, includes the latter among the birds of Lapland, but we cannot place much faith in his ornithological remarks; for if his description be at all correct, some very curious kinds, many of which must now be extinct, appear to have been met with in Lapland at his day.

There are, however, two other Lap owls which I never met with myself in this district—the Lap owl (*Strix Lapponica*, Retz.; "aapu," Lap.; "Lap uggla," Sw.), which does not appear to have been known until the end of the last century, and the Ural owl (*Strix Uralensis*, Pall.; "slag uggla," Sw.),

Respecting the first, I cannot but express my surprise that we did not find it at Quickiock, for the nest has been taken both at Iockmock and Gellivare, and further north, near Munio; and I can only account for the circumstance by the fact that the forests just round Quickiock are too small. The Lap owl is a true forest owl, and *builds* a large nest, generally high up in a largish pine, in the very deep forest. As to the Ural owl, a great mystery appears to hang over this bird, and especially over its breeding habits. By all I could learn, it is occasionally seen near Quickiock. It is not uncommon around Skellefteä, on the coast near which place I obtained a fine specimen of a female on my journey up; and it is also said to be common near Lepsala, in Lapland.

In the district around Quickiock the great shrike (*Lanius excubitor*, Lin.; "var fogel," Sw.; ".utsah ruoscha garanas," Lap.) was by no means common; and although we shot five or six young birds when the season was over, we only obtained one nest, containing five eggs. This was on May 13th. We shot the old female. The nest was placed in a small fir not high from the ground. It was one of the warmest and most comfortable nests I have ever seen, large and deep; built outwardly of dead fir-branches, and lined with a very thick layer of the pure white feathers of the willow grouse. The great shrike was the only species I ever met with in Lapland.

The cuckoo (*Cuculus canorus*, Lin.; "gök," Sw.; "giekka," Lap.) was as common in the fell valleys as in the lowlands; and I have heard its monotonous, but familiar and cheering call-note throughout the whole summer nights at the foot of the real snow fells, high over the limits of the forests.

The great black woodpecker (*Picus martius*, Lin.; "spill kroka," Sw.) was quite as common up here as in the middle of Sweden. We took the first nest on May 5, which is about two weeks later than we find them in the Wermland forests. As far as I can remark, five is the full number of eggs, which vary much in size, sometimes being very little larger than those of the green woodpecker (*Picus viridis*, Lin.), which bird I never saw in Lapland.

The three-toed woodpecker (*Picus tridactylus*, Lin.; "tschaitne," Lap.; "tretäig hackspett," Sw.)—Of all the woodpeckers this is the commonest in Lapland, and goes up the fell sides as far as the fir forests extend; but, common as it was, I was unable to obtain more than four nests (three with eggs, and one with young). In two instances the full number of eggs was three, and I never saw more than four in one nest. This species appears to be a much later breeder than that last described; they showed no signs of going to nest until about June 5. I fancy most of the woodpeckers are partial migrants, for in our Wermland forests we often in the winter kill both this and the grey-headed green woodpecker (*Picus canus*, Gm.), and the white-rumped woodpecker (*P. leuconotus*, Tem.), but we never find the nest of either in Wermland; but since my return (on Oct. 11) I shot a *Picus tridactylus*, a bird of the year, which must have been bred near Gardsjö. I never met with either the grey-headed or white-rumped woodpecker in Lapland, although I saw one of the latter sitting on a fence by the roadside, between Umeä and Piteå, on our journey up. The egg of the three-toed woodpecker is rather less than that of the great spotted woodpecker, and more tapering towards the small end.

The great spotted woodpecker (*Picus major*, Lin.; "store hackspett," Sw.), and the lesser spotted woodpecker (*Picus minor*, Lin.; "tsitsach tschaitne," Lap.; "mindre hackspett," Sw.), were both met with here, but the greater spotted was the rarer of the two. I consider the egg of the lesser spotted woodpecker a most difficult one to obtain, well authenticated. They appear to go to nest late, and I have always obtained the eggs out of a hole in a small dead fir or aspen. The num-

T

ber usually five, sometimes six. The collector should be very careful in the identification of the eggs of all the woodpeckers. The egg of the wryneck is doubtless often substituted for that of the lesser spotted woodpecker, but, on placing two genuine *fresh* eggs side by side, the difference may be easily detected, for the egg of the wryneck has a more elongated form, and the white colour, although perhaps purer, has not so much of that beautiful shiny gloss which characterises the eggs of all the woodpeckers.

I never saw the wryneck (*Yunx torquilla*, Lin.) in Lapland.

The raven (*Corvus corax*, Lin.; "korp," Sw.; "garanas," Lap.) was very common on the fells. I saw only one pair of the hooded crow (*Corvus cornix*, Lin.; "vuort sches," Lap.) at Quickiock; they appeared as spring migrants, early in April. I cannot say whether they would have stayed to breed with us, as both were shot and brought to me by a boy as great rarities here.

The rook (*Corvus frugilegus*, Lin.; "räka," Sw.)—This is a rare bird in Sweden, and supposed to be confined to the very south of the country. I never met with it in the middle of Sweden. Judge of my surprise, therefore, when one morning, early in May, I saw two birds stalking about a wet meadow, which I knew could be no others than a pair of my old friends the rooks. They remained with us about three days, when, I suppose, not liking the appearance of the place, they migrated a few miles further south; but they might just as well have remained where they were, for in a few days they were brought in to me by a boy who had shot them. This was adding a new fact to the Swedish fauna. For what purpose they had travelled up here was hard to say; but the fact of this single pair of rooks being met with so far north, proves how much the habits of birds may be altered by circumstances, for no bird is perhaps more thoroughly gregarious than the rook. Now, if these birds had come up here to breed, it must have been like the carrion crow—in a solitary manner.

I never saw the magpie (*Pica caudata*, Ray) up at Quickiock, but they are occasionally met with at Iockmock.

Although I never met with the nutcracker (*Caryocatactes guttatus*, Nilss.) up here, I am pretty certain that it breeds in Lapland, for the Laps know the bird and have a name for it; but the breeding habits of this strange bird seem at present to be shrouded in an impenetrable mystery.

I never saw the jay (*Garrulus glandarius*, Briss.) up here, but it seems occasionally to visit these forests, for they describe a larger kind of "lafskrika" at Quickiock, which, in some years, is pretty common, and which, they say, breeds later than the common *Garrulus infaustus*. It can be no other than the common jay.

The Siberian jay (*Garrulus infaustus*, Nob.; "gnofsak," Lap.; "lafskrika," Sw.)—We come now to a peculiarly northern bird, and one which is as familiar to the Laplander as the miner and mocking-bird are to the wanderer in the Australian bush, for go where you will in the Lap forests this cheerful, bold bird is sure to be your companion—now hopping on the ground before you, now floating from one tree to another, or, perched on the lower branch of a fir, it will sit and utter its melancholy "mew" till another of its comrades is attracted to the spot, when it instantly gives chase, and a battle royal appears always to take place. In some of its habits the lafskrika resembles its congener, the common jay, but it is not half so noisy, and a much more companionable sort of a bird, although it never comes so near the houses. It is one of the boldest birds that I know, and I never liked to shoot one, for there was something of a cheery welcome to the stranger in the free, unsuspecting habits of this bird. It is, nevertheless, a very savage bird of prey; and I once actually saw a lafskrika give chase to an old willow grouse—a bird ten times its own weight. It never could have been for the purpose of killing and eating it. I do not think these birds are nearly so gregarious as the common jay, and, in my opinion, much more carnivorous. I cannot say how it may be in the depth of winter, but certainly those we saw together after the breeding season were families, and when we arrived in the spring the birds had paired. I cannot agree with the accounts which some naturalists give of the extreme difficulty in finding the nest of this bird. It is true that they breed in April, when the snow lies deep in the forest; and a man without "skiddor" cannot get on at all, except just in the very early morning after a sharp night's frost. They are, moreover, very quiet in their breeding habits, and, as old Major Bagstock would say, "Sly! devilish sly!" for once I watched one (evidently building) come hopping, with a stick in its mouth, towards me. As soon, however, as it caught sight of me, it dropped the stick and flew back like an arrow to the place from whence it came. But when once built, there is little difficulty in finding the nest by any one who has a pair of good eyes in his head, for it is very large, never placed very high in a small fir, and generally in a most conspicuous situation, often by the side of a pathway in the forest. I am certain, if I had wanted them, I could easily have procured a dozen nests in these forests. The first nest that we took in Lapland belonged to this bird (on April 21), with three eggs, and this, I think, is about the number; for although I found one nest with four eggs, and once shot an old female from a nest of three, out of which I took another *full coloured* egg just ready for laying—they say here that the lafskrika begins to sit as soon as the first egg is laid, and I fancy this is the case with the crossbills—all the other nests contained but three eggs, and these often sat on. I never met with the Siberian jay out of the forests save on one occasion, when we were eating our dinner on a tolerably high fell, at the foot of an old dead fir which had been stuck up on its highest peak as a kind of landmark, when a lafskrika perched on the top of it and watched us at our repast, all the while uttering its long plaintive mew as if begging for an invitation. In the middle of June I shot strong flyers. The nest is thick and large, formed outwardly of dead fir branches, and thickly lined inside with feathers. The egg is a little smaller than that of the jay, ground colour pale bluish grey, mottled and dashed all over, especially at the large end, with darker grey and light brown.

I shot two specimens of the starling (*Sturnus vulgaris*, Lin.; "starre," Sw.) close to the priest's house, on April 26, before the snow had begun to go, but I never saw another.

There is no northern bird whose breeding habits have been shrouded in such mystery as the waxwing chatterer (*Bombycilla garrula*, Veil.; "sidensvans," Sw.; "bæljerastasch," Lap.). So many different accounts have been given by men who had evidently never met with the bird in the summer season, that the thanks of every naturalist are due to the indefatigable exertions of the late Mr. Wooley for setting at rest the *quæstio vexata*. It is difficult to believe half one hears up here; but he must evidently have been in "the thick of them," for he is reported to have obtained upwards of 400 eggs up near Munioniska, at least with the assistance of the Laps. I was, however, not so lucky, for we never saw the waxwing while we were at Quickiock; and the only nest I obtained was from a collector there, with two eggs, which was taken the year before about an English mile from Quickiock, and the old female snared on the nest. In some seasons, however, they are rather common here, but the waxwings appear to be as uncertain in their summer as in their winter migrations, for even in the tracts around Munio, from which Mr. Wooley obtained so many eggs in 1855 or 1856, in some seasons hardly a nest is to be found. The nest is large, with thick walls, not very neatly or artistically built; outside, sticks, grass, and reindeer moss mixed, then a layer of fibrous hairy moss (*Usnea barbata*); lined inside with coarse grass, but no feathers. The eggs, four or five in number, resemble those of the *Sylvia turdoides*, nearly as large as those of the common bunting, but shorter, the ground colour pale bluish-white, thickly speckled all over with purple, black, and brown spots, but leaving the ground colour of the egg very visible. They go to nest early in June. It is strange that out of all the Swedish naturalists who have travelled in Lapland no one had discovered the nest of this bird; and as for the fabulous prices which are said to have been offered for the egg of the waxwing, I do not believe there is a man in Sweden who would have given 5s. for it, even before it had been well authenticated by Mr. Wooley. The Swedish naturalists in general care very little about eggs; in fact, they will pay very little in money for a specimen of any kind. I fancy the waxwing is one of those silent birds that take care never to betray the locality of their nest; and these Lap forests are so interminable that a man may wander mile after mile, and only by chance hit upon the nest of any bird except the very commonest, unless he knows well the habits of the bird.

Although Löwenhjelm includes the night-jar (*Caprimulgus Europœus*, Lin.; "natskära," Sw.)

in the list of Lap birds, I never met with it at Quickiock, nor did I ever hear of one having ever been seen there.

The swift (*Cypselus apus*, Ill.; "torn svala," Sw.) was very common around Quickiock, and I often saw them hawking over the very high fells. I think the swift was the latest summer migrant that arrived at Quickiock, and when we left on August 21 some were still there. We had the swallow (*Hirundo rustica*, Lin.; "ladu svala," Sw.), the common martin (*H. urbica*, Lin.; "hus svala," Sw.), and the bank martin (*H. riparia*, Lin.; "strand svala," Sw.), more common, I think, up here than even in Wermland.

The pied flycatcher (*Muscicapa atricapilla*, Lin.; "svart och hoit flugsnappare," Sw.) was much commoner up here than its congener the common flycatcher (*M. grisola*, Lin.; "gra flugsnappare," Sw.). I never saw the pied flycatcher on the very fells, but as far up as the birch region extends. I used, however, to find the nest principally in small dead birch stubs by the river side.

The common thrush (*Turdus musicus*, Lin.; "sang trast," Sw.) was not nearly so common as either the redwing or fieldfare; and a boy brought me in two nests of the common thrush, which he wanted to sell me as great curiosities here, and he valued them as much as nests of the pied grosbeak; in fact, it might, as well as the misselthrush (*Turdus viscivorus*, Lin.; "dubbel trast," Sw.), be considered rare in this district. I only took one nest of the missel-thrush here (and it was considered a great rarity), and that was on July 9, with four fresh eggs. I was surprised at this, for I always considered that, both in England and in the middle of Sweden, this bird was among our earliest breeders.

The fieldfare (*T. pilaris*, Lin.; "bjork trast," Sw.; "baflerastes," Lap.) was, next to the brambling, the commonest bird in these forests, and its hoarse, laughing cackle (for I never heard this bird make the faintest attempt at a song) followed us wherever we went in the fir forest (and I never saw the fieldfare breeding anywhere else). These birds are, in fact, the greatest nuisance to the collector in these woods. They did not breed *here* in colonies, for, although the nests are seldom far apart, we never found two in the same tree. I think no thrush's egg is subject to so much variation as the egg of the fieldfare, and it would be almost impossible to describe it better than that it much resembles the egg of the blackbird, but is usually more highly coloured. We took our first nest on May 25, and our last on July 7; but at this time some of the young were flyers.

The redwing (*T. iliacus*, Lin.; "rödvinge trast," Sw.; "miestag rastes," Lap.) appeared to be nearly as common as the fieldfare, with which they associated much in the breeding season; and, quite contrary to its habits in Wermland (where we always find the nest solitary, and in the thickest bushes), it bred here in company with the fieldfare, and we always found the nest in the same situation—in a small fir, never very high up, and always close in to the stem. The nest is smaller and more neatly built than that of the fieldfare. Although the eggs of the fieldfare vary much in size, it is rarely that they are so small as those of the redwing; and I can hardly see how one egg could ever be mistaken for the other. The egg of the redwing is always smaller, neater, and purer in colour than that of the fieldfare. It has, moreover, when fresh, a peculiar green tinge, which, however, fades soon after the egg is blown. You rarely see an egg spotted like that of the fieldfare—they are (generally) of a uniform green colouring, which soon fades to green-brown. Of all the northern songsters, perhaps the redwing stands first on the list, and is with justice called the northern nightingale, for a sweeter song I never wish to listen to when this rich gush of melody is poured out from the thick covert of a fir in the "silence of twilight's contemplative hour," or often in the still hour of midnight when all else in nature is at rest. But as soon as the breeding season commences this beautiful song ceases, and is now changed to a kind of call—"Twee, twee, twee, twee, tweet," ending with a little trill. (I fully agree with Morris when he says, "We have always thought the endeavouring to express the notes of birds by syllables a very unsatisfactory method.") During the season you rarely see the bird, but, hidden in a fir, it utters this monotonous loud call, and as soon as you approach the tree it quietly flies to another. The note was quite new to me, and I was most anxious to find out what bird uttered it; and I shall not easily forget the trouble I had before I solved the mystery. We took our first nest on May 22. In the autumn, when they migrate down to Wermland, they have a very pretty song early in the morning.

The ring ouzel (*T. torquatus*, Lin.; "ring trast," Sw.) was not a common bird here; but a pair or two were distributed here and at the bottom of the fells. We took two nests—the one from a tree, the other from the ground—as late as July 2. Of all the thrushes, perhaps the wild desultory carol of the ring ouzel is loudest and clearest.

The water ouzel (*Cinclus aquaticus*, Bech.; "strom starre," Sw.; "guoikgarek," Lap.) was very common in all the rivers at the foot of the fells, and, if they did not remain here all the winter, must have been very early spring migrants, for we saw them when we arrived, running along the ice by the sides of the waterfalls, or sitting on the snow banks, uttering their low, plaintive little song, which always sounds to me like nothing but a rehearsal. It is a cheerful little bird, and, were it not for the belief that it is a great enemy to the spawn of fish, must be a favourite with every northern angler.

The wheatear (*Saxicola œnanthe*, Nob.; "stensquatta," Sw.). The whinchat (*Saxicola rubetra*, Bechst.; "busksquatta," Sw.).—Of the two the wheatear seemed far more common here, and was generally spread over all the lower fells. I fancy it used to go much higher up than its congener the whinchat.

Of the common little Warblers, the only ones I could clearly identify in this district were the following (but I may add that, in these mossgrown, stubby firs, and thick willow plantations, it is difficult to detect these little, mice-like birds, especially as they were a class of birds we did not care much to look for).

The garden warbler (*Sylvia hortensis*, Bechst.; "träd gard sangare," Sw.); the willow warbler (*S. trochilus*, Lath.; "löf sangare," Sw.)—much more common than the last—and the chiffchaff (*S. abietena*, Nilss.; "grän sangare," Sw.); the redstart (*S. phœnicurus*, Bechst.; "rödstjert," Sw.)—very common both in the lowlands and by the side of the fells; 'and the hedge sparrow (*Accentor modularis*, Cuv.; "jern sparf," Sw.), which appeared to be entirely confined to the lower fir-woods, and, unlike the hedge-sparrow in England, altogether to shun the companionship of man.

I never saw the robin here; nor could I identify either the reed or sedge warblers; but, as I have before said, I might have overlooked them.

The blue-throated warbler (*S. suecica*, Keys and Bl.; "blä häke sangare," Sw.; "gjelanælgo," Lap.).—Contrary to my expectations, this handsome little warbler was rare in this district, and very local. I think they arrived the latest of all the warblers, for I did not see one till early in June, when they appeared to come dropping in singly, stayed a few days in the lowlands, and then made their way up at once to the flat swampy meadows at the foot of and between the fells. Here, among the stunted willow-bushes, always near water, you might see the female creeping from branch to branch like a mouse, while the male, perched on the top of a high bush or a dead tree, would trill out his clear, loud, rich song.

The note of the blue-throated warbler is certainly louder and more varied than that of any other warbler, and it well deserves its Lap name of "saddan kiellinen" (or hundred tongues)—totally different from anything I ever heard before; in fact it is quite impossible to describe it on paper. The nest is most difficult to find, and I only procured two (on June 27), on one of which I caught the old female. Both were built *in the* ground, quite open, with no shelter of a bush, and one I had to cut out with my knife. The nest was altogether formed of dry grass, deep cup shaped. Eggs, in both cases, six, pale bluish-green, minutely spotted with rusty brown, giving the eggs quite a rusty appearance. We shot the young flyers in the end of July. The habits of this warbler are certainly far more aquatic than those of the redstart, and on August 3rd, 1863, while beating a reedy meadow in Wermland for double snipe, I shot one example of the female blue-throated warbler.

Of the pipits, I only met the common meadow pipit (*Anthus pratensis*, Bechst.; "ang piplarka," Sw.), and we used to find this very high up on the fells.

Of the tree pipit I never got a specimen here. I never could identify the red-throated pipit (*A.*

cervinus, Pall.) on these fells, although it is met with a little north.

The continental white wagtail (*Motacilla alba*, Lin.; "ring arla," Sw.) was scarcely so common here as the yellow wagtail, "gularla," which abounded in all the lowlands. The yellow wagtail did not make its appearance till the 17th of May, or nearly three weeks later than the white wagtail. I never saw up here the common variety of the yellow wagtail (*Motacilla neglecta*, Gould), which is our common one in Wermland; all that I met with here were the *Motacilla borealis*, Sund. In all the males I killed, the head was black, with or without a white streak over the eye. The call-note and habits of this wagtail resemble much those of the *Motacilla neglecta;* and it is hard to say whether we are justified in considering it as a distinct species, or anything more than a northernly form. If, however, the grey-headed yellow wagtail is to be considered as a distinct species from Ray's wagtail, I think this *M. borealis* (Sund.) is also entitled to be considered distinct; but we are all yet much in the dark respecting the European wagtails; and perhaps after all, which I think highly probable, we have but three distinct species of the wagtail in Europe.

Of the titmice, as may be supposed, we had plenty of individuals in these forests, although fewer species that I had imagined, the only two which I could identify being the marsh tit (if our *Parus borealis* is identical with the *Parus palustris* of Britain,) and the Siberian tit (*P. Sibiricus*, Gm.; "Sibiris mes," Sw.). I believe it is, however, admitted now that this *Parus borealis* (De Selys), is nothing more than the northern form of the *P. palustris.* To me the note appears very different, and I invariably find the nest of the *P. borealis* in the deep forest, never by water, built always of the inner fibres of the bark of some dead tree, probably the willow or alder. They both appeared to associate in the winter; but the Siberian tit could be detected in a moment by its louder call-note; the habits of both and the localities they frequented were much alike. The nest of the Siberian tit, like that of its congener, was always placed in a stub, the nest built of the blue fur of some species of field-mouse; a very thick wall, but flat, and with a little moss at the bottom outside; the eggs six or seven, in shape, size, and colouring much resembling those of the crested tit (which I was surprised to find did not come up so far north as this). The Siberian tit seem to go to nest later than the *P. borealis*, for the first nest we obtained was on June 5, whereas I found nests of the other as early as May 20.

I never but once saw the golden-crested wren

(*Regulus cristatus*, Ray; "kungs fogee," Sw.) up here. This was a single example, which I shot on May 8; and on the same day I saw one specimen of the tree creeper (*Certhia familiaris*, Lin.; "trad krypare," Sw.). But, as I never again met with either, I think we may conclude that they are very rare here. I never either saw or heard of the nuthatch (*Sitta Europea*, Lin.) in Lapland.

The skylark (*Alauda arvensis*, Lin.; "sang lärka," Sw.) was one of our earliest spring migrants, for I saw a pair in the end of April. They kept close to our house for a few days, when they disappeared, and I never saw any more, nor did I hear of a nest being taken here.

But the shore lark (*A. alpestris*, Lin.; "berg lärka," Sw.; "ruoscha alap," Lap.) was the common fell lark, and on this year they appear to have been more common around Quickiock that usual. On April 28 I shot the first, a single specimen, close to the house; and after that, small flocks of them kept dropping in for about three weeks, when they all left us and went up on to the fells to breed. When in the lowlands they kept in small flocks on the bare patches of cultivated land which the snow had left by the river side; and their habits were exactly the same as those I watched on the coast of Scania in the winter of 1849-1850.

They were not at all shy, but very restless, sweeping in small flocks just over the surface of the ground, uttering their feeble single call-note. They never flew far and soon pitched again. That they came in tolerable quantities may be gathered from the fact that in about three weeks I obtained more than fifty specimens, and, strange to say, every one, except one single example, were males. By all Swedish naturalists the shore lark is considered very rare in Sweden; but I think it must have been overlooked. I consider the Swedish name "berg larkä," or rock lark, much more appropriate than our British name of "shore lark." The colours of this bird appear to be much brighter and richer in the spring than at any other season. There is little difference then between the male and female; but a female which I shot on July 2 had a very pale yellow forehead; horns scarcely perceptible; top of the head and forehead only speckled with black, a little darkish on the forehead; throat very faint yellow; the black shield on the breast small, and not nearly so dark as in the male; back all speckled with blackish-brown, not pure light chestnut, as in the male. The female which I shot on April 20 had the ovary small, but very distinct. The colours were much brighter than in the summer, and it much more resembled the male, save that the yellow was not so brilliant, although the black was nearly as deep. But one thing I remarked in the spring, that in twenty-four hours after the bird was killed the yellow colour appeared to fade. When skinning them in the spring, I always observed a faint, musky smell about them. Sommerfeet describes the nest and egg thus: "They breed as well close to the sea as further inland; not always among grass and moss, but in gravel, and among the dead leaves which have fallen from the birch bushes. The nest is built of grass, and I never saw any feathers in it. Their three to five eggs are in general yellow, or yellow-grey, with yellowish-grey or grey-blue and brown spots, often crowded at the large end. You find them breeding early in May, and also in July."

Strange to say, I can neither describe the nest nor egg of this bird; for, although we never went on to the fells in the summer without seeing them, and in the middle of July we shot many young, we were never able to find a single nest, much as we searched localities where we felt certain that the bird bred. I cannot help thinking that on these fells the old female builds her nest in crevices of rocks, and often far in under stones; for I have more than once seen her come out of such places, and by her habits it appeared as if she had just left the nest. By the end of July both males and females were in deep moult.

Of the buntings, we had—the yellow bunting (*Emberiza citrinella*, Lin.; " gulsparf," Sw.), very common; and if they did not remain here all the winter, they came before us in the spring.

The black-headed bunting (*E. schœniculus*, Lin.; " säfsparf ").—A summer migrant, common in the willow bushes by the river side.

The ortolan bunting (*E. hortulana*, Lin.)—Very rare. I could only find one nest.

And the two northern buntings—the snow bunting and the Lapland bunting.

Although they did not appear to remain here throughout the winter, we observed small flocks of snow bunting (*Emberiza nivalis*, Lin.; " snö sparf," Sw.; "alap," Lap.) during our whole journey up north of Hernosand; and very soon after we arrived I shot specimens at Quickiock in nearly pure winter dress; they appeared to leave the lowlands for the fells early in May. During the summer they were always higher up on the fells than the shore lark. We never could find a nest of the snow bunting, although they bred commonly on our fells, and we shot the old birds in summer dress as well as young flyers in the end of July. But I shot one young flyer as early as July 6. I do not so much wonder that we did not find the nest of this bird, for the wildest and most desolate spots on the fells appeared to be their summer home.

On these fells there are thousands of acres (we may say many miles) covered with nothing but loose, shingly slate and ironstone, and boulders of erratic rock, which are most difficult to traverse; and here we always saw the snow bunting during the breeding season, although when the young could fly they appeared to draw down lower on the fells.

The Lapland bunting (*E. Lapponica*, Lin.; "lapsparf," Sw.; "tschappis vuoolasch," Lap.) appeared to arrive later than any of the others, and, unlike the shore lark, did not rest in the lowlands, but went straight up to the fells at once; for I don't think we saw six examples at Quickiock the whole spring; whereas in the middle of June they were literally swarming in certain places on the fell meadows—so much so, that in one night we took thirteen nests, from all of which we shot the old birds. They seemed, however, to be very local; and it was long before we could discover their breeding place, for we never saw them on the high fells. At last we found a low flat at the foot of the highest snow-fells (but still, perhaps, 2,000 feet above Quickiock). This was covered with rough tussocky grass and patches of willow bushes, and studded with innumerable lakes and water-courses, and proved a rich tract to us— a real "Tom Tiddler's ground"—for here we found the nests of the Lap bunting, blue-throated warbler, broad-billed sandpiper, Temminck's stint, wood sandpiper, phalarope, scaup duck, and long-tailed duck. If we had only pitched our tent in this fell meadow for a month, no telling what varieties we should have met with. Independently of this, it was one of the sweetest spots that could well be imagined —a real oäsis in the desert; and I never enjoyed a summer ramble as I did in this wild tract. There are certain circumstances in life, as well as places, which leave too lasting an impression on the mind ever to be obliterated, and this fell meadow forms one of the brightest flowers in the field of memory as regards my Lapland journey.

When I first searched this spot I was attracted by a soft loud pipe, very much resembling the call of the golden plover, but fainter. I was certain, however, it was not that, for it seemed to come from the low ground, and in the evening was all round me. It was long before I could make it out, for I never could see the bird, till at last one rose. I shot it on the wing, and it was a male Lap bunting. The mystery was solved, and we had no difficulty now in finding the nest, which was never far off. I soon became more familiar with their habits. The female rarely rises, except you tread close to the nest, but runs away on the ground much like the pipit. The male sits on a stone or heap of earth, uttering this monotonous, plaintive whistle till disturbed, when he rises in the air, much after the manner of the common bunting, soars for a while, and then suddenly drops down to the ground, as we see the skylark into a field of young wheat at home. While in the air, the song of the Lapland bunting is as rich and clear as that of any of our songsters—not so shrill as that of the lark, but far sweeter and more varied, for in this song the clear flute-like note of the corn bunting is blended with the varying strain of the skylark, and I thought I never listened to a sweeter melody. Oh, how often have I at such times envied the feelings of the true naturalist, who can listen to the artless song of the little bird without wishing it in his game bag, and watch its habits without hoping soon to see it lying on his skinning table! There must, however, be collectors, or our knowledge of the feathered race would stand still; but depend upon it, the study of the animal creation loses half its innocent charms as soon as we make it a matter of pounds, shillings, and pence. "Bosh!" I fancy I hear the surly critic exclaim; and so it may be, but it is nevertheless true.

The nest of the Lapland bunting, as far as I could see, was always placed on the ground, generally sheltered by a tussock of grass, occasionally under a small bush, built invariably altogether of fine grass, loosely and without much care. The eggs vary much in colour; and like those of the meadow and red-throated pipits, become paler with age. They combine the characters both of the bunting and pipit, and often resemble those of the black-headed bunting, but are more clouded than streaked; and I have seen them very like those of the meadow pipit. This is one of the small eggs that requires very careful identification. Six appears to be the full number. By the end of July we shot strong flyers, although most of the nests we took were about the 27th June.

I never saw the common sparrow (*Fringilla domestica*, Lin.) at Quickiock, though I observed them common at Iockmock on our way home; and probably as cultivation spreads, this impudent little bird will follow the plough.

The chaffinch (*F. cœlebs*, Lin.; "bofink," Sw.) was common up here, but not nearly so much so as its congener,

The brambling (*F. montifringilla*, Lin.; "berg fink," Sw.; "vintan," Lap.,) was certainly the commonest of all the small birds in our forests during the summer; and the flocks which we used to see on the bare patches of cultivated land early in May (when they first arrived) were past all belief. Every forest was soon filled with them, and their monotonous call-note, " cree, cree," was heard from every tree. In some parts of the north the brambling is called " har sparf," because they say that the greyling or " harr " come up from the deeps as soon as this bird appears. When they first arrived they seemed to be in full summer dress. We took our first nest on June 2. As far as I could see, the nest was always placed in a small fir, generally six to ten feet from the ground, very like that of the chaffinch, built outwardly of moss and fine grass, thickly lined with feathers of the willow grouse, deep and cup-shaped, but hardly so neat and pretty as that of the chaffinch. Six eggs appear to be about the full number, though I have often seen seven in one nest. The eggs are very like those of the chaffinch, but generally a trifle smaller, darker in the ground colour, and the purple lines and dots more coloured. Still the greatest caution is required in identifying the eggs, for where both these birds breed in the same district the nests may easily be confounded; and this was a nest which I would always take myself, and see the old bird. I got plenty of these nests, and could have had as many more had I wanted them.

Like the mealy redpole, there was a little mystery regarding the breeding of the brambling. We took our first nest on June 2, and again as late as

August 3 I took two nests with fresh eggs. Could it be possible that these birds bred twice in the season?

I never could hear the brambling make the slightest attempt at a song, although I do not deny that it can sing.

At Quickiock, when we first came up, we saw large flocks of the mealy redpole (*F. borealis*, Tem.; "gra siska, morisk," Sw.; "om oltsitsasch," Lap.) It was exceedingly common in the district, and seemed to have remained here all the winter. Of the mealy redpole we have two forms, if they are not distinct species, in the north; the one is the *F. linaria Alnorum*, Sund., from its partiality to the seeds of the alder (*Betula Alnus*), which is called the "läng nabbad," or long-beaked form, the beak being $3\frac{1}{2}$ lines in length. This is the common mealy redpole. The other is the *F. linaria betularum*, Sund., so called from its partiality to the fruit of the birch (*Betula alba*), which is called the "kort nabbad," or short-beaked form, the beak being only $2\frac{1}{2}$ lines long. This form seems to be almost confined to the north, and is rarely seen south of Stockholm. I never met with it until I came up to Quickiock. But in the winter of 1862 I shot four specimens of the short-beaked bird at Gardsjö, South Wermland, out of a large flock of the common mealy redpole. The difference in the size of the beaks of the two birds is very apparent, and I always fancied the short-beaked bird was duller in plumage than the other. Besides these, I shot two specimens of a mealy redpole, nearly white. I would suggest a comparison between this short-beaked form and our lesser redpole, which at present has not been identified in the north. I observed that the red breast of the male birds became much deeper and more vivid as the season advanced; in fact, they did not appear to be in full summer dress till many of the young were flyers. I think the nest of the mealy redpole is one of the most beautiful I ever saw; perfectly cup-shaped; built of fine sticks, then a layer of fine grass, and lined inwardly with the white down of the willow, and white feathers of the willow grouse, forming one of the prettiest little mementos of the Lap forest that I know; the eggs often as many as six, sometimes pale light blue, unspotted, generally much resembling those of the lesser redpole, and very little larger.

I saw the common linnet (*F. cannabina*, Lin.) once or twice in the meadows, in the end of July, but I never took the nest.

The bullfinch (*Phyrrhula vulgaris*, Tem.; "domherre," Sw.) was rather common just around Quickiock. We, however, never saw them till

July, and I obtained a nest with fresh eggs as late as August 2.

The common crossbill (*Loxia curvirostra*, Lin.; "korsnabb," Sw.; "batsak lodde," Lap.). We saw very few crossbills in these forests, and I don't think they breed here, for they used to appear only at uncertain periods. I never saw the parrot crossbill here. All that we killed were the common bird. I don't think that the parrot crossbill has so high a northern range as the other.

I have been lately much interested in the study of the change of plumage of birds, and the three which I have turned my attention to have been the crossbills, the pine grosbeak, and the ptarmigan. This has proved a most interesting study. The reader will find my remarks regarding the grosbeaks and ptarmigan in the proper place; and I will now proceed to notice the different changes of plumage in the crossbills, of which little appears to be known even at this advanced stage of the science of natural history. I may add that my observations respecting all these three birds are the result of the actual examinations of scores of specimens, both in the fixed and intermediate plumage; and I do not believe that any naturalist living has paid more attention to this subject, than myself or had better opportunities of examining the birds in a state of nature.

As regards the crossbills, I can clearly prove, by specimens killed in a state of nature, that they have four distinct dresses, assumed at different ages, and these I will shortly describe. The first dress, after just leaving the nest till up to the first moult in the autumn (in September), is greenish-brown, with dark longitudinal streaks down each feather; and in this first plumage there is little difference between the male and the female. In the nest plumage the beaks of the young birds are straight; but the mandibles soon begin to cross each other after leaving the nest; and in young birds of the year killed by me in November, the beak was nearly as much crooked as in the older birds. Sometimes the point of the under mandible crosses to the right, sometimes to the left.

As soon as the first autumnal moult is complete, the females are easily distinguished from the males. The young striped feathers are very apparent in both, all through the winter and following spring; but all the under parts are tinged in the young males with yellow orange, and in the females with bright yellow. In the males the heads and rumps are orange, in the females only tinged with yellow.

In not one single young male of the year which I have shot in the winter (and the birds of the year are easily distinguished at this season by the presence of the dark striped feathers) was there the slightest indication to lead one to suppose that he would become red before the next moult. The question is, when will that moult take place? some fancy in *May*, some in the ensuing September. I think it very probable that a change in colour takes place in May, for it appears to me that this orange colour gradually reddens without moulting. And so much do the shades vary that scarcely two young males are exactly alike. It is impossible to say how long this young plumage lasts, but I am inclined to think certainly until the second autumnal moult of the bird, perhaps gradually becoming redder, and probably in many birds even longer; for early in November I have killed young males of a beautiful orange-red colour, which, from their size and general appearance, and the total absence of the dark striped feathers of youth, could not have been birds of the year. These orange birds might certainly have been bred very early in the preceding spring, but I think not; and I almost feel confident that this orange-red colour is a gradual transition to the red dress, or else that the mature male crossbill owns two dresses—*i.e.*, that some birds of the same age are orange-red and others deep red. Of one thing, however, I am perfectly convinced, that *none* of the young males obtain the full deep-red dress at the *first* autumnal moult. In the year 1863 I obtained the males breeding in the same woods in three different dresses—1st, in the early striped dress above described (these were evidently birds of the year); 2ndly, in this orange-red dress; and, 3rdly, in the deep-red dress.

I am at present of opinion that this orange-red dress is a transition gradually assumed between the first autumnal dress and the deep-red plumage in which we usually see the male crossbill depicted, and which I consider their standard livery, and worn by them longer than any other.

I may remark, however, that in our forests we meet with far more of the deep-red birds than of these orange-plumage males.

Respecting the bright yellow-green dress which the old male crossbills occasionally assume (but which, although so rare that we very seldom meet with it, we must nevertheless still consider as *normal*), it is hard to say at what age it is assumed, but we may reasonably infer at a very advanced period of life *in a state of nature;* though it is said that as soon as either a male crossbill or grosbeak is confined in a cage, it changes from red to bright yellow-green at once, and this colour it wears till it dies. This may or may not be the effect of confinement, but as I have killed the old birds of both in this yellow-green plumage, in a state of nature, I for one do not hesitate to pronounce it normal.

This latter dress can never be confounded with the yellow-orange plumage of youth by any one who has had opportunities of comparing the two.

In the summer the red dress of the male crossbill appears to become darker, and the only change that I can observe in the female is that the yellow shading on the head and rump become brighter with age, but always brightest in the breeding season.

So much for the changes of plumage. I will now make a few remarks on the habits of the crossbills. I fully agree with Thompson that " he is inclined to consider the crossbills as a wandering tribe, having no proper home, but who pitch their tent and take up their residence at a place just so long as it suits them, without contemplating a return to any particular region."

This is peculiarly the case in our forests. They appear to leave us as suddenly as they come, and as soon as the breeding season is over they leave for other districts, and we see very few, often none, in the summer. It is not every year that we have them, and it is singular that we rarely ever have both the parrot and common crossbill breeding with us in the same year. I take it all depends upon the state of the cones on the pines and firs. When there are plenty of fir cones in the autumn, it is pretty certain that we shall have the common crossbills breeding with us that winter, and the same with the parrot crossbills when the cones on the pines are plentiful. But this appears to happen in our forests only about every third or fourth year. One curious fact I have observed, which is this, that if we see large flocks of crossbills in our forests in the autumn (they generally appear about September or early in October), we shall have very little snow that winter.

The pairing season begins about the middle of January, when both male and female have a very pretty song: that of the female, however, much the faintest. Were it not for the difference of the landscape, we might almost at this season imagine ourselves in the tropical forests of the south, when we watch a little flock of these birds feeding, flitting from cone to cone, or climbing over them with their backs downwards, like the parrots, their bright-red or orange plumage reflected in the rays of the afternoon sun (at which time they are generally busiest feeding), which even at this inclement season gilds the tops of the firs for an hour or two before sinking below the horizon.

They go to nest often in the end of January, always by the middle of February. The nest of both species is placed (almost invariably) in a small pine, near to the top, close in to the stem, never in a deep forest, but always with us on a stony rise, where the pines are small and wide apart. The parrot crossbill generally goes to nest a little later than the common one. By the middle or end of April the young birds are strong flyers, and we *never take a nest with eggs after that month.* The nest of both species is much alike (that of the parrot crossbill thickest and largest), built outwardly of dry fir sticks, lined thickly with moss and grass. The eggs much resemble those of the green linnet, but are always larger. The egg of the parrot crossbill is often scarcely larger than that of the common bird, although usually it is thicker and has a finer and bolder character. The full number of eggs appears to be three, and it is very rarely that we find four in a nest. Some naturalists say that the crossbills breed at all seasons, from December to June, and that the winter nest is domed, with a hole in the side to go in at. All I can say is (and I have had now some years' experience with these birds), that I consider their breeding season as regular as that of any other bird, at the period I have before stated; and as for a domed nest, I never saw such a thing. I have often wondered why nature should have neglected this provision as regards the crossbill, for in the end of March, 1863 (in which year I took above thirty-five nests out of our woods), when the weather was very stormy and rainy, I found more than a dozen nests, in which the unfledged young had perished through the inclemency of the weather.

The pine grosbeak (*Corythus enucleator*, "tall-bit," Sw.)—I was much pleased on arriving at Quickiock to see small flocks of pine grosbeaks in the fir forests, close to the village, which appeared to have remained here throughout the winter, at least I saw frozen specimens which had been killed in February, but these might have migrated and returned again, for I have always noticed that when the grosbeak come into our Wermland forests in the winter, they usually appear early in November and leave us in February. By the first week in May they had paired, and we took our first nest on June 4, with three eggs, in a small fir, about ten feet from the ground, on the side of a small fell, in by no means a large wood; and I may here observe that all the nests we took were built in small firs, never high from the ground, or in deep woods, and generally in rather conspicuous situations; the nest always placed close in to the stem. All the trees in the Quickiock forests are so small and stunted, and the branches so bare, that scarcely any bird, except the very small ones, builds its nest out on the branch. The old female was very silent, and by no means shy. The male was red. In all, I found five nests, of which two had four eggs (which I take to be the full number, although, as the crossbills, they appear to sit sometimes on three), and two had young. The nest is neither large nor deep, but very compactly and cleanly built like basket-work, the outside walling of very fine fir branches and thin cranberry fibres tightly interlaced, lined with fine stiff grass and a little hair. The eggs vary much, both in size and colouring, but are usually about the size of those of the hawfinch, but a little thinner, pale blue-green ground, blotched and lined with light purple and dark burnt-umber spots and pricks, always thickest towards the large end; average size 1 inch by $\frac{3}{4}$. The nest is very neat and strong without being pretty, and very different from the warm nest of the Siberian jay or great shrike, or the thick mossy nest of the waxwing. Morris's figure, taken from Thieneman, although not correct, nevertheless gives an idea of this egg. He says the nest is lined with feathers—there was not a single feather in either of the five nests which I saw.

I think the nest and eggs of the pine grosbeak one of the neatest and finest which we took in Lapland.

I had now good opportunities of examining the different stages of plumage in the grosbeak, and I did not neglect them. I could now distinguish the sexes by dissection, and I soon found that my conjectures formed last winter were right, and that all the ash-green birds which I shot then were not females, but that the male has an intermediate dress between the nest plumage and the deep-red (which last dress I fancy they do not assume until the third year), so like that of the female, that it is hard to distinguish one from the other. In all these young ash-green males which I shot in April or May the testes were never so fully developed as in the old red males. Two questions now remained to be answered: was this ash-green dress really intermediate between the nest plumage and the handsome red dress in which we see the old male grosbeak always depicted? and did these young males breed? Both these points I solved entirely to my own satisfaction. On June 14 I took a nest with four eggs hard sat on, and shot both old birds. The body colouring of both is nearly the same—ash-grey; in the male slightly tinged with reddish-brown, most on the breast, head reddish-yellow; in the female, the tinge on the breast and head (especially) is much more yellow; and this is the only difference in the plumage of the two sexes, at this age. This is the usual dress of the *female* at all seasons; but that it is only intermediate, and assumed by the male before he comes to his red dress, I proved by three specimens shot on or about August 4, all in deep moult. They were all young ash-green males, and the red feathers were shooting out all over them under their ash-grey body plumage; in fact, many had already appeared on the head and back. But even now I do not think that they assume this fine deep-red livery at once, for I have shot male birds with a deep purple tinge on the red, very different from the fine carmine-red which we all have supposed to be the full mature dress of the pine grosbeak. Only one more state of plumage was wanting, and my series would have been complete—but this, I am sorry to say, I was unable to obtain—and this was an old, bright-green, yellow male, the last dress of all. I never met with this in the forest, although I have seen it in a cage; but I shall never feel satisfied until I have shot such a bird in a state of nature, for I do so much wish to upset the dogma of our *savans*, who contend that this last bright yellow-green dress, both in the crossbills and grosbeak, is not *normal*, but only the effect of confinement. I have killed the old male parrot crossbill from his nest in this dress, and why not the pine grosbeak? Now I will ask what are we to consider as the true adult plumage of the grosbeak? and can a bird be called adult as soon as he is able to breed? I can prove three distinct dresses in the male of this bird at different ages, in all of which they can breed; first, olive-green tinged with yellowish-red; second, true carmine-red (I think we can hardly call the purple-red a distinct dress, as most probably it changes with age, and I cannot prove that the birds wear it for a year); and lastly, a bright yellow-green dress, which is only observed in the very old males, and which, when once assumed, never changes. Now, are we to wait till they have assumed this last yellow-green dress before we consider them mature, and must we contend that no man has arrived at maturity till his hair becomes grey? I can prove that the grosbeak can breed in both of the first two dresses; and as I shot the old bright green parrot crossbill breeding, it is reasonable to suppose that the grosbeak does the same. I am not at all surprised at these young ash-green males breeding, for I believe, although I never myself could prove it, that some of the parrots in Australia (of which bird the grosbeak and crossbill are the European type), breed in this intermediate yellow-green dress; but what I am surprised at is this, that no naturalist, as far as I can see, has noticed this first ash-green plumage in the male grosbeak. Nilsson leads us to suppose that the first dress is carmine-red, and that after this they assume the bright yellow-green dress to which I have above alluded. But he mentions nothing of this first ash-green plumage; and that he never remarked it, is pretty certain, when he refers in his "Synonyms" to the grosbeak in Wilson's plate (p. 73, Am. Ornithology), which he (Nilsson) says is a younger male, and this figure of Wilson's, in my edition, represents a purple-red male. I fancy Kjœrbolling, the Danish naturalist, had some idea of this change. Although we see far more of these ash-green males than of the red, it seems that we rarely find them breeding; for out of five nests which I took, four belonged to red males. The plumage of the young grosbeak appears to vary in the nest as well as in the first dress, for you occasionally see the young birds with a tinge of red on the olive-green body, but in general they are altogether dull olive-green.

The food of the grosbeak is not, as in the crossbills, from the seed of the fir *cones*, but the small buds or embryo of the young branches which shoot out from the lateral branches of the fir. But they can pick out the seeds from the cones, both of the pine and fir, quite as cleverly as the crossbills. They feed as well on the fir as on the pines, and every nest which we took was placed in a *fir*.

Very different are the breeding habits of this bird from that of its near relation, the crossbill. As soon as ever they begin to build, the sweet song of the male entirely ceases, and he assiduously assists the female in gathering sticks and fibres for the construction of the nest. Not a note do they utter except a gentle "cluck," as if conversing together in an under tone; and nothing in their note or habits indicates the proximity of the nest. Not so the crossbill male; all he appears to have to do with the building part of the business is to sit on a high fir close to the nest, and cheer his mate in her labours by a loud clear song. Thus the nest of the crossbill is very easy to find, that of the grosbeak difficult. The note of the male grosbeak, both in winter and early spring, is delightful, clear, and flute-like; and I have observed them on a frosty winter day sing in the air while floating from one tree to another, after the manner of the woodlark. But you often hear both male and female keeping up a very low pretty little twitter (without breaking out into a song), as if conversing; as in the crossbill, the female can sing, but not so loudly as the male. You principally hear the song early in the morning, and in egg collecting, one hour in the morning before ten o'clock is worth any three after. It is a very fine, bold, tame bird, rather foolish than otherwise, for here boys often snare them from the tree, with a hair noose, on a long pole. It is an excellent cage bird, but must not be kept too warm, or it will soon die.

The Turtle Dove. Strange to say, a pair of turtle doves (*Columba turtur*, Ray; "turtur dufa," Sw.) were shot at Quickiock a few years since, on the ground right in front of the priest's house. We never, however, saw a wild pigeon of any kind in Lapland, nor do I believe, except as an extraordinary instance, that any of the family come up so far north.

The capercailzie (*Tetrao urogallus*, L.) was very common in these forests. The largest male which I shot up here weighed 11lb., and this is about the common size of a large male in Wermland; so, contrary to the usual opinion here, I do not think the capercailzie in Lapland are so much smaller than those in Wermland.

The hazel grouse (*Tet. bonasia*, Lin.; "hjerpe," Sw.) was also very common round Quickiock, and I observed that in those which we shot here the plumage was lighter and prettier than in the Wermland hazel grouse. I may add that in these forests, which are thin and scrubby, the sport is much better than in the dense Wermland forests, and a man can now and then get a flying shot.

The ptarmigan (*Lagopus alpina*, Nilss.; "fall

ripa," Sw.; "keron," Lap.).—It is, I now believe, generally admitted by naturalists, that the British, the Scandinavian, and the Iceland ptarmigan are one and the same bird; it is probable, however, that climate may have an influence on the plumage, and the reader will therefore bear in mind that my remarks apply only to the ptarmigan which we killed on the Quickiock fells, and not to the British bird, which I never saw in a state of nature. This remark is called for from the circumstance that Mr. Gould, who looked over my ptarmigan skins (which presented every stage of plumage to which the Quickiock ptarmigan is subject), observed that not one was so black as those he had received from Snee-hatten, near the Dovre fell, Norway. My remarks and descriptions, however, are strictly correct as regards the Quickiock ptarmigan, and few men have had a better season's experience with them than myself. This was one of my principal objects in visiting Lapland, and I obtained specimens during every week of my stay. I came up when they were in the pure white winter dress, and did not leave until the blue autumn plumage was complete; in fact, many of the white winter feathers were already beginning to appear. No man in Britain could have had so good an opportunity as I had here, for nowhere would he be allowed to shoot the old birds as we did in the spring, old females from the nest, and young chirpers that could scarcely fly. Above 150 specimens passed through my hands, in every stage of plumage; and I will now proceed to lay before the reader a statement of facts and the inferences which I draw from them. It is singular that the ptarmigan should not be met with in Ireland.

We are led to believe that both the ptarmigan and willow grouse are found in North America, and probably both are identical with the European birds. Wilson, in his "Ornithology" of 1832, edited by Sir W. Jardine, does not figure either; but in a note Mr. Douglas mentions the ptarmigan as very rare, and the willow grouse, he says, inhabits the far countries from the 50th to the 70th degrees of north latitude, within which limits it is partially migratory. Frank Forrester does not notice either in his " Game Birds of the United States and Canada."

In both the willow grouse (*Lag. subalpina*, Nilss.) and the ptarmigan the winter plumage is exactly the same, pure white, with fourteen black tail feathers; and to the casual observer they appear to be one and the same bird; but the willow grouse is a larger and plumper bird, the beak is thicker, and the male ptarmigan has a black streak through the eye, which is wanting in the willow grouse, as well as in the female ptarmigan. Moreover, in the willow grouse the fifth wing-feather is always longer than the second, in the ptarmigan it is always shorter; and in the winter season the only distinguishing marks between the female ptarmigan and willow grouse, are the difference in the wing-feathers, and that the willow grouse is a more robust bird, with a much thicker beak. I may add that very few of the white grouse, which are sent from the north to England in the winter to the London markets are the real ptarmigan, but willow grouse. The true ptarmigan is seldom taken in snares, for the wild snow-covered regions which they frequent in the winter are rarely accessible to man; and although at this season they may come lower down on the fells, they are never seen in the forests which the willow grouse frequents; whereas the latter bird, at no season shy, in the winter becomes still tamer, and comes right down into the bushes close to the dwellings of man. Thousands are then caught in snares, and those snares in use at Quickiock are formed thus: after cutting all the branches from a young birch, about six feet or eight feet long, a horsehair snare is fastened to the top end, which is bent down, and stuck into the snow, so that the snare stands about a hand over the surface. A little hedge of birch branches is built up on each side, and along this hedge they stick up birch branches covered with fruit and catkins as a bait for the birds. They set these as soon as sufficient snow has fallen, and as more snow falls they raise the snare. Nilsson says that ptarmigan are occasionally taken in these snares, but from what I could hear this is never the case at Quickiock. A Lap settler will perhaps own several hundred of these snares.

In July I weighed one willow grouse and two ptarmigan. The willow grouse weighed just 16oz., or scarcely so much as the red grouse, but the two ptarmigan only 20oz. English.

When we first arrived on the fells (April 16) some of the ptarmigan were still in pure white winter dress; others were just beginning to assume the summer plumage, and here and there a summer feather was shooting out on the head and neck. In about a month's time many of the summer feathers had appeared in different parts of the body of both males and females, and about May 22 the ovaries of many of the females were in a very forward state, but the change in plumage seemed to go on slowly. On June 5 we took our first nest, with ten eggs, and the old female (which I shot as she rose) showed nearly as much of the winter as of the summer plumage. By June 10 the males were, however, greyish-black on the head, back, and chest, the belly and under part pure white. The black colour darkest on the breast.

The change from the winter to the summer dress is clearly a *true moult*, and not a change of colour in the feathers. It is most difficult to say what is the real summer dress of the ptarmigan, for they appear to be in a continual state of change or moult during the whole summer, and bear no one dress for any length of time; and so irregular is the moult or change, that you scarcely ever see two exactly alike or in the same state of forwardness, for in the same day in the end of July you may kill some in the early summer dress, and others with many blue autumn feathers. Up to July 9 I observed that all the old males which I killed were dark brownish-black on the back, speckled with lighter brown, especially on the head, breast, and sides; belly pure white, but the dark breast is much more conspicuous in some than in others. By July 20 the whole body colour had become much lighter, and by the end of July was evidently changing to blue-grey, but still speckled with brown, especially on the head. By the 6th of August the majority of the males had assumed a totally different dress—head still speckled with yellowish-brown, back bluish-grey, watered with black and white; belly pure white; and this was the plumage of the males on August 18, when I killed my last.

This blue watered dress appears by degrees to become fainter, in fact mere grey-blue, until the end of September, but the white winter feathers keep gradually showing themselves under the blue autumnal dress. I observed, in two specimens shot early in October the year before, that one was half blue and half white—*i.e.*, that half the body appeared to be covered with the blue autumn dress, the other half with the white winter plumage, some of which, if not all, were perfectly new feathers, for I observed blood-shafts to many of them; in the other specimen, very few of the blue autumn feathers remained. From what I could hear, for I did not stop up long enough to judge for myself, I should say that in many, perhaps most, the pure winter dress is complete by the third week in October.

Much as the males vary in plumage, the females appear to vary still more, and only to have a standing dress for about three weeks in June, just when they are laying, and this early summer dress may be described thus : body blackish-brown, every feather broadly edged with yellow, brown, and white, giving the bird a very light yellow-brown appearance; breast much lighter; belly *never* pure white, as in the male, but, as well as the sides and

Y

breast, covered with black zigzag lines on a rusty yellow and white ground, the white colour most apparent on the belly. By the second week in June this dress was complete in most, although the birds vary much in shading, scarcely two being exactly alike, when it all at once became much darker. In fact we may describe the summer dress' of the female ptarmigan thus: throughout the whole of May the ground plumage was white, here and there speckled with mottled rusty yellow and black feathers, which, as in the males, appear first on the head and neck, then on the back. By the third week in May the body is thickly speckled with these mottled feathers (some intermingled with the white, others shooting out from the skin under them), so we are not at all surprised that early in June a sudden change takes place, and all at once the bird assumes its early or first summer dress as above described. This appears gradually to darken as the season advances, the dark brown colour occupying much more space, the yellow feather edges becoming much fainter, and by the beginning of July the female has assumed a totally different and much darker dress. About the end of July we see some small blue feathers shooting out among the rusty brown ones, and this appears to be a *true moult*, and not a change in colour of the feathers. The bird now assumes a beautiful dress, far more handsome than in the male—brown-red, variegated with blue-grey, which often on the back appears in patches. But they vary so much in colour and in the distribution of these blue feathers over the surface of the body that it is impossible to give a correct description. Moreover the birds vary so much in the forwardness of this blue dress that on the same day you may kill an old female in the perfect dark summer dress, and another beautifully mottled with blue. I have seen many very handsome "almond tumblers" in my day, but I hardly ever saw one to beat some of the female ptarmigan I killed in the end of July. I fancy both male and female retain this blue dress longer than any other. It gradually becomes lighter as the season advances, till at length the old female is quite blue (but still always with some rusty mottled yellow feathers at the sides), and about the middle of October the blue dress gives place to the pure white plumage of winter.

Now, which are we to call the true summer dress of the ptarmigan, the nuptial dress, or this blue plumage, which is not assumed till after the season of incubation (although before the young birds are strong flyers), but still long before autumn, and which is retained by the birds longer than any other?

By August 4 the young were strong flyers, and

by August 12 fit to kill. Their plumage in the downy state is rusty yellow, with minute black spots. The first dress after that is black mottled with rusty yellow, and white, above; underneath, pale rusty brown, with blackish wavy lines; wings grey-brown. Early in August they assume another dress, and moult as it were for the second time; the birds are then about ten inches long. The whole body plumage is now grey-blue finely streaked with black, and white pinion feathers now appear in the place of the brown ones of the first dress. The grey plumage gradually becomes lighter, as in the old birds, till like them they assume their white winter livery in the autumn, and by November 1 there is no perceptible difference between the old and young birds.

It appears, therefore, that the Swedish ptarmigan owns three distinct dresses in the course of the year, and so many curious and puzzling changes that they almost seem to have a different dress for every summer month.

The question now arises, How many times can the ptarmigan be said really to moult in the course of the year? I don't mean change colour, for a change seems to be going on all through the summer, *but actually to moult;* and my opinion is as follows (and here let me observe that this opinion is not grounded on supposition, but on the careful examination of specimens in every stage of plumage, both fixed and intermediate):—

It is quite clear to me that the change from the pure white winter dress to the mottled plumage of spring is *an actual moult*, and no change of colouring in the feathers, for in all the specimens I obtained from the middle of April to the end of May, the variegated mottled feathers were to be seen, of all sizes, shooting out from the skin, with blood-shafts among and under the white feathers in all parts of the body, some very small, and quite hidden by the white plumage; others full-grown, and occupying patches on the white ground. In not one of the specimens killed at this time could I observe the slightest indication of a *white feather gradually changing colour*. That the spring dress, however, when once assumed, may change in shading of colour before the blue autumn dress appears, I think very probable.

Now, with regard to the blue autumn dress. Although I was at first of a different opinion, I am now inclined to think that this dress is also assumed by a *perfect moult*, and not by the early brown and black mottled feathers becoming blue, for in most of the specimens killed late in July, or early in August, I observed these blue feathers (evidently new), many of them quite small, shooting out of the skin, with blood-shafts under and among the darker body plumage, while patches of blue feathers were already full-grown; but, again, not a single indication of a brown-mottled feather becoming blue. It is therefore clear that, if some of the mottled spring feathers should change their colour to blue, a greater proportion of this blue autumnal dress is obtained by a regular moult.

And now, with regard to the change from this blue autumnal dress to the pure white of winter; I am now decidedly of opinion that this is also a true moult—in fact, that it is the usual autumnal moult peculiar to the feathered race. I certainly may, however, remark that in the birds I killed in August, many of the blue feathers were white half-way up from the bottom, and with broad white edges, as if they were gradually becoming white; so I do not wonder that the general opinion should be that these blue feathers gradually whiten, the transition appears so easy and natural. But then, on the other hand, in some of the birds killed as early as the second week in August, I observed some new white feathers shooting out under the blue; and, in the two specimens to which I have above referred as killed in the end of September and October, the white feathers were apparently *all* new, and what blue feathers remained were loose and ready to fall off. I did not remain long enough on the fells this year to obtain specimens myself to prove clearly how the autumn change went on, but I hope to do so another season.

To sum up all, however, my present opinion with regard to the change of plumage in the ptarmigan is this—that they *moult* three times between March and November; and, although this opinion is given advisedly, it is grounded wholly on the results of my own experience and close examination of many specimens. I have never yet spoken with any one on the subject who appeared more competent than myself to give an opinion, and as for the descriptions which I have read of the different stages of plumage in the ptarmigan, they are all far too general to be of the slightest assistance in determining a question which is of so much interest to the naturalist. If, however, at a future day I should see good reason to change my opinion, I shall be too happy to convict myself; for, as some old writer quaintly observes, "No one need be ashamed of owning that he was wrong, which is only saying, 'I am wiser to-day than I was yesterday.'"

Even in regard to the young birds of the year, I have observed the new blue feathers shooting out under the darker dress, as in the old ones; and if, as we have every reason to suppose, the change from the autumn dress to the white winter plumage is a moult, these young ptarmigan appear to moult three times in less than four months.

The exact measurements of the Swedish ptarmigan, taken carefully from fresh-killed specimens, in Swedish measure (a mere trifle shorter than the English) are these:—Male, 14 to $14\frac{1}{2}$ in. long; 20 in. breadth of wing; $\frac{5}{8}$ in. beak from forehead; 8in. wing from carpus; $4\frac{1}{2}$ in. tail; $1\frac{1}{4}$ in. tarsus; $1\frac{3}{8}$ in. middle toe; female half an inch shorter, and the other measurements proportionately smaller.

The ptarmigan may truly be said to be a child of snow, for you never meet with them off the real fells, although I have occasionally flushed them from the fell sides, just where the willow bushes end. Their real home is the higher fell tract, and in the middle of summer on their very highest snow-clad summits. In the spring they come down to the lower fells to breed, but you never find them there in the end of summer. The pairing season here appeared to begin early in May, and lasted a fortnight or three weeks, and during this time the hoarse laughing love-call of the old male might be heard at very earliest dawn on any of the fell tops. This is soon answered by the finer "i-i—ack—i-i—ack" of the female, and the love chase commences. This is the time when many are shot off, for they are now too engrossed with each other to heed the shooter, who lies behind a stone on the pairing ground, and picks them off as he pleases.

Both the ptarmigan and willow grouse are strictly monogamous. Some naturalists appear to have an idea that both, when pairing, have a kind of "lek" or play, like the capercailzie and blackcock, both of which birds are polygamous. I can only say I never saw anything of the kind. The ptarmigan, certainly, have their favourite pairing grounds on the fells, and here the birds assemble at daylight in the early spring, in small flocks, but widely scattered all over the place. The old males utter their peculiar love-call, which is answered by the female, and they draw together; but although there are several males in the neighbourhood, each one seems to have his particular stand and his own favourite female, and if by chance another male intrudes on his ground he drives it off. But I firmly believe that one male treads only one female.

I never could discover a playing place of the willow grouse, nor do I believe any such existed in the Quickiock forest. At early dawn the birds were scattered all over the forest, and the hoarse love-call of the males resounded on all sides. This would soon be answered by a female, and the couple would join. The willow grouse is easily brought within gun-shot by imitating the call of the other sex.

As soon as the female willow grouse wants to lay, she seems to be most anxious to get rid of the company of the male, and you will see him chasing her all over the forest, she all the while trying to avoid his importunities.

Early in June the female commences to lay, forming an artless nest on the bare stones, in the heather, or under a small bush; always, as far as I could see, above the very top edge of the willow region, but never on the snow fells. Here she lays generally seven to eleven eggs, subject to much variation in colour, but usually rusty yellow covered all over with black or brown blotches and spots heaped together. It is not easy to distinguish the egg of the ptarmigan from that of the willow grouse by the colour, but the egg of the ptarmigan is always a little the smallest, and more pointed at both ends. I once found seventeen eggs in a nest of the ptarmigan, and, if they were the produce of two birds (which I doubt), only one female was in the neighbourhood, and as she rose from the eggs I shot her. You occasionally find in the nest of the ptarmigan one small egg, scarcely larger than a musket-ball. This the Laps never take, for they fancy it is the egg of a *snake!*

As long as the female continues to sit, the old

male watches in the vicinity of the nest, like the willow grouse; but as soon as the young are hatched off, he leaves them to the care of the mother, and joining a lot more "bachelor friends," they seek the tops of the highest fells (leaving the female and young brood lower down in the fell valleys). Here we used to find the old males in small packs (I rarely saw more than nine together) throughout the whole of July, generally basking on the sunny sides of the fells on the bare patches which the snow had left. They were then by no means shy, especially if the day was hot and damp, and the easiest birds in the world to find; for as soon as the shooter enters their territory, one or more would perch on a large boulder of rock and commence a hoarse crow. This could hardly be for the purpose of warning the others, for they do not seem to rise at this challenge, only to squat closer, and it is by no means difficult to creep up to the sentinel himself and shoot him from the perch. But when the weather is boisterous they are the shyest of the shy, always rise out of shot (and you cannot hear them crow), and if they only get the wind in their tails they will often take a flight of two English miles before they drop. Early in August the young will be strong flyers; the old female then takes them higher up on the fells, they are joined again by the old male, and the whole family keep together till the autumn snow falls, when several families pack, and large flocks are met with in the lower fell tracts during the whole winter.

So beautifully has nature adapted the different changes of colour in the ptarmigan to the season and aspect of the landscape which surrounds them, that of all birds I think they are the most difficult to see on the ground, as Thompson prettily observes:—" Of all British birds this is perhaps the most interesting in consequence of the changes of plumage, every one of them beautiful, through which it passes. We hardly draw on the imagination by viewing its plumage as an exquisite miniature of the seasonal changes which the mountain undergoes—a miniature, too, drawn by a hand that never errs.

" In summer we look upon the beautiful mixture of grey, brown, and black, as resembling the three component parts of ordinary granite, felspar, mica, and hornblend, among the masses of which the ptarmigan generally resides. Late in autumn, when snows begin to fall upon the lofty summits, and partially cover the surface of the rock, we find the bird pied with white, and in winter, when they present a perfect chrysolite of snow, it is almost wholly of the same pure colour."

I have marked young birds down to an inch on

a bare fell, without a patch of covert, and although they were squatting within ten yards of me, I have had the greatest difficulty in seeing them; and truly do they need some protection, for although, perhaps, the ptarmigan has less to fear from man than any other game bird, it has, nevertheless, many enemies—the fell fox and the weasel creep upon them when crouched on the ground, and the gyr-falcon and peregrine strike them down with unerring aim when in the air; but so swift and strong on the wing is the ptarmigan that in a fair chase I have seen them distance the falcon. Although they furnish food for falcons, weasels, foxes, and owls (which swarm on these fells during the summer), so prolific are they, and so wide and inaccessible is the extent of barren country over which they range, that their number on these fells is incredible and never likely to diminish as long as the fell tracts retain their original wild character.

In the summer the food of the ptarmigan seems to consist entirely of leaves, flowers, and fruit of the fell shrubs. The young live much on insects, and in the winter the frozen fruit of the crowberry and cranberry afford them amply supply of food, and there are always bare places, even on the highest fells, from which the wind has blown the snow.

The willow grouse (*Lagopus subalpina*, Nilss.; "skogs ripa," Sw.; "riefsak," Lap.).—Some naturalists seem to have a faint opinion that the willow grouse is nothing more than a variety of the red grouse (*Tetrao scoticus*, Gould); but any one who has had the least opportunity of studying the habits of the two birds in a state of nature, will at once scout such an idea, for, although there may be a slight resemblance between the two in their summer dress, there it ends; and I perfectly agree with Dr. Bree's remarks, in his "Birds of Europe," "that its affinities are more with the ptarmigan than the red grouse, but it is distinct from both." That it certainly is; for in its habits it resembles neither. But even in the colouring there is one material difference, between the willow grouse and the red grouse, which would, in my opinion, alone mark a distinct species. In the red grouse, the wing primaries are always dusky brown; in the willow grouse, at every season of the year, they are pure white.

It is true that the seasonal change in the plumage of the willow grouse may be owing to climatic influence, but this is no reason why the wing primaries should be white at all seasons, or that the belly in the summer should be always so much lighter than the back, in fact, often pure white. I will now ask, as regards the habits of the two birds, did any one ever see a red grouse perch in a tree ? Did he ever find a nest *in the forest?* or did he ever know the red grouse even accidentally to frequent the small birch, willow, or fir forests that lie remote from the fells themselves ? In all these particulars the willow grouse differ from the red grouse, and in so great a degree that you never by any chance (at least I never did) find them on the open moors or fells, never higher up than the willow and birch bushes afford them a good shelter. And I may notice another striking difference in the habits of the two birds. I have always in August and September found that the red grouse are partial to dry situations, whereas at this season of the year the willow grouse invariably select the moistest places they can find; small belts of willow bushes by the side of the forest streams, often on wet woodland mosses, or morasses, but never out of covert; and I consider their name of willow grouse to be most appropriate. It has been suggested that, if the willow grouse were introduced into England, their colour would gradually change, and they would become more like the red grouse. This might or might not follow, but I do not see that this fact would at all prove the identity of the two birds, unless indeed the willow grouse were also to change its habits as well as its plumage in its new home, and leaving the shelter of the forest, at once take to the open moors. But I feel certain in my own mind that such would *not* be the case, for why do they not leave the lower forests in this country, and go higher up to the moors and fells which border on them? Or, why, on the contrary, do not the red grouse of Scotland come down from the moors into the lower forests?

I see Dr. Blasius allows the willow grouse to be a distinct species, but then he makes the British red grouse to be nothing more than a variety of the ptarmigan; thus I consider upsetting the laws of nature even in a still greater degree.

I wish, if we are not to consider that constant and striking differences in the habits of life between two birds of the same genus are not to justify us in considering them as distinct species, some one would just tell us in plain English what constitutes the difference between a variety and a species.

Surely it is scarcely consistent in us to set down the willow grouse as nothing more than a variety of the red grouse, or the red grouse as only a variety of the ptarmigan, when we retain in our Fauna as distinct species, the two nightingales, the lesser white-throat, the willow warbler, the pied wagtail, the grey-headed yellow wagtail, the tree pipit, the short-toed lark, the fire-crested wren, the lesser redpole, the tree sparrow, the parrot-crossbill, and some other birds which I could mention. In all those which I have named, the differences existing between them and their nearest relations in the same family are no more striking than between the willow and the red grouse, or the red grouse and the ptarmigan; in fact, in many, not nearly so striking, for their habits in life are in almost every case the same. Much as we may deprecate the foolish custom of manufacturing species, we should nevertheless be careful how we fall into the opposite extreme.

Of all the northern forest game the willow grouse is by far the most common; and, as they frequent the low forests of fir and birch at the bottom of the fells, often close to the villages, these birds, and not the ptarmigan, form the principal food of the northern settlers. In the winter they are met with (at least in the Quickiock district) scattered all over the meadows and low grounds wherever the willow or birch affords them shelter; but, as spring advances, they gradually draw up again into the forests. The pairing season took place about the same time as with the ptarmigan, but the female appears to go to nest a little earlier, for I took the first nest (with eight eggs) on May 28. The nest—very artless and carelessly built—is always in the forest or under the willow bushes by the sides of the fells, never in the open; the eggs generally from eight to eleven; and, as soon as the young can fly, the old females take them up higher on to the fell sides, but never above the willow and birch region—*i.e.*, never on to the fells themselves, although I have often found them in the fell valleys in July, by the side of water-courses where the willow luxuriates in rich profusion.

The food of the willow grouse during the summer consists almost entirely of the leaves of several plants, especially of the lesser willow (*Salix herbacea*, Lin.), which covers all the low meadows and marshy grounds at the bottom of the fells; the bleaberry (*Vaccinium myrtillus*, Lin.), and the flowers and seed of the viviparous knot-grass (*Polygonum viviparium*, Lin.), which is on this account called in Norway "rype gräs;" during the autumn their principal food consists of the berries of the bleaberry, etc.; and in the winter and spring they seem entirely to live on the catkins of the birch (both the dwarf and the common), and the stalks of the bleaberry bushes.

I have killed the willow grouse on the sides of the Œstmark fells, in about 60° N. lat., where they are tolerably numerous, and this I take it is their most southern limit in Sweden (the most southern range of the ptarmigan in Sweden appears to be about 62° N. lat.)

Although in Sweden the willow grouse has a lower southern range than the ptarmigan, it is confined entirely to the north of Europe, whereas the ptarmigan has a much more southern European range, being met with in many of the mountainous districts in Switzerland, Savoy, etc.

Early in August they appeared again to come lower down, and in the season when the young birds were fit to shoot, I generally found them on the small swamps in the forests, or in the bushes round the little streams which intersect these woods in every direction. In fact, it seems to me that, in the summer, water is indispensable to the habits of the willow grouse. The call-note of the willow grouse is much louder and hoarser than that of the ptarmigan, and resembles the sound "ka-wau-ka-wau." In one material respect it differs in habits from the ptarmigan; for not only does the male willow grouse watch his mate with the greatest care during the period of incubation, but when the brood is hatched off he never leaves them, he is always with them; and if by chance an intruder comes upon the nest or young brood, he bustles up, uttering his hoarse cackle, and if he is not able to drive away the enemy, he tries every artifice in his power to lure him from the spot. Beautiful as it is to witness the strong feeling of love which nature has implanted in the breasts of all the feathered race towards their helpless young, in no one bird is it displayed more strongly than in the willow grouse. I remarked that when the young were just cheepers, we used to find the broods much in the little foot-tracks that run through the forest; and one afternoon, in the very end of June, I came through the forest in a "bee line" down to Quickiock from the fells, *and without beating the woods,* in a distance of less than ten English miles my dog sprang about twenty-five broods, and I don't believe that the same brood ever rose twice. This will give some idea of their numbers in these forests.

The willow grouse is subject to far less variation of plumage than the ptarmigan, for although both sexes vary much in the shading of the colouring, they have but two distinct dresses. The winter dress is pure white, with fourteen black tail feathers; and the summer dress may be described thus:—*Male,* head and neck red-brown, often chocolate, *with a black chin;* body, black ground covered with red-brown wavy lines; belly, white. *Female,* head, neck, breast, crown, and sides rusty yellow, with black transverse bars; back, shoulders, rump, and the two middle tail feathers speckled with rusty yellow transverse bars. The female may be distinguished at a glance from the male by the under tail-coverts, which are rusty yellow, with black transverse bands; in the male they are red-brown, speckled with black, and only one bar in front of the white tip. The young at first are red-brown, speckled with black and white, primaries brown-grey. In August, however, they much resemble the mother, for white wing feathers usurp the place of the brown, and the black feathers appear. In this month the old birds also shed their wing and tail feathers, and also their claws. At all seasons in the old birds the wing primaries are white, and the fourteen tail feathers black with white tips. Old Pennant seems to have had some idea that the willow grouse was distinct from the ptarmigan. An old male willow grouse is a magnificent bird in his summer dress, as he rises in the forest, and goes away as straight and sharp as an arrow, but is by no means a difficult bird to kill. In the north this bird is preferred to the ptarmigan for the table, but I never could detect any difference when cooked, except that it is larger.

Nilsson says that both sexes *moult* in July and August: and so they do as far as the wing and tail feathers are concerned; but although the body colour appears to change in August, I do not think it a regular moult. There is, however, not the slightest doubt in my mind that the change from the speckled summer dress to the white plumage of winter is a true moult; and as early as August

16 I shot an old male, on the back and rump of which many of the white winter feathers were appearing among the brown, and these were certainly new feathers. In the end of April they began to assume the summer dress by *a true moult*, which was complete by about the end of May, as in the ptarmigan, the summer feathers always first appear on the head and neck, and when these parts are in full summer dress the body very quickly changes colour.

Analogous to the change of plumage in both the ptarmigan and willow grouse is the shedding of the claws, which in winter are long, nearly straight, concave underneath, and white; in the summer much shorter, brown, and flat. This takes place, at different times in different individuals, from the end of June to the middle of August. Cabanis is of opinion that this happens twice in the year; Mewes, on the contrary, distinctly says that the claws are shed only *once* in the year, and I agree with him. The new claws are at first about 8mm. long. I have measured the claw of a ptarmigan killed in December 21mm., and in one which I shot on June 22, the claws (evidently new ones) measured 10mm. This is doubtless another of the wise provisions of nature to enable these birds to scratch down to their food under the snow. They appear to grow longer as the winter increases, and to shorten, probably by scratching in the snow, towards summer; but I have seen them very long in the willow grouse in June, and I always observe that the claws of the ptarmigan which I shot about the same time were much shorter.

I do not see any reason why willow grouse should not thrive in Scotland as well as in Sweden —provided always, nevertheless, as the lawyers say, that the vegetation at the foot of the fells is the same. I think them much more likely to answer than hazel grouse, and they would afford much more real sport to the shooter; for when they are sprung in the forest they never settle in a tree, which the hazel grouse invariably do, but drop again within a short distance. But there is one remark I will make as regards the procuring of living birds and animals from foreign countries. If the Acclimatization Society are in earnest, their only plan would be to send to those countries from which they require specimens, proper men who understand their business, to collect them. It is all very well for amateurs to promise to procure clutches of eggs and birds, etc., and perhaps one out of ten will succeed; but no dependence can be placed upon a man unless it is made worth his while, and unless he gives his whole and sole attention to it; I know I always find in my collecting that amateurs promise, paid men perform. It seems easy enough for any man who is residing in a tract where the birds breed all round him, to procure a clutch of eggs and send them away; and so it would be, perhaps, in Britain, where no man lives further than a few miles from a railway station. But in these countries transport is not so easy; and although there is no trouble to procure the eggs, the trouble is to get them well to England.

There is a great doubt in my mind whether eggs sent over from this country would incubate when they reached England. But I see that Thompson, in his "Natural History of Ireland," mentions the fact of eggs, which had *been partly incubated*, hatching off after they had been taken *twelve* hours from the nest, but not longer. There are two birds in this country which many English sportsmen are desirous of obtaining—the willow grouse and the hazel grouse. Why don't they subscribe £100, and send over for a season a regular gamekeeper who is used to the management and rearing young birds? He would have no trouble to obtain what he wanted, and, doubtless, then the affair would be managed, and a good breeding stock would be obtained. £100 ought to pay all expenses; and what would this sum be when divided among a dozen of our rich game preservers? Depend upon it that this is the only plan to adopt. No one has a better chance of procuring eggs and birds than myself; and, as I have over and over again stated, I should be most willing to help the Acclimatization Society as far as possible, but my time is too much occupied, and I will never undertake a thing unless I can carry it through. Moreover, I am never at home in the breeding season. One thing must be borne in mind, that the willow grouse will never thrive in flat forests away from the fells, for the low forests on the sides and at the foot of the fells are as much the true home of this bird as the snow-capped fells are of the ptarmigan. As to the hazel grouse, they come much further south away from the fells than the willow grouse, although in the Quickiock district they seem to frequent the same forests as the willow grouse, but never so far up on the fell sides; but it is strange that although known in Germany, the hazel grouse is a stranger in the south of Sweden. I think one thing is pretty clear, that young fir plantings are not suited to the habits of the "hjerpe," but old fir forests, in which there is much rotten timber and many stony rises.

No disease appears as yet to have ever been known among the northern grouse.

Although the willow grouse will occasionally

perch, I never saw the ptarmigan settle in a tree.

In the winter the willow grouse pack, after the manner of the ptarmigan, and they say that then such flocks will sometimes settle in the birch-trees as quite to whiten them.

We now come to the Waders, and I may here remark that. I was greatly disappointed in the country around Quickiock, for I never saw fewer waders in any part of Sweden than here, and all the rarest seemed to go right up on to the high fell meadows to breed. The large valley of the Torneä and Munio rivers is without doubt a better district for waders than this.

The ring plover (*Charadrius hiaticula*, Lin.; "storre strandpipare," Sw.; "bovidat," Lap.) was not uncommon on the sides of the river just when the ice went; but in the breeding season they appeared to draw up on to the fells, and I have seen them high up on the very edges of the snow.

I never saw the little ring plover (*Ch. minor*, Mey.) here, nor do I believe that it breeds further north in Sweden than Wermland; but I often obtain the nest on the shores of Lake Wenern.

The dotterel (*Ch. morinellus*, Lin.; "fell pipare," Sw.; "lafol," Lap.).—This is peculiarly a fell bird, and next to the golden plover (*Ch.*

apricarius, Cuv.; "bitschus," Lap.), which swarmed on all these fells, I think was one of the commonest birds on our fells, and it is found as well on the snow-covered tops as on the lower fells, but always among the stones, never on the fell meadows. They were by no means shy, especially in the breeding season, and their soft whistling call-note, "kirley-kirlz," often betrayed the locality of the nest, which is generally nothing more than a little dry grass in a hole scraped on the bare fell; but once, and once only, I took a nest made of fine dry grass and a few ptarmigan feathers. I never found more than three eggs in a nest, and, as I have taken these hard sat on, I fancy three is the full number. We took our first nest on June 7, and our last on June 28; but by the middle of July many young were strong flyers. I know no egg which is likely to be mistaken for that of the dotterel—ground colour dark stone, thickly blotched all over with black patches.

I never could identify the grey plover (*Ch. Helveticus*, Bon.) in this neighbourhood, although I have good reason to *believe that it breeds here*. I offered a great price to the Laps if they could bring me the nest and bird of a plover *with a back toe*, but I never had the luck to obtain it. As a guide to the young naturalist, I may here notice that in the summer dress the grey plover differs little or nothing from the golden, but the small head will always distinguish the grey plover at all seasons.

I never met with the crane (*Grus cinerea*, Bech.) in this district.

Both the curlew (*Numenius arquata*, Lin.; "stor spof," Sw.) and the whimbrel (*N. phæopus*, Lath.; "sma spof," Sw.) are met with here; but I never saw any other than the whimbrel, and this bird was sparingly distributed over the lower fell tracts. "Gutsch kastaf" is the Lap name for both curlew and whimbrel. I never found more than three eggs in the nest of the whimbrel. They breed sparingly on our fells.

Not a single species of heron or stork appear to come up here to breed.

That the bar-tailed godwit (*Limosa rufa*, Briss.; "roströd lang näbba") breeds in this neighbourhood is pretty certain, although I never found the nest; but I fancy that both the godwits, although they may breed here and there in Lapland, breed principally more to the east.

Temminck's stint (*Tringa Temminckii*, Leisl.; "Temminck's strandvipa," Sw.; "vizardalle," Lap.) was rare in this district, and I only met with two pair. The one I shot by the river-side in the early spring, and the other with their nest on a fell meadow, close to where I found the nest of the broad-billed sandpiper. The nest was placed on a tussock of rushy grass in a swampy part of the meadow, nothing more than a few bits of dry grass. Eggs, four; very pyriform; chocolate-brown covered with a deeper shade of small fine spots all over. This stint does not appear to be confined to the northern tracts of Scandinavia, for I have taken the nest in Wermland. Strange to say that we none of us can find out the breeding-place of the little stint (*T. minuta*, Leisl.), nor have I ever seen a well-authenticated egg of this bird. We meet with them not only on all the Swedish coasts during the periods of migration, but even occasionally inland. I fancy their breeding haunts must be somewhere on the northern coasts of Norway, for early in August they are seen all along the Norwegian coast, and often in considerable flocks. There is a great resemblance between these two stints, but they may be always known from each other by this infallible mark: in Temminck's stint the shaft of only the first wing primary is white, of all the others the shafts are brown; whereas in the little stint the shafts of all the primaries are white in the middle.

The dusky redshank (*T. fuscus*, Leisl.; "tscappis tschoavtscho") seems a stranger here, but breeds further up in the valley of the Munio, from whence I have received eggs which are considerably larger than those of the common redshank, with somewhat the character of the great snipe's egg.

The common sandpiper (*Totanus hypoleucos*, Tem.; "drill snappa," Sw.) was very common on the lower rivers, but I never met with them on the fells. I shot one specimen of the purple sandpiper (*T. maritima*, Brün; "svart gra strandvipa," Sw.) early in the spring by the river side; but, as I never saw another, I do not fancy that these fells are the breeding place of this bird, which are very common further north. The redshank (*T. calidris*, Bech.; "rodbent snappa," Sw.) was very rare. The dunlin (*Tringa alpina*, Lin.) I could never identify in this district; and the green sandpiper (*Tot. ochropus*, Tem.) is certainly a stranger to the north of Scandinavia, although I have received the four eggs of this bird laid in a thrush's nest from as far north as Gefle. It is a curious fact, and one which did not appear to be known to any naturalist until I noticed it, that the green sandpiper, unlike the rest of this tribe, invariably, as far as I can see, lays its four eggs in another bird's nest, generally that of a jay or crow, often a mile from water, and often twenty-five feet up in a fir tree. I never took them on the ground, as noticed by all other naturalists.

The ruff (*Machetes pugnax*, Cuv.; "brushane," Sw.) was very common on the fell meadows, and early in July we used to shoot the males with very fine ruffs on them.

But the finest and perhaps one of the commonest of our waders here was the greenshank (*Totglottis*, Bech.; "glutten," Sw.; "vikkla," Lap.), which came up here among the earliest in the spring, and left certainly the earliest in the autumn. As I had now a good opportunity of studying the habits of this bird in the breeding season, I was much struck with its resemblance to the green sandpiper. The wild nature of the bird, its loud shrill cry, "chee-wheet, chee-wheet," as it dashes through the air with the speed of an arrow, and its partiality for woodland lakes and streams, all prove that it is more closely allied to the green sandpiper than any other of the genus, and, save that I always took the eggs from the ground, the habits of the one bird seemed exactly to resemble those of the other. The eggs of the greenshank are often laid far away from water. I took a nest once upon a stony rise right in an open forest, about one hundred yards from a little beck, laid on a thin layer of leaves. The eggs, always four in number, are very large, pyriform; ground colour stone yellow-green, dashed all over with dark brown and pale purple-grey, especially at the thick end. I observed as soon as the young were hatched off, the old birds would lead them down to some grassy swamp in the forest, and I have met with three or four families in the same spot. It is now that the wild cry of this bird is heard to perfection if you enter the swamp with a dog; and it is a pleasing sight to see how little fear the old birds display in endeavouring to beat the intruder from the spot. No trying to allure him away by sham pretences, as the lapwing and many other birds do, but a downright courageous attack, which never ceases till the dog is fairly beaten off. I have often seen the greenshank settle in a tree.

The wood sandpiper (*Totanus glareola*, Tem.; "grönbent snappa," Sw.; "utsea tschoavtscho," Lap.) was very common here; and far different are the quiet unobtrusive habits of this little bird during the breeding season, to the boisterous, noisy behaviour of its congener, the green sandpiper. Early in the summer the wood sandpiper has a new pretty little song, which it trills out when seated on a tussock of grass or when rising in the air in the vicinity of the nest. I have much oftener seen this bird seated on a tree or a rail than the green sandpiper, although that bird will occasionally perch.

Every endeavour to procure well-authenticated eggs of the knot (*Tringa Canutus*, Lin.), the curlew sandpiper (*T. subarquata*, Tem.), or the sanderling (*Calidris arenaria*, Leach), in Scandinavia have entirely failed; although I feel pretty certain that one or other of them breed in some of the secluded fell tracts, for I have shot both the knot and pigmy curlew in full summer dress on the coast of Skane as early as the first week in August.

As I before observed, this is a very bad district for the snipes. The only nest I obtained was that of the common snipe (*Scolopax gallinago*, Lin.; "makkastak," Lap.; "enkel becassen," Sw.). I killed one single example of the double snipe (*S. major*, Gm.; "dubbel becassen," Sw.) in the spring, and, strange to say, I flushed it in a dry open fir wood, far away from any water. This was the only specimen I saw, and I never met with the jack snipe (*S. gallinula*, Lin.) in this district.

None of the rails or crakes appear to come so far north.

Of the phalaropes, I could never detect the grey phalarope (*Phal. platyrhinchus*, Tem.) in this district; but the little red-necked phalarope (*P. hyperboreus*, Lath.; "smä nabbad sunsnappa," Sw.; "svapalas," Lap.) was very common in the higher fell meadows. It is curious to watch these little birds on a summer evening, in small companies of six or eight, chasing each other over a fell lake, into which they would suddenly drop, and swim over its surface, ducking, diving, flapping their little wings, evidently in high enjoyment. We always used to find the eggs close by the margin of the water; and, like all the small waders, the female never rises from the eggs until she is nearly trod upon. The difference in length between the two species (nearly two inches), and the different shape of the beak, will at once distinguish the two phalaropes.

The broad-billed sandpiper (*Tringa platyrhincha*, Tem.; "bred nabbad strandvipa," Sw.) Till within the last few years, this sandpiper appears to have been entirely overlooked in Sweden, but I do not think it is so very rare. Twelve years ago I shot three specimens in August, in the very south of Sweden; since then I have shot them in Wermland, and now I have taken the nest in Luleä Lapland. Of all the sandpipers, this certainly is the most unobtrusive and shyest in its habits; and its custom of creeping among the grass like a little mouse, causes it to be very seldom seen. When flushed, which is never until you nearly tread upon it, it rises with a faint single call-note, flies for a very little distance, then suddenly drops, and it is next to impossible to get it up a second time without a dog. I only found one nest of this sandpiper. It was in a high fell meadow, where I obtained so many of the Lap buntings, and I shot both old birds. The eggs were four, very pyriform; ground colour grey-brown, covered all over with minute spots of light umber-brown, nearly hiding the ground colour; size, $1\frac{1}{4}$ in. by $\frac{7}{8}$ in. The broad-billed sandpiper may, however, be considered as among our rarer sandpipers, and I can never account for the fact of some of our sandpipers (the whole of which class lay the same number of eggs) being so much rarer than the others.

I have seen the common tern (*Sterna hirundo*, Lin.; "fisk tarna," Sw.) and the common gull (*Larus canus*, Lin.; "fisk måse," Sw.), both at Quickiock, the latter high up over the fell lakes; and I shot one specimen of the lesser black-backed gull (*L. fascus*, Lin.; "sill måse," Sw.), flying over the Tana river; but they were all three rare, and, except Buffon's skua (of which more hereafter), these were the only species of this family I saw in this neighbourhood.

Buffon's skua (*Lestris Buffonii*, Boie; "skaiti," "haskil,". Lap; "fell labbe," Sw.). Owing, as it was supposed up here (but this was not my opinion) to the quantity of lemming which swarmed on these fells this summer, the Buffon's skua was unusually numerous in this neighbourhood, and from first to last I obtained more than thirty specimens of old birds, besides many eggs, and some young. But from all I could hear, this was a very unusual occurrence, and years may elapse before they will appear again in such numbers on these fells, although never a year passes without some being seen. It appears, therefore, that the northern stretch of this large fell range is the summer home of this skua, which in winter is occasionally met with as far south as the British Channel. I cannot hear of their breeding, however, further south than "Peleekaisin," perhaps 100 miles south of Quickiock. All the Laps with whom I spoke were well acquainted with this bird. We got our first nest on the 3rd of June, and continued to take fresh eggs until the end of the month. I myself never but in one instance saw more than two eggs in a nest. Once I obtained three; and as I have taken a single egg from a nest hard sat on, it appears that they do not always lay two, which, however, we may take to be the general number. The nest is nothing more than a few pieces of dried hay laid in a hole scratched in the ground, always in the vicinity of water, and I never saw it on a real snow fell. Although these birds live in colonies, you do not find the nests close together. None breed close to Quickiock, but on the fells about thirty miles to the west they breed in great quantities. No bird is more tame and fearless than this skua during the time they have eggs, for they come sailing close over your head when searching for the nest, performing the most beautiful airy gyrations, their long sharp wings and pointed tail giving them a singular and pretty appearance when in the air. Their cry is a loud dismal shriek—"i-i-i-ah, je-ah, je-oh, je-oh!" and might be heard day and night over their breeding-place. But as soon as the young were hatched off, their nature seemed to be entirely changed, and then they never approach within gun-shot, but wisely do not betray the proximity of the young (which always manage to hide themselves very cleverly) by any gestures of anxiety.

Of all the specimens which I opened, in the inside of one alone did I ever see the remains of a fell lemming, and in only one other were there the remains of a small mouse. Their principal food appears to be the common crowberry (*Empetrum nigrum*), a large beetle, and small crustacea. I never saw anything except crowberries in the inside of the young ones. The Laps have an idea that they will kill and eat the young ptarmigan. I have certainly seen a skua chase an old ptarmigan, but I fancy this was more from wantonness than anything else. I could scarcely distinguish the male from the female by the plumage. In one example the long middle tail feathers measured 13 inches, and extended 9 inches beyond the rest. Much confusion has existed respecting the different members of this group, and I believe it is due to the assiduity of Bonaparte that much of this mystery is cleared up, and that this skua is identified as a distinct species. Perhaps no class of birds are subject to so many changes in plumage, owing to age, and different shades even at the same season of the year, as the skuas; and I cannot help here quoting Wilson's very excellent remarks on this subject: "The changes of plumage to which birds of this genus are subject have tended not a little to confound the naturalist; and a considerable collision of opinion, arising from an imperfect acquaintance with the living subject, has been the result. To investigate thoroughly their history it is obviously necessary that the ornithologist should frequently explore their natural haunts; and to determine the species of occasional or periodical visitors, an accurate comparative examination of many specimens, alive or recently killed, is indispensable. Less confusion would arise among authors if they would occasionally abandon their accustomed walks, their studies, and their museums, *and seek correct know-*

ledge in the only place where it is to be obtained—in the grand temple of nature." I cordially agree with this latter remark of Wilson's. The young that I killed much resembled in plumage the young of the common skua (*L. cattaractes*, Ill.); the tail was perfectly *green*, no one feather longer than the others.

On carefully comparing specimens of the eggs of Buffon's skua with those of Richardson's skua (*L. Richardsoni*, Sw.) I could see no very apparent difference in the size. Those of Buffon's skua may perhaps be a *trifle* the smaller, but they vary in size, and I have seen them quite as big as those of Richardson's skua; while in one nest which I took, the two eggs were at least one-third smaller than any I had ever seen. One thing I remarked, that the egg of Buffon's skua is generally thicker and blunter at the large end than Richardson's. As to colour it is much the same in both, and subject to the same variations; but the oologist should be very careful how he admits the egg of Buffon's skua into his collection without a careful identification.

I could never detect the pomarine skua (*L. pomarina*, Tem.; " ave haskil," Lap.) breeding in this district. But many of the Norwegian Laps knew and described the bird well, and it is my opinion that this species breeds more on the north-west coast of Norway, and does not come so far inland as Buffon's skua.

I have, I believe, an authentic egg of the pomarine skua in my collection obtained from Greenland, and this is more pointed at the smaller end than the egg of any other skua I ever saw. It exactly agrees in shape with Mr. A. Newton's coloured figure in the Proceedings of the Zoological Society, and perhaps this pointed shape is a characteristic of this egg.

The wild swan (*Cygnus musicus*, Tem.; "vild svan," Sw., "neift scha," Lap.)—I never saw the wild swan in the vicinity of Quickiock, but I obtained two full nests from Iockmock, the one containing seven, the other five eggs. They appear never to go right up on to the snow fells, but to breed in the inland lakes that lie in the meadows at their feet.

The bean goose (*Anser segetum*, Gm.; "skogs gas," Sw., "tschuonga," Lap.)—I never was able to find the nest of this goose, and the only egg which I obtained I took out of an old female which I shot down at Quickiock in the end of May. But this goose does breed here, and, unlike the fell goose next described, appears never to go up on to the high fells, but to breed in the wood lakes, whence its Swedish name of "skogs gas," or wood-goose. The egg which I obtained was just ready for laying, pure chalk white, 3¼ in. by 2¼ in.

The little white-fronted goose (*A. minutus*, Naum.; "fell gas," Sw.; "kasak," Lap.)—This little goose, which appears to be a distinct species from the British white-fronted goose (*A. albifrons*, Bechst.), which latter bird, however, Nilsson includes in the Swedish fauna, giving it the Lap name of "kasak," and, moreover, telling us that it is the common fell goose of Sweden. Here he certainly is wrong, for I never could meet with the common white-fronted goose in Sweden; and I believe it is very rare even up at the North Cape. The Laps all have a name for the *minutus* but not for *albifrons*. I believe there has been some confusion regarding the Latin synonyms of these two birds, and I should certainly always recommend the common white-fronted goose to be called the *Anser albifrons* (Bechst.), and the lesser white-fronted goose the *Anser minutus* (Naum.). It is easily distinguished from the common white-fronted goose by its smaller size, measuring scarcely 22 in.; by the much smaller beak, and especially that the lamellæ in the beak, which, in *A. albifrons* are plainly to be seen along the whole mandible, in the *A. minutus* are not visible. The only species which I met with at Quickiock were these small geese (*A. minutus*, Naum.), and I could never hear that any geese bred here besides this and the bean goose. Although I never took the nest myself, it was certain they bred on the fells, for any night when we were camping out, we could hear the cry of this goose, which much resembles its Lap name "kasak, kasak," apparently from the highest snow-capped fells; from whence I infer they breed high up on the fells, as we never saw them in the fell meadows. The egg, which I obtained through the kindness of Mr. Alfred Newton, from the Munioniska district, is more ivory white than that of the brent goose (*A. bernicla*, Ill.), which I have received both from Greenland and Spitzbergen, being about $2\frac{1}{4}$ in. by $1\frac{7}{8}$ in.

The grey goose (*A. cinereus*, Mey.) does not appear to breed here; and I believe both the brent goose and the bernicle (*A. leucopsis*, Bechst.) pass over Scandinavia to breed either in Spitzbergen or East Finland; at least I could not hear of any black-beaked goose having been yet detected breeding in Lapland.

The common wild duck (*Anas boschas*, Lin.; "gräs and," Sw.; "dorsa," Lap.) is one of the rarest in the district, and I don't believe I ever saw more than three pair here. They call it here the "is and," or ice-duck, because they usually make their appearance early, before the ice has left the river. This egg was brought to me as a great rarity, and the boy who took the nest wanted double the price for it than for that of any other duck.

The teal (*A. crecca*, Lin.; "krick and," Sw.; "schik-sa," Lap.) was tolerably common.

The shoveller (*A. clypeata*, Lin.; "sked and," Sw.) is said to have been once or twice killed here, although I never saw it.

The widgeon (*A. Penelope*, Lin.; "blas and," Sw.; "snartal" Lap.) was the commonest of all the ducks here; and, perhaps, next to this—

The pintail (*A. acuta*, Lin.; "syert and," Sw.; "vuou asch," Lap.) I always found the nest of the pintail in the small willow plantations that skirt the foot of the fells. It is an early breeder; the first nest I obtained on June 4. The first nest of the widgeon, however, on May 29. The egg of the pintail much resembles that of the long-tailed duck, both being of a dark clay colour; but as they breed at different seasons, and in such very different localities, there is no fear of ever confounding the nests of the two.

All these species breed in the lowlands, and I never recollect seeing one in any of the fell meadows.

Of the diving ducks, first on my list must stand—

The golden eye (*A. clangula*, Lin.; "knip and," Sw.; "ts choadge," Lap.); and this was, perhaps, as common as any duck here. I never took the nest of the golden eye from the ground, always in "holkar" or tubs set up in trees, or in hollow trees themselves. The egg of the golden eye varies very much in colour and size; and it is remarked here, by the old settlers, who watch the habits of this bird closely, for its eggs afford them a good supply of food, that the old birds always lay the fewest, finest, and largest eggs (and this, I think, holds good with most birds). An old golden eye, they say, will rarely lay more than five eggs, whereas a young bird will lay as many as fifteen. When fresh taken, I think the egg of the golden eye one of the handsomest of all European ducks' eggs.

The tufted duck (*A. fuligula*, Lin.; "viggen," Sw.; "lilla lorte," Lap.), although I never saw it here, is said occasionally to breed in this neighbourhood; but local names puzzle one, and in this district they call two species of duck "viggen;" for instance, the tufted duck is the "sma viggen;" the scaup the "stor viggen," or large viggen.

The scaup (*A. marila*, Lin.; "hvit buk," Sw.; or white belly; "fjeltak," Lap.) was not uncommon, and I have met with them breeding both in the low grounds and on the fell meadows. The egg of the scaup resembles that of the pintail in colour, but is larger and thicker, measuring $2\frac{5}{8}$ in. by $1\frac{1}{4}$ in.

The common scoter (*A. nigra*, Lin.; "svarta," Sw.; "storra sorto," Lap.), (so named from its wholly black colour) is commoner than the velvet scoter, and always, as far as I could see, laid its eggs in the low grounds. The egg of the scoter is deep yellow-brown, $2\frac{5}{8}$ in. by $1\frac{7}{8}$ in.

The velvet scoter (*A. fusca*, Lin.; "sjo orre," Sw. and Lap., or the blackcock; "kolska," Fin.) (from the white speculum on the wing, which resembles that of an " orre " or blackcock).—Contrary to the last, they say this duck leaves the lowlands, and retires to breed on the fell lakes; and, although I was never able to find the nest myself, I often used to see the birds on the small fell lakes, evidently breeding. The egg of the velvet scoter, which I received from Munioniska, has an ivory tinge much clearer than that of the common bird—$2\frac{7}{8}$ by 2 in.

The long-tailed duck (*A. glacialis*, Lin.; "alfogel," Sw.; "hanga," Lap.) made their appearance on the Tana River towards the middle of May, and after remaining there a short time, they retired up to the fell lakes to breed. Before breeding, we always saw them in small flocks; and I think of all ducks these are the most restless, for they are never still, but continually chasing each other about, uttering a pleasing note, which Nilsson likens to the tone of a clarionet—"a agleck, a agleck." The only nest which I obtained of this bird was on the same fell meadow where the Lap buntings bred. I was walking down a narrow trackway by the side of a fell lake, and I nearly trod upon the old female, which was sitting on her nest, right in my very path. Although her head was turned towards me, she never attempted to rise, and I caught her on the nest. This was on the night of June 27. The nest contained seven fresh eggs, in colour resembling those of the pintail, but a little smaller. On the next morning, I saw two young broods of this duck on the water, apparently a few days old. During the breeding season the old males appear to leave the females, and congregate in small flocks; and even in the end of June we used to see occasionally six to eight males on the river down at Quickiock.

The goosander (*Mergus Merganser*, Lin. ; "stor skrake," Sw. ; "gussagoalse," Lap.) was not nearly so common as the merganser; and I used to observe that they much frequented the streams at the bottom of the waterfalls. The only two nests I obtained of the goosander were both on the bare ground. The egg may be distinguished from that of the merganser, which it rather resembles, by its larger size (at least, it is considerably thicker), by its clearer colour, and by its peculiar shape, being pointed alike at both ends.

The red-breasted merganser (*M. serrator*, Lin.; "sma skrake," Sw.; "vuofta goalse," Lap.). On our journey up we saw a merganser on April 14, in the open water at a waterfall in a river over which we passed. This bird was far commoner than the last. All the eggs which we obtained were taken on the ground.

The egg of the smew is very rare in the north. I may mention that one of the late Mr. Wooley's best collectors has informed me that in ten years' collecting, in the Munio district, he has only succeeded in obtaining eight eggs of the smew. It is described as breeding in holes, and the egg is so like that of the widgeon, that the only way of detecting the difference is by examining the texture of the shells under a microscope.

In vain did I make the most diligent inquiries after the smew (*M. Albellus*, Lin.; "sal skrake," Sw.); I never could detect it breeding here. The settlers, however, certainly had a confused notion that such a bird is occasionally seen on these waters, but I fancy they confounded it with the red-necked grebe (*Podiceps rubricollis*, Lath.; "gra strupig dopping," Sw.), which bird breeds sparingly as far north as this, and I obtained one nest with six eggs. I fancy this grebe must have a more extended range in Scandinavia than any other of the tribe, for I never heard of any other grebe being much within Lapland; and it is only of late years that this bird has been detected breeding so far north.

Both the black-throated diver (*Colymbus arcticus*, Lin.; "Dofta stor lom"), and the red-throated diver (*C. septentrionalis*; "sma lom;" "gakkur," Lap.) were common up here, and I fancy that the black-throated went further up on the fells than the other. And these conclude my list of the birds which *I am certain are met with* in the Quickiock district, of which, as a reference for the naturalist, I add a list, affixing an asterisk to those whose eggs I obtained. There may of course be others which I overlooked, but certainly not many:—

Norwegian jer falcon*
Peregrine
Merlin*
Kestrel*
Sparrow hawk*
Goshawk
Golden eagle
White-tailed eagle
Osprey*
Rough-legged buzzard*
Snowy owl*
Eagle owl
Hawk owl*
Tengmalm's owl*
Lesser European sparrow owl
Short-eared owl*
Great shrike*
Cuckoo
Great black woodpecker*
Three-toed woodpecker*
Little spotted woodpecker*
Great spotted woodpecker
Raven
Rook

Hooded crow
Siberian jay*
Starling
Creeper
Bohemian waxwing*
Swift
Swallow
Martin
Bank martin
Pied flycatcher*
Common flycatcher
Common thrush*
Missel thrush*
Ring ouzel*
Fieldfare*
Redwing*
Water ouzel*
Wheatear*
Whinchat*
Garden warbler*
Willow warbler*
Chiff chaff*
Redstart*
Hedge sparrow*
Blue-throated warbler*
White wagtail*
Yellow wagtail*
Meadow pipit*
Tree pipit
Siberian tit*
Marsh tit*
Skylark
Shore lark
Yellow bunting*
Black-headed bunting*
Snow bunting
Lap bunting*

Ortolan bunting*
Chaffinch*
Brambling*
Mealy redpole*
Common linnet
Bullfinch*
Crossbill
Pine grosbeak*
Capercailzie*
Hazel grouse*
Ptarmigan*
Willow grouse*
Ring plover*
Dotterel*
Golden plover*
Whimbrel*
Temminck's stint*
Redshank
Ruff*
Common sandpiper*
Wood sandpiper*
Broad-billed sandpiper*
Greenshank*
Double snipe
Common snipe
Red-necked phalarope*
Common tern
Common gull
Lesser black-backed gull
Buffon's skua*
Wild swan*
Bean goose*
Lesser white-fronted goose
Common wild duck*
Teal*
Widgeon*
Pintail*

Golden eye*	Goosander*
Scaup*	Merganser*
Common scoter*.	Red-necked grebe*
Velvet scoter	Black-throated diver*
Long-tailed duck*	Red-throated diver*

Considering it was my first season, and I knew nothing of the locality or fauna of the district, I was very well satisfied with what I saw and obtained at Quickiock. But if I spend another season there, which I hope I shall, I trust to do far better, especially in eggs. I will obtain much more assistance, and I will take up a small tent and camp on the fells during the whole month of June, for it is impossible to work these fells thoroughly if you have to bear up a day or two's provisions, and keep going backwards and forwards to and from the village.

CHAPTER X.

A CHAPTER ON THE ORNITHOLOGY AROUND VARDOL, IN EAST FINLAND, LYING CONTIGUOUS TO THE NORTH CAPE.

FROM Quickiock to the North Cape, as the crow flies, will be about four degrees, or 240 English miles; and the wild, barren tracts lying on either side of the great Torneä river, which enters the Bothnia at Torneä, or the great Tana river, which flows into the Polar Ocean at Tana fjord, a little to the east of the North Cape, are probably richer in the rare ducks and waders during the summer than any other portion of the European continent.

I have already noticed all the birds which I met with in the Quickiock district, and a list of the birds which are found in the tracts lying between this place and the North Cape will render my notes on the ornithology of Lapland complete and very useful to the naturalist who studies that most interesting subject, the geographical distribution of species. Of course, from my own personal observation, I can say nothing of the fauna north of Quickiock; but the following notes on the ornithology of the country around Vardol, by the Rev. C. Sommerfeet, for the last ten years priest in the parish of Nasby, in the Varanger fjord, a keen collector and an excellent ornithologist, may be safely relied upon as being correct.

I may, however, notice that four of the rarest species, such as the waxwing, pine grosbeak, and some of the rarer waders, do not appear to go up so far, but their principal breeding localities seem to be more in the valley of the Munio and around Enara, in East Finland. Still, from its contiguity to the fells, I do not think that any station in Lapland for the general collector beats Quickiock. The only fault which I find with the place is that it is rather the fashion here to visit it in the summer, and consequently wages and all things are dearer than in any other part of Lapland.

The coasts of East Finmark are washed by the Polar Sea, which encroaches upon the land by many "fjords," or bays, of which the largest are Laxe fjord and Tana fjord on the north, and Varanger fjord on the east. The most northerly part of East Finmark consists of two islands—the one north of Hops and Eids fjords, the most northerly point of which is Nord Kyn; the other, Varanger Næs, surrounded by Tana fjord, Tana river, and Varanger fjord, on the east point of which lies Wardoe, the most northerly town or village in Europe. These large islands, and a great part of the "Fast" land which lies contiguous to Hops and Eids fjords, consist of a tolerably flat table-land dotted with higher mountains, having on its surface long stretches of shingle and gravel, without the least signs of vegetation, not even lichens, although on the snow mosses which lie here throughout the whole year we find the so-called "red snow" (which singular phenomenon in nature is attributed by the celebrated Swedish professor, Agardth, to the agency of a species of algæ (*Protococcus nivalis*, Grev.), and of which Berkeley, in his "Introduction to Cryptogamic Botany," observes—" In the very confines of the order, we thus become acquainted with the striking resemblances which are exhibited by certain states of algæ and infusoria—resemblances which are so close as to be perfectly convincing that we must greatly modify our notions of the distinctness of animal and vegetable life if we wish them to agree with fact, and not with mere arbitrary theories."

On this table-land we find large mosses, or morasses, partly flat and even, partly filled up with greater or smaller hillocks of turf, with deep holes of black mud between them. This flat is divided by many rivers, the banks of which are fringed with birch and willow, while in the meadows we find a far richer vegetation of Alpine flora than we should have supposed. These rivers have their rise from the fell lakes, of which there are many of a tolerable size—*i.e.*, "jeris jaure" ("jaure" is the Lap. term for a lake), and "naste jaure." In most of these lakes we find fish, crustacea, and the larva of insects (probably of mosquitoes), so that both the water-fowl and waders here find a rich supply of food.

In this, the wildest and barrenest tract of East Finmark, the gyr-falcon, the snowy owl, the snow bunting, the wheatear, the purple sandpiper, one or other of the skuas, the godwits, gulls, cormorants, guillemots, razorbills, oyster-catchers, Arctic terns, the ring dotterel, Temminck's stint, and the rock pipit, breed; while further inland we find in the summer the fieldfare, redwing, shore lark, merlin, greenshank, wood sandpiper, dunlin, and some of the aucks.

Further south we also meet with a flat, desolate tract, but not nearly so wild and barren as this, for here we have lichens and grass, plantations of birch and willow, not only along the sides of the rivers, but even in the meadows, which are also much more fruitful, especially in Lyd Varanger and Tanadalen. In Lyd Varanger, that portion of East Finmark which lies on the south side of Varanger fjord, we meet with some small fir and pine forests, the Oriental fir, birch, alder, and willow, but, for the most part, large tracts of heather and morasses.

The great Tana river stretches above twenty-six Swedish miles from S.W. to N.E. to Polmak, and from thence, six miles further, it flows into Tana fjord, a broad, and, in seasons of flood, a mighty river. On both sides of this river are forests of fir and pine mixed together; while on the Norwegian frontier, birch, alder, aspen, mountain-ash, and bird cherry take their place; and we then come to the real fells, whose tops are covered with perennial snows, from both sides of which fall many large rivers down into Tana fjord. The whole tract on both sides of Tana river is richer to the naturalist than any other part of East Finmark. These large rivers silently flowing through wide-stretched valleys, which are flooded in the spring, but which in the summer are covered with rank grass and willow bushes, the deep birch forests thickly blended with many species of willow, and the wild, solitary character of the whole landscape, where human foot seldom wanders, renders it a peculiarly fitting home for the rarest birds which are met with in East Finmark, and the flycatcher, the bullfinch, the rosy bullfinch, the greenshank, the wild swan, the scaup duck, the gyr-falcon, the Siberian jay, the three-toed woodpecker, thrushes, finches, and warblers, breed here in great quantities.

Respecting the climate of East Finmark, we may divide the year into eight months of winter and four months of summer. The winter sets in generally early in October with cold, stormy weather, and so sudden are the changes in the temperature here that the thermometer often in twelve hours will fall from freezing point to 24° of cold (Reaumur), although the usual winter temperature is between 15° and 20° R. Seldom does it stand for a week more than 20° R., and this is always followed by a northerly storm, although in Varanger fjord 32° cold R. has been known. Spring usually sets in early in May with mild and beautiful weather, and by the middle of May the snow begins to melt. The birds of passage arrive about the middle of May, although the snow bunting and rock pipit sometimes appear in the end of April. During the cold, snowy, windy weather, which always sets in just before the ice begins to go in the rivers, the little wanderers assemble in large flocks in the neighbourhood of houses, where they endeavour to get a scanty sustenance. The true summer sets in late in June, but the principal part of the song birds lay their eggs in the middle of that month, the shore lark and the fieldfare in the beginning. The summer heats at Vardol is often 24° R. in the shade, but from ten to five a fresh sea breeze generally blows. The cold autumn weather generally begins about the end of August, although the night frosts often set in between the 4th and 11th of that month.

In mild summers, with an early spring, the Siberian jay, the shore lark, and the mealy redpole lay at two different times, the first time in the end of May, the second in July. It is hard to say whether it is the same individual bird that lays twice, but it is not improbable, from the long period that elapses between the two layings.

East Finmark owns a tolerably rich ornithological fauna, for in Sommerfeet's list he mentions 138 species, viz. :—

Accipitres	14
Passeres	44
Gallinæ	3
Grallæ	26
Anseres	51

It will not be uninteresting to compare this with my list of the birds of Quickiock, about 4° more to the south.

ACCIPITRES.

With the exception of the kestrel, the list of hawks is the same. The gyr-falcon is one of the commonest of the falcons. It does not appear certain that the peregrine breeds in East Finland, but is seen there early in the autumn and spring. All except the merlin, the peregrine, the osprey, and the sparrow hawk remain during the winter.

He does not notice either the lesser European sparrow owl or Tengmalm's owl. The Lap. owl is only occasionally met with in autumn, and does not appear to breed further north than Enara. The eagle owl appears only once to have been accidentally shot here in the winter. The short-eared owl is a summer migrant. The snowy owl and the hawk owl remain throughout the year.

It is strange that the Ural owl is never seen here. They have an idea up here that the snowy owl always carries away its eggs if they are touched. It appears to breed here in May.

PASSERES.

The cuckoo, not seen every year.

The only woodpeckers noticed are the lesser spotted and the three-toed, both which remain throughout the year.

The starling is accidental, but a young bird

appears to have been shot up here in December, 1846.

Of the crows, he mentions the raven, the hooded crow, and the magpie (rare), as remaining here throughout the year.

The Siberian jay also remains during the year.

The waxwing does not breed here, and is only very rarely seen in the autumn.

Of the swallows, he notices all except the swift, as summer visitors.

Both the flycatchers appear to breed here.

The great shrike is a summer visitant.

The fieldfare, the redwing, and the ring ouzel, are all summer migrants. The water ouzel remains throughout the winter, and these are all the thrushes that he notices.

Three wagtails are summer migrants: the continental white wagtail, the grey-headed yellow wagtail (which I never identified at Quickiock), and the black-headed yellow wagtail (*M. borealis* Sund.), which is commoner than the *M. neglecta*.

He mentions three pipits as summer visitants: the meadow pipit, the water pipit (*A. rupestris*), and the red breasted pipit (*A. cerernus*, Pall.)

The latter is common. The eggs of this pipit so much resemble those of the meadow pipit, that it is very hard to distinguish between the two.

The wheatear is a summer migrant, but the whinchat is not noticed.

Of the true warblers he mentions only three. All summer migrants:—

The willow warbler (commonest of all), the blue-throated warbler (common), the redstart (rare).

There is a doubt if the hedge sparrow comes so far north. He notices only one titmouse, the Siberian tit, which remains throughout the year.

The skylark is rare. The shorelark very common. Both are summer migrants.

The yellow bunting (rare), the black-headed bunting (rare), and the Lap bunting (common), are only summer visitors; but the snow bunting remains throughout the year.

The common sparrow has once been seen. The tree sparrow is rare (in the summer). The brambling is a common summer migrant. The mealy redpole remains throughout the year, and the *Fringilla canescens* has been killed here.

The bullfinch is a rare summer visitant, and although the scarlet bullfinch (*P. erythrina*, Tem.) has been occasionally seen, it is not known with certainty to breed here. The common crossbill is very rarely seen in the district, but appears to breed here. The parrot crossbill evidently does not come so far north as any part of Lapland.

GALLINÆ.

The turtle dove has once been shot at Vardol. The capercailzie, the ptarmigan, and the willow grouse remain here throughout the year.

They have neither the black grouse or the hazel grouse so far north as this.

GRALLÆ.

The golden plover and the dotterel very common in the summer. The ring plover rarer.

Strange to say, Sommerfeet distinctly says that to his knowledge the grey plover has never been seen in this district. But as Morris figures the egg taken by Mr. Tresham, in East Finmark, we must conclude that they do breed here.

The turnstone and the oyster-catcher are both summer visitants to the coast around the North Cape.

The crane is seen very rarely (in the autumn) in Varanger, but does not appear to breed here. In fact, I fancy that the crane is chiefly met with in the midland and eastern parts of Sweden.

The curlew and the whimbrel are both summer visitants. The knot is certainly rare, but that it breeds here he hardly doubts, as it is seen on the flats between Varanger fjord and the Tana river, in June. The little stint is only seen here during its spring and autumnal migrations. Temminck's stint, the purple sandpiper, and the dunlin are all common in the summer. But neither Sching's sandpiper, the broad-billed sandpiper, the pigmy curlew, or the sanderling have been noticed here at any season. Although Sommerfeet feels certain that both the pigmy curlew and the broad-billed sandpiper breed here.

The ruff is a common summer visitant.

The common sandpiper, the redshank, the dusky-redshank, the greenshank, and the wood sandpiper, are all summer migrants to this district.

The common godwit and the bar-tailed godwit, are both summer visitants. Sommerfeet has, however, never seen the egg of the latter taken here, although it breeds near Enara.

Both the common and the jack snipe are met with here in the summer.

The red-breasted phalarope breeds here. But not the grey phalarope, although the latter has been shot here in the end of August in full summer dress, and also in October in pure winter plumage.

Two specimens of the coot were shot on Vardo in October, 1857.

ANSERES.

The fulmar petrel is seen here at all times of

the year, but, strange to say, does not appear to breed.

The only species of tern met with here is the arctic tern, which is a common summer visitant.

The ivory gull is seen off these coasts very rarely in the winter, especially after a northerly storm.

The kittiwake comes in May and leaves in October; the Iceland gull is supposed to breed on Vardol; the common gull, the herring gull, the greater black-backed, the lesser black-backed, remain up here throughout the whole year.

The common skua is only accidental. The pomarine skua is yearly seen here in spring and autumn, and without doubt breeds here.

Richardson's skua is common in the summer, and Buffon's skua not rare. None of them, however, remain throughout the winter.

Sommerfeet remarks with regard to the breeding of the different skuas here :—The pomarine skua breeds inland a little way from the sea, for example, on Varanger Nas; Richardson's skua on islands in the sea, and on dry places on the Fast land, but does not appear to go long into Varanger fjord. Buffon's skua breeds on the morasses and little islands in the fjord, and also on the mosses by the sides of the rivers.

The wild swan is a summer migrant.

The white-fronted goose is rare. The lesser white-fronted goose more common. The common wild goose is seen here in the spring on the way to a breeding place—Tamsoe, in West Finmark.

The bean goose and the *Anser arvensis* (*Brehen*) breed in many places in East Finmark. The bernicle goose has only once been shot in Naesby, and the brent goose is seen only during their migrations in the spring and autumn to and from Spitzbergen, where they breed. Not one of the geese remain here during the winter.

The sheldrake has on only one occasion been shot in Varanger fjord.

Steller's western duck is seen here at all times of the year. Its egg, however, has never been found here, although they probably breed in Eastern or Russian Finmark.

The king eider and Barrow's Iceland duck are only occasionally seen in the autumn. But the pintail, the teal, the common wild duck, the widgeon, the scaup, the scoter, the velvet scoter, the golden eye, the long-tailed duck, and the common eider are all regular summer migrants to this district, where they all breed.

It is not certain whether the tufted duck comes up further north than Enara.

Both the goosander and merganser breed here,

and in mild winters an occasional merganser will remain.

Both the cormorant and the shag remain off the coast throughout the year.

The great northern diver is only seen in spring and autumn. The black-throated diver often remains off the coast through the winter, and the red-throated diver is a regular summer migrant.

The Sclavonian grebe (*Padiceps Arcticus*, Bov.) is the only grebe known here.

The common, the ringed, the black, and Brumich's guillemots remain off the coasts throughout the year. The ringed guillemot appears the commonest.

The little auk is only a winter visitant.

The puffin is only seen during the summer, as also the razor-bill.

The great auk has been seen off this coast, but can hardly now be reckoned in the fauna of the north coast of Finland or Lapland.

It will be seen by the above list that out of the 138 birds enumerated as belonging to the fauna of Vardol, nearly 120 breed here.

I may here add that the names given by the natives to the different species of birds up here are Finnish, and many of them differ from the Lap names in use at Quickiock, although the word Finmark is used by the Norwegians in the same sense as the word Lapmark is used by the Swedes. My Lap names used in the birds of Quickiock, will pass current in both places to a certain degree. But an Englishman makes such a mess often in the pronouncing of foreign names, that the collector should always have a few coloured plates with him of the birds he most wishes to obtain, to show to the natives.

CHAPTER XI.

THE JOURNEY DOWN, AND CONCLUSION.

Our journey down to Luleå was a very different affair from our journey up, and twice as troublesome and expensive, for we had to travel the whole 200 miles by water and on foot. We required two boats and four rowers, to each of whom we paid 1 rix-dollar per mile. Had we been able to row the whole way, it would have been easy enough; but the water communication is impeded by so many rapids and falls, over which no boat can ascend or descend, that there we are continually obliged to leave the boat and walk; and for this reason there can never be a direct water communication from Luleå to Quickiock. Our first day's journey was well enough, and we had very little carrying. I may add that my collection filled about twelve boxes, besides gun and trunk; and as each bearer's burthen is fixed at 40lb., we required about six bearers besides my lad. For this you pay each bearer 1 rix-dollar per Swedish mile. We had no difficulty in getting either boat or bearers, and everybody was very civil to us. At one place one of our bearers was a woman, and she stumped away manfully under her burthen for about two Swedish miles. It was rather unfortunate for us that it was just the time at which school was opening at Luleä; and at every place we stopped we were requested either to take a boy down in our boat ("Oh! he don't weigh anything"), or a trunk or portmanteau ("which would not take any room"). I had already saddled myself with the charge of one lad—the priest's son at Quickiock; and, if I had wished it, I could have had the honour of bringing into Luleä three or four more. I never was able to practise thoroughly the Roman matron's lesson to her son, "My child, learn to say nay!" and I am certain I can trace half my troubles in life to the sole circumstance of not bearing in mind old Johnson's motto, that "a good-natured man is next to a fool." However, I always try, if I can, to help a fellow creature, and as this is a poor country, they are glad to catch at any chance to save a penny. The weather was delightful during our whole journey, and scarcely an accident happened on the road worth recording. Only once were we in a little danger. We came to a small wood-lake about two English miles across. The boats on the river were excellent, but on this lake we found only two boats, and these, having been laid up high and dry all the summer, had their planks started by the sun, and were hardly safe. However, my head man—for I took one man whom I knew well, all the way down from Quickiock to Iockmock—said that he thought they would carry the baggage over, and, as by crossing this lake we saved the bearers nearly four miles, we launched the boats. They did not seem to make much water, so we packed our things in, and seating myself on the top of one load, and my lad on the other, we put to sea, and sent the bearers round the lake. The rowers at first remonstrated, and said that it was not safe for us two to accompany them. I was, however, determined to sink or swim with my collection, and insisted on going; and lucky it was that we did so, for the boats leaked so much when we got into the lake, that it took all the time of myself and the lad to keep baling out the water. Had the least wind sprung up we must have gone down, for we were loaded up to the very gunwales, and even in smooth water it required the greatest care and steadiness to keep the boats right. I did not perceive the danger until we were out in the lake, and as I did not then like to "show the white feather," I would not turn back. I could see by the faces of the rowers that, although there might be but little fear there was a good deal of danger. However, not a word was spoken; I kept on baling, and we managed the boats so well that not a drop of water touched any one of the boxes, for I had taken the precaution to put cross sticks under the lower ones, so that they should not touch the bottom of the boat. We reached the opposite shore in safety, and glad enough I was, for any old collector can imagine my feelings when crossing that lake in a rickety boat, which would hardly hang together, laden with the hard-earned treasures of four months' collecting.

We came to Iockmock on the afternoon of the second day, and slept again at the good old priest's, (who, however, had improved in the "world's wisdom" since we went through in spring, as he now charged us just double for our accommodation), and on Saturday afternoon rowed over a small lake to his son's, a settler near here, where we slept. During our absence they had nearly finished a new road for about four miles from Iockmock to the great Luleä river, and we had only to row and bear our things one Swedish mile to the high road, where we got carts and two horses to carry them for four Swedish miles. Although we had to pay 2 rix-dollars per mile for each horse, and walk ourselves, it was better than paying bearers, for we had not nearly so much trouble, and at six P.M. we reached, a village by the side of the great Luleå river, about eighty English miles from Luleå. If we could only obtain boats here we could row all the way down to Luleå, and not have to shift our things (with the exception of about five English miles bearing). We luckily met with a most accommodating settler, who provided us with a large boat and two rowers at the rate of 3 rix-dollars the Swedish mile; and, as a hint to the traveller in the north, I will say that it is as well to be a little liberal. One shilling more or less to a peasant makes but little difference to the traveller, and if he chance to come the same road again, it is not forgotten. We had another school-boy palmed upon us here, but the old settler was really such a good sort that I could not do less than take charge of his son. I may here mention that the boats on these rivers are very long, and both ends are sharp, and rise high out of the water. They always have two rowers, who sit face to face; the man in the bow rows, and the other at the stern backs water with a pair of short oars—in fact, steers the boat—and in going down these rapids the whole management of the boat falls on him. The oars are very small, and, instead of rowlocks, run through a twisted willow band or loop. The women here can row just as well as the men. We left this settler's at nine in the morning. We rowed through the whole night, each one taking his turn, and reached Luleå on the Tuesday afternoon, the journey of thirty-two Swedish miles having occupied six days. We had to wait in Luleå three days for the Stockholm steamer, which came up on Friday, and reached that place on the afternoon of September 4th, having been about a week on the road from Luleå, for the autumn had now set in, and the steamers are obliged to make short days' runs. In the summer the steamers run up to Luleå in three or four days; and one boat, the Volontaire, which goes through without calling at any station, does it in less.

During our journey down from Quickiock, I had an opportunity of seeing Lapland in her summer dress, and more lovely scenery on both sides, as we floated down this magnificent river, I never wish to see. I was surprised at the richness of the vegetation by the river-side, and the crops of barley were really astonishing, although I feared, this year, they would never ripen. As I lay upon the baggage in the boat, I mused on the past, the present, and the future. I wondered how many centuries had elapsed since this rocky, iron-bound land was thrown together, and what changes it had undergone. Then, as I gazed upon the clear unclouded sky above my head; the placid, waveless river on whose bosom we were floating; and the magnificent scenery which rose on all sides around us; I could not help thinking that, notwithstanding the wild character of the land, and the inclemency of the climate in the winter, such a country as this could never have been formed to be entirely forgotten, and to lie for ever a desert on the face of the globe; but that possibly in the lapse of centuries, owing to that change which, as geologists tell us, is gradually but surely going on in the surface of the world, the appearance of this land may be entirely changed, and instead of standing as a wilderness on the face of the globe, Lapland may become a fertile region when the wave rolls over the richer and more cultivated countries of the south. Yet even these wild, and what we call barren countries, are, doubtless, necessary and important links in the great chain of creation; for, as old Acerbi truly and philosophically observes, "The imagination of the traveller through Lapland will be exalted to an ecstacy of a melancholy kind—a pensive sadness, not without its charms and usefulness; that profound solitude and silence which everywhere reigns will every instant suggest the question, What good end do these places serve? to what purpose all that beautiful scenery of lakes, rivers, rivulets, and cascades, if these deserts, as would seem to be the case, are never to be peopled by human beings? This question will never be solved by man while he retains the persuasion that he is the lord of the creation, and so long as he indulges the idle and presumptuous prejudice that everything exists only for him. . . . Those birds which make the woods resound with their song, which swarm in marshes, on rivers, and in the air, and which in summer retreat, by a long-continued flight to Lapland, from all parts of Europe, in order to provide themselves with breeding-places—have not those creatures a natural right of multiplying their species as well as man? Persecuted everywhere else by human snares and industry, refined by fictitious wants and 'desires, ought they not to have an asylum where they may deposit the fruits of their loves?"

A rather jovial incident (twenty years ago I should have called it "a lark") wound up my Lap trip. As I was sitting at supper in the inn at Luleå on the night we arrived, my attention was attracted by hearing English spoken at a side table; and not having heard the old language so long, I introduced myself after supper, and joined the company, which consisted of two Swedish captains, who spoke English very fairly, and a stout, weather-beaten, jolly, good-looking fellow—a true sample of the British merchant-skipper. Any intelligence from home in a foreign country is always welcome; and though the most important piece of news which he could tell me was that "Jem Mace was matched to fight Tom King again," still there was something English about that, and we discussed the merits of the two men quite as warmly and enthusiastically under the polar circle as in Mace's own parlour. It appeared that the skipper's brig was lying in the harbour laden with timber, ready to sail the next morning, and he was (true sailor-fashion) enjoying his last night on shore. The girl, however, came to warn us at eleven that it was time to close, but, to borrow the skipper's phrase, we had not half "spliced the main brace." So I proposed an adjournment to my private room, and by dint of a little flattery and cajolery we persuaded her to take down a bottle of brandy and "the materials;" to which she at first objected, saying, she knew what we Englishmen were when we got together—most probably we should set the room on fire. Where the carrion is there will be the "vultures;" and our company was soon increased by two or three other skippers, and last of all by a burly Russian captain, who claimed an introduction on the score that his brig had been burnt by an English man-of-war during the late Russian war. A jolly night we spent of it, and great was the Babel; for I have invariably observed, that when a parcel of foreigners and Englishmen get drinking together, each one seems to feel bound, out of compliment, to address the foreigner in his own native language. For instance, I tried Finnish with the Russian, he tried English, and the English skipper tried Swedish— and I must say that one was about as good as the other. The English skipper was as good a singer as ever I heard, and the pathos which he threw into "Nelly Gray," and some other of those sweet nigger melodies, was really worthy of a better audience. Of course we wound up with "The Red, White, and Blue," at which the Russian took offence. "I like not de blue." He spoke feelingly, for he said it was "von —— Admiral of de Blue" who burnt his ship. Luckily we had but one bottle of brandy, and as there are no "finishes" in Luleå, we were perforce obliged to be "merry and wise." However, I agreed to go on board with the skipper to wind up, and see him off, and come back with the pilot boat. He took a great fancy to a large reindeer skin and a pair of very neat small horns which lay in my room, and I gave them to him, just to show them at home that he had been in Lapland. Tying the skin around him, forming a hood over his head, and fixing the horns on the top, out we sallied, and a curious figure he looked rolling down the quiet street of Luleå, in the grey hazy light of morning. The weather had come on squally, and so heavy a mist hung over the river that we could not see a boat's length before us. We pulled out in a rickety little dingey to the brig, which lay some distance from the shore, and it was some time before we could find the ship. "Brig ahoy!" met with no response, till at length we saw the hull of the "timber drogger" looming right ahead. When we ran alongside, all was silent as death, and we would not wake any of the crew. In fact, that would not have been an easy task; for while the skipper had been enjoying himself on shore, the crew were doing the same on board, and every man, especially the old mate, had turned in considerably more than half seas over. "Now," said the skipper, as we climbed up the chains, "I'll have a lark with my old mate." So we groped our way quietly down into the cabin—a little confined place, redolent of pitch and bilge-water—and as soon as we had struck a light, the skipper, clad in his rein-skin and horns, went up to the mate's bunk, and, shaking him roughly by the arm, roared out in a voice of thunder, "Now turn out, old fellow, I've come for you at last; I've been wanting you a long time." Never shall I forget the ludicrous scene that followed. After staring wildly for a few seconds at the strange apparition that met his astonished gaze, the old mate sprang out of bed and rushed to the companion ladder in his shirt, in order to escape on deck. Out went the light. "Pull him back by his leg," roared the skipper, which I managed to do; and I had better have left him alone, for he immediately turned on me, and, pinning me down on the table, began hammering away at my head as I lay under him. If I had wished, I could not have defended myself, for I was so convulsed with laughter. In the mean time, the captain (who had sprung into his cabin, cast off the skin and horns, and lit a candle) came to the rescue. And if the old mate's astonishment was great when he woke and saw the strange figure by his bedside, it was far greater now, when he saw only two human beings like himself in the cabin. The pantomime—and I never saw a pantomime in my life half so good—did not take so long to act as to describe. It was all a mystery to him; but he went back to his bunk a sober man, and all he begged of us was, not to be left again in the dark; so the captain and I sat up yarning in his cabin till the pilot came aboard. In the morning, the old mate, who soon got excellent friends with me, took me on one side, and told me confidentially that it was all a mistake about Saätan being black; he was grey—he could swear it, for he had seen him in the night. I pooh-poohed the whole thing, said he must have been dreaming; but it was no use. He said he never dare sail in that brig again—in fact, he was getting old, and had some serious thoughts of knocking off the sea altogether; and begged me, if possible, to procure him a live bear or some other wild animal, as he thought he could get a good living by leading it about England. At five the pilot came aboard, and the anchor was soon apeak, the cheery voices of the British crew bringing back to my mind scenes in foreign harbours now many thousand miles distant. I went out to sea with him about twenty miles, and on leaving in the pilot-boat a beautiful leading wind had sprung up, and was steadily carrying the old brig out to sea; and as the dear old British flag faded away in the distance, I inwardly wished her a good passage, and hoped, to use the skipper's phrase, that "she'd bump home in something under a month."

We had not many passengers on the Stockholm boat, but there were three young men standing together on the poop when I came on board, who deserve a passing notice. The manly, open countenance; the wiry, well-knit form; the neat, well-fitting dress (with nothing of the swell or dandy about it); and, moreover, the quiet, determined air, all bespake the well-bred Englishman. I could have picked them out of a thousand foreign youths as sons of the old country, as well as if their native land had been written on their foreheads. We soon got into conversation, for there was nothing of that haughty pride about them which too often characterizes the travelling Briton.

There was no nonsense about these three young fellows, and there was a refreshing and truly English welcome conveyed in the quiet, half-knowing nod, and "How are you, old fellow, this morning?" when we met at the breakfast-table. The greeting was, perhaps, not quite so demonstrative as when two foreigners meet, but it was equally sincere. "I wonder," once asked a foreign lady of me, "whether there was ever a really polite Englishman." "Certainly not, in your acceptation of the term," I answered; "for we generally mean what we say."

It seems that these young travellers had been by sea coastwise right up to the Alten, near the North Cape, and come down on foot all the way to Tornea, through the very wilds of Lapland, without an interpreter, and not knowing a word of the language. I thought I had done great things getting up as far as Quickiock, and yet these three seemed to make nothing of their travel; and I could not help admiring the quiet, unassuming manner in which they alluded to the troubles and hardships they had undergone—and these could not have been a few. Well may *foreigners* wonder at the true pluck and determination of character in the Englishman; and from what does this spring? Why, in a great measure from the manner in which the British youth are brought up. The love of manly exercises and field sports is, as it were, a part of their nature, and by becoming a proficient in any one of these the lad gains a feeling of self-dependence. "The will to do, the soul to dare," becomes too deeply implanted in his breast ever to be uprooted—and what is the consequence? The lessons learnt on the Thames, the Cam, and the Isis, in the cricket-field, or across country, are never forgotten; and when such men in after-life are placed in situations of danger or difficulty, it is easy to see the advantages of early training. One of these young striplings was captain of a Cambridge boat. The only anxiety which the youngest seemed to feel was, that he should not be home in time for the best partridge shooting. And as for the eldest, no wonder he took things coolly, for he was "an old bushman" in truth; and a man, who could travel (as he told me he had done) alone through a country peopled with wild and savage "Maories," was not likely to see much fear in wandering through a quiet country like Lapland. No fear of Old England going to the wall, as long as she can keep up the breed of young men like these.

We were about seven days between Luleå and Stockholm. We left for Carlstadt the morning after we arrived in Stockholm, and two days' journey brought us back to that good old town, having been in all about sixteen days on the road; and when I unpacked my collection, I had the satisfaction of finding that not one egg was broken or a skin injured. The trip cost little more than £100 in all. The journey was far less troublesome than I had anticipated, and left upon my mind a very different impression from that which the same journey seems, some years ago, to have impressed on the mind of a querulous old Frenchman, who wound up a description of his trip to Lapland in this manner: "Thus ended a course which I would not have left unmade for all the gold in the world, and which I would not for all the gold in the world make over again."

I shall now take my leave of the reader, in the hope that, if he has borne with me to the end, he will have derived both amusement and instruction from the perusal of my Lap notes, and have obtained a slight insight into the fauna of this wild and interesting land. It were impossible from the experience of a single season to give anything more than a general outline of the fauna of any country : this is all that my notes profess to do. I have stuck to the truth throughout, relying on my own personal observation for *matériel*, except as regards the ornithology of the district round the North Cape. I have carefully avoided going over beaten ground, and I think much new, and, to the ornithologist, interesting matter will be found in the foregoing pages. Should a perusal of what I have written induce any brother naturalist to follow my steps, I will promise him that he will not be disappointed.

The ornithologist and oologist will see, by reference to my list of birds, what treasures lie hidden in the wilds of Lapland; and to the botanist and entomologist this is indeed as sacred ground. It is not, however, only to the naturalist or collector that this country offers such peculiar attractions. There are many other men who, without being collectors, are nevertheless quite as true lovers of nature, and whose sole delight is in wandering among wild natural scenery —men who, to quote the words of a pleasant sporting writer, can "look upon a fine quickset hedge without inwardly wondering how they would 'go at it;' or gaze with admiration upon a wide stretch of meadow land without suggesting what a devilish good two-mile gallop might be made there." And to such men the varied scenery of a Lap landscape will present features of a new and altogether different character from anything they have ever seen before; and to spend midsummer night on a high fell, within the polar circle is, to such men, alone worth the trouble of a journey from England.

Any one, as I have before observed, can picture to his mind the principal beauties of a fell landscape. One mountain so much resembles another, that the painter's pencil can probably nearly imitate the reality of this part of the scene; but a far more difficult task would it be for any painter to convey a just idea of the beauty of the landscape of a true fell valley.

Here is indeed a rich field for the botanist; and I really think, if I were asked how the full sum of earthly happiness was to be obtained, I should answer, "Place a true botanist" (for of all pursuits that of the botanist is, perhaps, the most innocent and charming) "in one of these fell valleys, on a fine day in July, and leave him to wander free and unmolested, with no other companion than that most delightful of all books, 'Sowerby's Wild Flowers.'" I am no botanist myself, and scarcely know the scientific distinction between a buttercup and a daisy; but I know them both again when I see them so truthfully depicted in his pages—my companion in many a solitary ramble. What happy remembrances, how many visions of happy days long since numbered with the past, has that book conjured up in my mind! and how many heartfelt blessings must ever rest on the head of that man who can, by a few strokes of his pencil, recall to the wanderer's mind so many fond recollections of youth and home!

Youthful impressions are hard to eradicate; and perhaps of all our innocent loves that of wild flowers clings to us the longest. I can pass by the richest parterre with a very casual glance, and though I cannot help admiring the gaudy colours of the tulip, the dahlia, or the hollyhock, I scarcely care to take a second look at them. Many a year has now passed by since I plucked the violet, the primrose, the dog-rose, and wild honeysuckle in the sheltered lane of my own happy village; but if by chance I recognize one of them, or even a representative, in a foreign land, it seems like meeting with a dear old friend, and in an instant I am again at home. For,

> "What fond recollections the cowslip awakes,
> What sweet little islands twice seen in their lakes,
> Does the wild water-lily restore!
> What visions I read in the primrose's looks,
> And what pictures of pebbled and minnowy brooks,
> In the vetches that tangle their shore!"

Lasting will be the impression which the beauty of the Lapland landscape left upon my mind, and I trust that many others will gaze upon it with the same feelings of delight as myself. There is something cheerless in the word "wanderer;" but depend upon it, that the man who is tied to one spot, and whose whole life is solely engrossed in the cares and business of the world, becomes as it were a mere automaton, and although the one all-engrossing pursuit of money-making may absorb every better feeling, he must at length

"Weary at the oar
Which thousands, once chained fast to, quit no more."

And although there may be times when the wanderer will sigh for the comforts of a settled and domestic home, there are others when he would scarcely exchange his lot with the wealthiest in the land.

It is when wandering among scenes like those above described that the cares and troubles of the world are really forgotten. It is among such scenes that a man learns to feel his true position, and if he only tries to read the great book of nature aright, "to look up from nature unto nature's God," instead of regarding his time as thrown away, he may consider the hours thus spent as some of the happiest and most profitable in his life—hours upon which he can never look back in after years with a single pang of regret—hours which will render him a wiser and a better man, and the mere recollection of which will, it is to be hoped, in his declining days serve to "cheer the gloom of life's fast-ebbing scene," and afford him for the time being that true peace of mind which the world can never give, but which it, however, too often takes away.

THE END.

www.ingramcontent.com/pod-product-compliance
Lightning Source LLC
Chambersburg PA
CBHW030604300426
44111CB00009B/1094